CHINESE LIVES
An Oral History of Contemporary China

CHINESE LIVES
An Oral History of Contemporary China

ZHANG XINXIN AND SANG YE

Edited by W. J. F. Jenner and Delia Davin

Translated by the editors and
Cheng Lingfang
Gladys Yang
Judy Burrows
Jeffrey C. Kinkley
Carole Murray
Geremie Barmé

PANTHEON BOOKS, NEW YORK

Library of Congress Cataloging-in-Publication Data

Zhang, Xinxin, 1953–
Chinese lives.
1. China – History – 1949– . I. Sang, Ye,
1955– . II. Jenner, W. J. F. (William John Francis)
DS777.55.Z45   1987   951.05   87-43060
ISBN 0-394-55928-2

Typeset in Great Britain, printed in the United States

First American Edition

Contents

PART FOUR: STATES OF MARRIAGE

PART FIVE: REFORMERS

PART SIX: PEASANTS

PART SEVEN: WORKERS

PART EIGHT: SERVICE

CONTENTS

CONTENTS

Map

Preface

Imagine Huck Finn, raggedly insouciant, holding forth in a big city subway. He is lugging an incredible popcorn machine, twice as big as himself. He sells the stuff. Though he's just come from a small peasant village, he's not put down by sophisticated wisecracks, "What's the joke? You townies do a lot of laughing. You laugh at anything. . . . Money stinks but I sure want to make some."

Imagine a couple on the make. In a posh restaurant, they spill out their tale of success, putting one another down in the telling. Mink farming is their game; *bourgeoisie* is their name.

Would you believe these are two portraits from contemporary China? Yet they are but small details in a huge, astonishing canvas of *Chinese Lives*. Street vendors; corner philosophers; old women remembering pre-Liberation days, forced prostitution, and bound feet; intellectuals suffering during the Cultural Revolution; family disputants; peasant day-to-day musings; hotshot youths, Westward-Hoing; dreamers of the ideal . . . they're all uninhibitedly here. In this stunning, delightful, disturbing, and altogether revelatory oral history of the People's Republic, we see a country as never before. It is truly a bottom-up history that's been a long time coming.

Two remarkably gifted interviewers, Zhang Xinxin and Sang Ye, have followed the tradition of Henry Mayhew's pioneering expeditions in Dickensian England. In wholly unexpected, free-and-easy style, they have opened up a China hitherto unexplored. "Open" is the operative word. The reticence we have so long come to expect from these quarters has given way to a refreshing, and surprisingly frequent, irreverent candor. Talk about talk! You'll find it in this work, flowing over.

You'll get an earful, an eyeful and a mindful. You'll get China.

Studs Terkel
1987

Editors' Introduction

Chinese Lives is the product of a chain of influences between China and the West stretching back a quarter of a century to 1962, when the Swedish anthropologist Jan Myrdal and his wife Gun Kessle spent a month in a Shaanxi village, interviewing over fifty of its people about their lives. The resulting *Report from a Chinese Village* inspired Studs Terkel to embark on the first of his books of oral history, *Division Street: America*. His later books, *Working* and *American Dreams: Lost and Found*, attracted much interest in Chinese translation, and gave two young writers the idea of a similar collection to record the feelings of Chinese people about their lives in the 1980s.

Sang Ye had been working as a journalist and columnist. Zhang Xinxin, best known for her fiction, was at the time the object of controversy over her stories, generally regarded even by her critics as extremely well written but seen by some as alarmingly frank about the attitudes of her generation. In 1984 they travelled around China interviewing people to form a composite picture of the modern descendants of the Peking Man of half a million years ago – hence the original Chinese title of the collection, *Peking Man (Beijingren)*. The interviews, which were always intended to form a book, started to appear in 1984 as a regular column in the New York Chinese-language newspaper *China Daily News*. At the beginning of 1985 the first fifty-eight pieces were republished simultaneously in five different literary magazines in China. The interviews, with their unvarnished reality, the sense they give of people talking the way they really do, had a sensational impact. Apart from the interest they aroused among critics, ordinary readers saw in them something much more true to life than almost anything published in China. Until recently most Chinese have preserved a cautious reticence about themselves in print and even in conversation. The openness and authenticity of many of these accounts allowed Chinese readers to reassess and set in a wider context their own lives and experiences, satisfying a deep need to come to terms with the tumultuous events of recent years. A round hundred of the pieces appeared in book form in China in August 1986.

Zhang Xinxin was born in 1953 in Beijing and is widely regarded as one of the most talented young writers in China. Her given name Xinxin, "Bitter joy" or "Pain then joy", refers to her mother's long and painful labour. In 1966, when she was thirteen, her formal education was interrupted by the outbreak of the Cultural Revolution. Three years later she joined the exodus of Beijing youngsters to farm the Great Northern Waste in China's Siberia. After a year there she became an army nurse. Prolonged hospitalization with kidney trouble gave her the chance to read extensively. Once recovered, she continued to work as a nurse for a time before becoming an administrator in the Communist Youth League. In 1979 she entered the Central Academy of Drama in Beijing, graduating in theatre-directing in 1984. During this time she directed a production of Arthur Miller's *Death of a Salesman*. She subsequently joined the Youth Art Theatre, worked in television and became well known as a performer through a series of programmes she wrote and presented about herself on a cycle tour along the Grand Canal.

Sang Ye was born in 1955, also in Beijing. His original name was Shen Dajun. His education too was disrupted by the Cultural Revolution, and in 1971 he began an apprenticeship in a small factory, becoming an electrician and then a salesman. He received technical training in Hongkong and wrote for the Hongkong press. He is now a columnist for the New York paper *China Daily News*. He has written a great deal of reportage and oral-documentary literature, much of which has been published in Hongkong.

Zhang Xinxin and Sang Ye collaborated throughout the writing of *Chinese Lives*. Some of the interviews were conducted by the authors together, some separately. Occasionally they used a tape recorder, but more often they took only brief notes. Each interview was written up by one of them and polished by the other. All were published under both their names, and all are presented to us as their joint work.

Western readers will find that many things which are initially unfamiliar will make more sense as the book goes on, but a little of the background knowledge shared by both speakers and readers in China should perhaps be sketched in here.

For some thirty years now the China of before 1949 has been dismissed as the "old society", known to the young only through stories, propaganda images and family tradition. It is now as remote from those under forty as is the Second World War. When these interviews were conducted only people over sixty could remember much of the Republic before the beginning of the war with Japan in 1937. The old lady in "Ancient Footprints" and the specialist in "Avionics" recall the 1920s clearly; two women recruited to work in the city, one into a brothel ("Her Past"), one into a silk mill ("Selling Flowers"), saw a seamier side of urban life in the 1930s.

The Japanese occupation of the north-east (Manchuria) in 1931 changed the life of a schoolgirl who became a guerrilla ("Bandit Turned Housewife"). For most Chinese the war against Japan began in 1937, when the major cities fell to rapid Japanese advance. Most city people had to stay under the occupiers; some, like the hairdresser in "Vieux Paris", moved inland to areas still under the rule of the Kuomintang (Nationalist Party) leader, Chiang Kaishek. In north and east China many villages were drawn into the struggle against the invader led by the Communists, among them the brother of the Shandong peasant in "Land".

The Japanese surrender in 1945 did not bring peace: it was followed by the civil war that ended with the communist victory. This victory and the founding of the People's Republic in October 1949 are almost always referred to in China by those who lived through them as "Liberation". Great changes then began. Land was redistributed in the villages; women acquired more legal rights in matters of property and marriage (though the realization of these rights often proved difficult). Communist officials, called "cadres" (*ganbu*) to distinguish them from the officials of the old order, were more honest and also more intent on controlling and transforming society. Galloping inflation was brought under control and the war-torn economy put back on its feet. Every effort was made to win over professionals, managers and technical experts, including those who had been working abroad. People like the distinguished engineer in "Avionics" were therefore accorded special treatment.

In the first years of the People's Republic everyone was assigned the socio-economic class status that governed their later fate. To be a worker or poor peasant was good. To be a landlord, or the child or grandchild of a landlord, was to bear a heavy handicap. A bourgeois

[xvii]

family background was not much of a disadvantage at first, but by the 1960s it too was a burden. Class origin remains important: it has to be declared on most official forms and has often been a criterion in the selection of candidates for university, for good jobs and for promotion. The ex-prostitute in "Her Past" was grateful to be allowed to enter the non-explicit "urban poor" on the forms she had formerly dreaded. Others were less lucky. The teacher in "Irreproachable Conduct", the factory worker in "Woolly Hat" and the landlord's son in "Bridges and Rabbits" all bore the scars of the discrimination, both official and unofficial, practised against those with "bad class origins".

Peace did not last long after the establishment of the People's Republic. In October 1950, when General MacArthur's thrust to the Yalu frontier threatened to carry the Korean War into China, Chinese forces started moving into Korea. To many people's surprise, the American forces were held, and the war ended in stalemate in 1953 with China's morale greatly enhanced. The Korean War intensified pressures inside China, however, setting off a number of campaigns against counter-revolutionaries, corrupt officials and business people. Nevertheless, the early 1950s were for most people a period of greater stability and prosperity than they had known before – or than they would experience in the years to follow.

The breakneck rush to collective agriculture in the winter of 1955–6 as the peasants were organized into co-operatives ended the private ownership of land. Less than three years later the co-ops were amalgamated into people's communes in the heady atmosphere of the Great Leap Forward, an ill-fated attempt in 1958 to break out of backwardness by mobilizing the whole population to achieve instant modernization through super-human efforts. Absurdly inflated grain yields were reported; home-made blast furnaces all over China consumed huge quantities of labour, wood and coal to produce worthless iron and steel; and the whole economy went out of control. The result was a famine that is now admitted to have caused many millions of deaths. The shadow of the Great Leap falls over several of the lives recounted in these pages – "Land", "Bridges and Rabbits", and "Going Back" among them.

With agriculture collectivized, private industry and commerce followed suit. Private firms were brought into joint state–private enterprises, the former owner, like the father in "Good Looks", often being kept on as manager.

The socialist transformation of the economy was accompanied in 1956 by the call to "let a hundred flowers blossom and let a hundred schools of thought contend". This produced a rising tide of criticism of Communist Party rule: criticism that was at first encouraged and then, after it reached its height in the spring of 1957, ruthlessly crushed. Hundreds of those who had spoken up, especially students, teachers and other educated people, were branded as "rightists" and punished with disgrace, exile or imprisonment. Such was the fate of "Lawyer" and of the songwriter in "Song of Praise". The narrator of "Schoolfriends" lost her rightist mother to a labour camp when she was eight, her brother had a breakdown when his mother's disgrace excluded him from university, and the family home was confiscated. In 1984 they were still hoping that it might yet be returned to them. This is the background to the warning given by the cautious "Section Chief": "people should watch their step, keep their cool, and not make trouble for themselves and their children." The price of silencing loyal dissent was to be a very heavy one for the whole of China when none dared point out the follies of the Great Leap Forward.

During the 1950s a new political system was created, strongly influenced by Soviet models. Party and government structures reached into every corner of society so that even the old peasant woman in the Taihang Mountains, whose village was too remote to have been much affected by previous regimes, was drawn into the new order ("Deep in the Mountains").

After the initial surge of peasants into towns and cities to build and staff the new factories of the First Five Year Plan (1953-7), the movement of population was subject to strict controls. Many new immigrants to the cities were sent back to their villages. From 1958 strict new regulations on household registration (*hukou*) made it very difficult for people to migrate from the place where they were registered, especially when this involved the exchange of a rural registration for an urban one, or a transfer from a provincial city to a great metropolis such as Beijing, Shanghai or Guangzhou (Canton). These measures, still in force today, have prevented the growth of typical Third World shanty towns around big cities, but have virtually tied the peasants to the land. Even city residents assigned to the country during the Cultural Revolution, like the young women in "Diploma" and "Schoolfriends", often had to scheme for years to get back to their old homes. Without urban residence rights, one cannot officially have a permanent city job. Neither does one receive coupons for grain, various foodstuffs and other essential supplies which have been rationed since the mid-1950s. For most of the time rations have been adequate, but they were severely cut back in the hard years which followed the Great Leap Forward. The old lady in "Selling Flowers" blames the death of her husband and his mother in this period on malnutrition. On the whole, however, the cities went less hungry than the stricken countryside, as the Shandong peasant in "Land" was all too well aware.

A third of a century of revolutionary upheaval has modified but strengthened the family, especially in the countryside. Through all the changes of rural life the basic unit has remained the household of parents and children, sometimes with one or both paternal grandparents. The family, not the individual, received the income from collective agriculture, and it now contracts for land. In the countryside there is some minimal community provision for the destitute with no relatives, but normally it is the family which supports those who cannot look after themselves. The family head is usually the oldest working male; and although in law daughters have the same obligation as sons to maintain their parents in old age, the custom that women marry out makes this difficult. In "Planning Her Family" a mother of six daughters explains that when a girl marries she is lost to another family – only boys can be depended on to look after their parents in old age and see them decently buried. She describes her willingness therefore to defy officialdom and pay a huge fine for breaking family-planning regulations in order to try yet again for a son. This is the rational economic base of the preference for sons which is so hard to eradicate. It is also a serious impediment to improving the social and economic position of peasant women.

Although freedom of choice in marriage is protected by law, many rural matches are still arranged by the couple's parents through a go-between. The financial dependence of young people on their families, the enormous cost of weddings and the large sums paid by the bridegroom's side to compensate the bride's family for the loss of her labour, make marriage in the face of parental opposition a near impossibility. However, even in the countryside the bride and groom now meet to approve each other before the wedding instead of marrying each other as strangers as they once did. This "freedom", of which the old woman in "Deep in the Mountains" is so disapproving, has relieved some of the miseries of the old marriage system.

The family remains basic to urban life too, although for those in regular work the individual wage, pension rights and sick pay confer some degree of independence. People like the "Virtuous Wife, Good Mother" may marry the partner of their choice despite their parents' disapproval. Her pragmatic, unromantic principles of selection, or the unashamedly materialistic ones of the bride in "Newly-weds", would not seem shocking in China.

In city and country alike, the pace of working life is leisurely, but hours are long and holidays few. In the city people work eight hours a day, six days a week, and the only public holidays are 1 January, Spring Festival (Chinese New Year) in January or February, May Day, and National Day, 1 October. Housework, childcare and daily shopping for food all consume much time; this burden still tends to fall more heavily on women, even though in the city many work full-time outside the home. An active grandparent can be a great help. Labour-saving appliances such as refrigerators and washing machines are still rare enough for their owners to feel they are worthy of mention ("Hard-earned Money" and "Bandit Turned Housewife"). There is little money to spare for leisure activities, though for city people a day in the park, a visit to the cinema, a meal out or an evening with friends or relatives are common recreations. Only in the 1980s has a television become a normal household possession. Young people have few places to meet and let off steam; some complain of boredom. The sort of vandalism that set "Son" on the path to the labour camp is seen as a growing problem.

Travel for pleasure is only slowly becoming a part of the pattern of everyday life. For the honeymoon couple in "Golden October" it will probably be a once-in-a-lifetime treat, while the newly rich peasant couple in "Ten Thousand Yuan" regard it as a reward for their efforts. Economically successful enterprises sometimes use trips as bonuses for favoured employees like the chemical worker in "The Human Factor". This young man explains that his wife usually stays overnight in a hostel provided by her office because poor transport makes a daily commute impractical. Other urban couples are sometimes divided by much greater distances if the husband or wife is transferred to some remote posting, although where possible this is now avoided.

Primary education, normally beginning at seven, is available to all city children and to most children in the country. Secondary education, which starts at thirteen, is divided between junior and senior middle school, each of three years. In the big cities most children go through junior middle; but in the countryside the school fees, the entrance exam, their families' need for their labour, or the distance to the school still keep the majority away. The entrance exams for senior middle are difficult to pass even in the towns, and only the luckiest children from the countryside overcome the practical and academic obstacles to getting that far. In senior middle school the emphasis is on fierce and competitive cramming for college entrance. The pressure on the city girl in "Second Try" is obviously painful, but perhaps she is luckier than the village boy in "Popcorn" who has to leave home to make his own living when only thirteen. If she makes it to college or university she will have joined an élite.

Most people in the city belong to a unit (*danwei*), usually their place of work or study. The unit is the community within which most of life is lived. Unmarried staff live virtually rent-free in a unit dormitory, married ones in a room or a small flat normally provided by the man's unit. Rations, health care, pensions and sometimes even schooling for the children of employees come from the unit. Once employees have become members of the permanent staff they are usually there for life. Dismissal is almost impossible except for a serious criminal offence; and it can be very hard to obtain a release from one unit to move to another. Almost any dealings with officialdom outside the unit require a letter from it. The close ties between employee and unit can give a comforting sense of identity. Employees who have a bad relationship with the unit leadership, however, may find that it affects not only their work but every aspect of their lives. As the teacher in "Irreproachable Conduct" shows, it is possible to fight back, but the struggle is unequal. Many people in this book asked to remain anonymous because they feared the consequences of offending their all-powerful leaders or annoying their colleagues. Even after retirement people depend on the unit rather than on the state for pension, housing and health care.

A place in a unit can be inherited by a son or a daughter on the retirement of either parent. "Mr Average" took advantage of this option, as did one of the young bus conductresses in "Forty Minutes", prudently but regretfully preferring the certainty of a job to a chance of getting into university. The crematorium worker in "At Your Service", almost it seems to his own surprise, has developed such a pride in his calling that he will not choose the escape route of taking over his father's higher-status factory job. It is difficult to find a regular urban job without family connections: on leaving school, many young people are expected to fend for themselves as small traders.

To go it alone without a unit in the city is very hard: the state provides little to the isolated individual, and the street committee, a civilian organization responsible for matters like public security, hygiene and welfare, offers much weaker support than a unit can. The young entrepreneurs in "Joining Forces" who ran their own restaurant for a while found it easier in the end to merge with a large collective concern.

All permanent unit employees are ranked on various national scales of grading for workers, cadres, technicians and so on. The advantages of higher rank include much more than higher salaries: access to more information, better medical care, superior housing and, at the top, the use of a chauffeur-driven car, all at little or no cost. With so much at stake, it is hardly surprising that so many people in this book are extremely grade-conscious.

For peasants, who make up over three-quarters of the population, things are rather different. In 1958 they were organized into rural people's communes. Each commune embraced several thousand households, and combined economic with administrative functions. It ran the militia, the police, education and medical care. Below the commune came the production brigade of several hundred households which often corresponded with a natural village, and below that was the team, consisting of perhaps twenty or thirty families. Although major decisions about planning and production were taken at commune level, their day-to-day implementation was the responsibility of the brigade and the team. With collective agriculture there developed a large number of official posts in the commune, brigade and team administration and in the parallel Communist Party structure. Practically all the peasants in these pages have something to say about rural cadres.

If the famines of 1960–2 emerge from these stories as the great horror of modern times for country people, the best and the worst of times for many city dwellers came during the Great Proletarian Cultural Revolution, Mao's extraordinary attempt to lead from on high a mass rising against the Communist Party machine. College and middle-school students responded for the most part with youthful enthusiasm to the calls from Mao in 1966 to form Red Guard organizations, to seek out and destroy the "ghosts and monsters" in Chinese society and to "criticize the small handful of people in authority taking the capitalist road". These were heady days for the young – mass rallies in the presence of the Great Leader, free travel by train around China to "exchange revolutionary experiences" with other Red Guards, and a licence to attack their former teachers, to raid the homes of the supposed bourgeoisie and to beat up their victims. Sometimes these beatings were fatal, and there were many suicides. Even now, when the terrible cost of the Cultural Revolution is clear, those who were among the first to rebel still recall the excitement, as does "Red Guard".

In 1967 the upheavals spread from the schools to factories and the countryside. Rival groups were allowed to help themselves to the army's weapons and they used them in factional struggles for power. Villagers too were split by hostile factions, and in many places this contributed to a weakening of collective agriculture and the prestige of village cadres.

In both city and countryside external calm was restored by 1969, often through the intervention of the army. The wounds of the Cultural Revolution, however, took much longer to heal. Within the units, colleagues who once belonged to rival factions that imprisoned, tortured and even killed each other now had to work together as if none of it had ever happened. Through the woman who lost her husband ("Staying a Widow") and the worker whose father committed suicide ("The Human Factor") we can understand something of the impact of the tragedy; its enormous scale is harder to comprehend.

The Red Guard students found themselves being packed off to the countryside or to border areas like Qinghai, Ningxia or the Great Northern Waste, China's equivalent of Siberia. Here they were supposed to be re-educated by the peasants and steeled and tempered by manual labour. Their resettlement was at first intended to be permanent and their registration was transferred with them to the countryside. The harsh monotony of rural life and the political backwardness of the villagers – for example in their attitudes to women – stunned the young exiles. If their idealism survived this experience, it was not usually strong enough to withstand the shocks of a succession of political changes at the top. The most astonishing of these was the death of Chairman Mao's designated successor, Lin Biao, when his plane crashed in Mongolia in 1971, apparently after a failed coup, an event which led many to question what the Cultural Revolution had really been all about.

The early 1970s saw a partial return to normality. People struggled to rebuild their lives, schools re-opened, and a few young city people began to filter back to their homes, often with great difficulty; the flood of returnees came later. Above all there was a sense of waiting. Newsreels showed that Mao was fading fast, and everybody wanted to know who would succeed him; an astute reading of campaigns, events and the Party-controlled press provided clues about the struggle being waged on high.

Mao's death in September 1976 was followed within days by the arrest of his widow and other members of what became known as the Gang of Four, a group closely associated with the extremist policies of the Cultural Revolution. Just over two years later Deng Xiaoping's reform plans were launched. Perhaps the most significant of these has been the contracting of land to the peasant household. Collective agriculture has virtually disappeared, replaced by a system in which the household is again the basic unit of production. Private enterprise in the villages, once condemned as capitalist, is now encouraged. Some peasants, like the couple who raise minks ("Ten Thousand Yuan"), are doing very well out of the new system; the success of others, as we learn in "Bridges and Rabbits", may be mere propaganda hype. However, there is no doubt that there has been a general increase in living standards in the villages.

Economic reform and liberalization have also taken place in the cities. There has been a striking growth in small private trading and some collective enterprises, like the building company led by "Builder", have benefited from the changes. Most factories and enter-prises are now required to make a profit and some find this very difficult. "Builder" would probably argue that state enterprises are held back by too much red tape, but the salesman in "Drinks and Smokes" reveals that bribery may play as important a part as efficiency in winning contracts.

As economic controls loosened, prices rose, though most of those in work received wage increases large enough to leave them better off than before. This, together with a new official encouragement of consumerism, home-building and dressing well, have produced much higher levels of spending and an unashamed acquisitiveness reflected in pieces such as "Ten Thousand Yuan", "Newly-weds", and "Hard-earned Money".

Translating and editing the English-language edition of *Chinese Lives* has been an absorbing task. As we got to know the book better we felt we were also getting to know the people whose stories it tells. Yet the task was also frustrating because translation was bound to lose some of the variety and individuality of the different voices. We could not have people from all over China speaking a single regional dialect of English, nor did we feel it would be appropriate to use a variety of recognizable forms from around the English-speaking world, making readers feel they were listening to Jamaicans, Geordies, Kentuckians, Dubliners and so on. We have also tried to avoid sticking so close to the Chinese idiom that instead of responding to the speakers' humanity, readers would be preoccupied by their exoticism. We hope that our linguistic equivalent of monochrome has not done too much injustice to the subtle shadings of the originals.

We have translated sixty-four from a total of well over one hundred pieces. We tried to choose those we thought would interest western readers most, and would also reflect the diversity of the original interviews and indeed of the experiences of the Chinese people themselves.

With the authors' kind consent we have also done some cutting and condensing in order to include more interviews than would otherwise have been possible. The original titles of some pieces would have lost much in translation or would have required explanation to make them comprehensible to the western reader; in such cases we have given them new titles in English. In some of the translations there has been some minor rearrangement of material, usually in order to make the chronology easier to follow, but nothing has been added and nothing switched between pieces. These changes were made after the original translations were done, and as editors we are responsible for them. The order and grouping of the pieces is ours.

Our early translations were made from pieces as they appeared in literary journals. When the book appeared in August 1986 some of these pieces had been slightly revised and we incorporated the revisions into our translations where this seemed appropriate. The book also contained pieces we had not previously seen elsewhere. Finally, the authors kindly made two of their interviews available to us in manuscript form. A list at the end of this book gives the Chinese sources and titles for the interviews and identifies the translators.

Italicized passages mark the authors' speaking in their own voices, or reporting interruptions to the interviews; footnotes are our own and we take sole responsibility for them.

We have used the metric system for most weights and measures; the few inconsistencies we have allowed ourselves reflect the mixture of old and new which still persists in China.

The basic unit of currency in China is the yuan, divided into 100 cents (*fen*). The exchange rate of the currency, officially called *Renminbi* (People's Currency), has generally fluctuated in the range of 2–3.50 yuan to the US dollar, or 3–5.50 yuan to the pound sterling. Of course rates of exchange are a poor guide to money values. A better indication, perhaps, is that one hundred yuan a month, a good wage in the city, will buy many times more ordinary food, clothing and services than the equivalent would in the West, but would not go as far towards a television set.

Our debts are many: to Zhang Xinxin and Sang Ye for entrusting us with their work; to our fellow translators for allowing us to take such liberties with their faithful renderings; and to Jennifer Kavanagh for putting together a very complicated package of international publishing arrangements. Li Kaining provided much expert assistance. We are grateful to Wendy Wolf for showing us how to turn a heap of translations into a book; to our other editors for their patience; to Alice Halliwell and Claire Brown for their typing and to our families for their tolerance of our obsessiveness, our unsocial hours and our demands for cups of tea.

We began this introduction by explaining that *Chinese Lives* was part of a chain of influences between China and the West. We hope that this translation will add another link to this chain and will give its readers an understanding of the courage and resilience of ordinary Chinese people.

D.D. and W.J.F.J.
April 1987

Chronology of Principal Events Mentioned in *Chinese Lives*

1911	Revolution that overthrows the Qing (Manchu) dynasty.
1912	Founding of the Republic of China.
1931	Japanese occupation of north-east China (Manchuria).
1937 July	Outbreak of war with Japan.
December	Nanjing falls to the Japanese.
1945 August	Japanese surrender.
1946 March	Outbreak of civil war between the Kuomintang and the Communists.
1947	Land reform begins in areas under communist control.
1949	Communist victory and establishment of the People's Republic, usually referred to as Liberation. Kuomintang withdraws to Taiwan.
1950–3	Land reform throughout China.
1950	China enters the Korean War as US forces reach the Yalu.
1951	Three Anti's (Sanfan) drive against bureaucratism among cadres.
1952	Five Anti's (Wufan) drive against corruption among business people.

1953	Ceasefire in Korea.
1953–7	First Five Year Plan leads to rapid industrialization.
1955	Campaign against the "counter-revolutionary clique" of the writer Hu Feng.
1955–6	High tide of collectivization in agriculture.
1956	Socialization of private industry and commerce.
1956	Under the slogan, "Let a hundred flowers blossom, let a hundred schools of thought contend", the Communist Party releases some controls on intellectuals.
1957 May	Hundred Flowers campaign leads to widespread criticism of the Party.
June	Anti-rightist campaign begins.
1958	Launch of the Great Leap Forward and the People's Communes.
1960	Withdrawal of Soviet experts as the Sino-Soviet dispute becomes open.
1960–2	Economic disruption following the Great Leap leads to serious famines and industrial contraction.
1963	First nationwide campaign to learn from Lei Feng.
1964	Socialist Education and Four Clean-Ups campaigns.
1966	Beginning of the Cultural Revolution. Formation of the Red Guards. Closing of schools and colleges.
1967–8	Factional fighting between rival mass organizations in many parts of China.
1968	Red Guards sent to the countryside.
autumn	Clean Class Ranks movement begins.
1971 September	Death of Mao's designated successor, Lin Biao, apparently when fleeing China after an unsuccessful coup, profoundly shakes many Chinese.

1972	Reopening of universities and colleges with students selected on political criteria.
1973 summer	Zhang Tiesheng submits blank exam paper.
1976 January	Death of Zhou Enlai.
April	Demonstrations in Tiananmen Square provoked by removal of wreaths placed to commemorate Zhou Enlai.
September	Death of Mao Zedong.
October	Arrest of the Gang of Four.
1977 summer	University entrance exams reintroduced.
1978 December	Third Plenum of the 11th Central Committee of the Communist Party of China launches Deng Xiaoping's reform plans, including the contract system in agriculture.
1979	One-child family campaign begins.
1980–4	Contracting of land to peasant households virtually replaces collective agriculture. Contract systems begin to be applied in industry. Most factories and other enterprises required to make profits. Growth in foreign trade and investment. Establishment of Special Economic Zones, like Shenzhen, to promote such growth. Changes in pricing systems lead to a hike in consumer prices. Rapid growth of small private enterprises. Rising living standards for most people.
1983	Campaign against "spiritual pollution" intended to restrict foreign cultural and moral influence.
1984	Anti-crime drive leads to many arrests and thousands of executions.

A Note on Pronunciation

We have generally used the Hanyu pinyin system of romanization. A few proper names such as Yangtse, Kuomintang and Sun Yatsen have been left in older spellings because their pinyin forms might be more difficult for our readers to recognize. Most letters in pinyin are pronounced more or less as the English-speaking reader would expect. Some exceptions are:

- c = ts
- i = ee after all consonants except c, ch, s, z, and zh, when it is a little like the unstressed indefinite article in English
- q = ch
- x = hs, pronounced quickly together
- z = dz
- zh = j

Authors' Note

Because of custom, character and understandable considerations, some of the speakers in this book asked us to omit their names and actual places of work. For similar reasons a few of the narrators may not have been entirely truthful. We have followed their wishes and have recorded what they actually said.

Zhang Xinxin

Sang Ye

1

LIVINGS

Popcorn

The underground railway in the evening rush hour. Crowded. A little boy with a carrying pole a lot taller than himself pushes his way into our carriage. Attached to one end of the pole is a corn-popping cylinder and portable coal stove; on the other is a box bellows standing half as high as an adult. His face is filthy with coal dust, and he leans nonchalantly by the doors. "Where are you going?" we ask and, showing his snowy white teeth, he replies:

Me? I'm going to Babaoshan. *(This sets off a roar of laughter in the carriage. In Beijing slang "going to Babaoshan", where the city's biggest funeral hall, crematorium and cemetery are, means dying.)* What's the joke? You townies do a lot of laughing. Laugh at everything. I'm staying in the Babaoshan hostel. Seventy cents a night, and more than twenty of us to a room. When one rolls over we all do.

I'm over thirteen. From a village in Fuyang county, Anhui. I didn't come here by myself — one of my big brothers and four other boys from the village are here too. We've each got a popcorn machine. During the day we split up and pop our corn, and we meet up again each night. We're all working for ourselves and keeping what we make.

I've been to school. I dropped out after the fourth year. My family contracted for some land. Dad said I'd be leaving school and coming home to farm. I didn't like school. It was boring. There are eight of us in the family: Gran, Dad, Mum, Big Brother, Second Brother, me, Little Brother and my kid sister – she's the baby. There's about thirty families in the village, all farmers apart from the soldiers. And the soldiers come back to farm after they've done a few years in the army. Soldiers had it made a few years ago. When they'd been in the army they could join the Party and be top men – Party committeemen, village doctors, running things, bossing people about. They were somebody. But not any more.

[3]

Now the land's divided up and contracted for, nobody can boss anyone else about, so being a soldier gets you nowhere. What I want is to make money. We're poor, and money's what we want. Money stinks, but I sure do want to make some.

The very first year we farmed our contract land the crops failed. The grain we got was next to nothing – never mind paying our taxes, it wasn't even enough to keep belly from backbone. That's why there's so many of us trying to make a living in the cities this year. Some of the men pop corn and some of them are in construction teams putting up buildings for the government. The women have gone to the cities as maids. None of us are beggars – at least, none from our village.

Begging's shameful; it don't get you nowhere. The government's banned it, and you don't make much. Besides, the government relief grain's enough to keep you going. We leave the village to work and make money.

Dad and my eldest brother stayed back in the village to work the land. I left with Second Brother. These machines cost a packet – eighty yuan each. We got ours with an agricultural loan. You grit your teeth and buy them, then pay the money off gradually. It's a good bargain. There's no interest to pay on agricultural loans in disaster areas – you've only got to pay the capital back. We borrowed 200 yuan, spent 160 on the machines, and had 40 left for our fares.

We left before they gave out this season's relief grain. Spring's when we're broke, so it's worth having two less mouths to feed at home. What a stupid question! Of course they don't do a head count when a family gets relief grain. We get rations for eight every time, which means two extra ones.

There were six of us in our group. We walked from Fuyang to Hefei. We had to carry the machines and the bellows, and they're heavy – twenty-five or thirty kilos. I'm the youngest, and I couldn't manage it. My brother had to help me. The others? Not them. It's every man for himself now – they wouldn't lift a finger to help me carry the stuff. I was lucky enough they let me go along with them: I could hardly expect them to help me carry it. One of us is the boss. He's been to Beijing before and he knew the way. We started earning when we got to Hefei. We worked there for a week and made enough for our fares to Beijing. Making money in big cities is easy.

Hefei's no good. Too many people trying to make money the same way. When I heard all those land-mines going off like crazy I knew we weren't going to be able to get by there. You know how the corn pops when there's a big bang, right? That's why the machines are called land-mines.

The first thing when I got to Beijing was I had to pay a fucking fine in the station. We thought all we had to have were tickets for ourselves. We didn't know we needed luggage tickets for the machines. We got charged for excess baggage. They gave us receipts, but that's no damn use to us. We don't work for the government – we can't claim it on expenses. So we tore the fucking things up.

As soon as we'd got out the station we all chipped in and spent over a yuan on a couple of bowls of noodles each. Then we started letting off our land-mines, and we made over two yuan each that afternoon. We found a place to stay that night but checked out the next morning. It was too expensive: 1.50 a night. We'd heard that the Babaoshan hostel was cheaper, so we moved there. I reckon it's a good hostel, and cheap too. It doesn't matter that it's such a long way out – you can get into town for ten cents on the underground.

Been in Beijing over three weeks now. I make over two yuan a day – over four on a good one. We carry our gear to outside an apartment block and shout, "Fresh popcorn!" Once you start popping you draw a crowd. One explosion works a lot better than a dozen shouts. They bring their own corn – all I do is pop it for twenty cents a time. For that I'll pop them a whole sack of corn – much cheaper than the state shops. Sometimes I don't ask them to pay, I'll do it for five pounds of grain coupons. City people are rolling in grain coupons. I need them when I buy food, otherwise I have to pay extra for my grain – five cents more for a bowl of noodles. Sometimes I ask for coal, especially from kids. I promise them a big handful of popcorn for free if they'll steal me a few lumps from home. Nobody counts their coal. That way I've got my fuel. The Beijing city government's got everything planned – you can't even get coal without showing your book. If you're from out of town and you ain't got no book, forget it. Okay. So I get the Beijing kids to steal it for me.

The way things are going now I'll be able to go on making money till the autumn harvest. I save over a yuan a day, more than forty a month, enough to buy 200 kilos of unhusked grain. That's not bad.

Government kids are real softies but I'm no match for them – their dads carry too much clout. Those kids give me a bad time. They call me a hick. I didn't used to know that word, but I do now. They take the piss out of me. Well, let them, the fuckers. I'll carry on letting off my land-mine. Would they be able to work their way out of trouble and make a living if Beijing had a famine? No. We'd have to feed them.

What really makes me want to throw up are those bigmouths who keep on asking me questions and giving me a load of crap about not going to school being a serious problem, some kind of fucking social problem. What's being broke got to do with anything social? I'm here in Beijing with a letter of introduction from my production brigade. The letter's got a big red official stamp on it. I'm not here because we're dying of starvation – I'm here to make money. As for school, I'll go if I feel like it, and I won't if I don't. Nobody's going to tell me what to do. I'm going to decide.

I'll be serious with you: our life's got a lot better since the Centre decided to divide the land and contract it out. You put your back into it, and you graft. Get rich and you're the greatest; be poor and you're the pits. We had floods the first year. It was terrible. But for that we'd have built ourselves a new house. That's another reason why I've got to earn. My dad said if we have a good harvest this year we'll build the new house come next spring. Then we'll be doing even better. My eldest brother's getting hitched, and it's about time my second brother fixed himself up with a girlfriend and got engaged. As long as the weather's all right we've got it made. But I don't reckon I'll ever catch up with Beijing people. From the way they throw their money about you can tell they've never been broke.

I'm much better at this than I was when I first came. I can pop rice and New Year cakes too. Dried-out New Year cakes are great when you've popped them. In small towns you've got to add a bit of colour and saccharine when you pop corn, make it red and green and sweet. Beijing's got stupid ideas, so you can't do it here. They want it white. They say colours and saccharine give you cancer. Load of rubbish. Who ever caught cancer from eating popcorn? And they won't let me pop corn at midday, so I don't disturb all those precious government officials' siesta. Beijing people are soft. Well, that suits me fine. I have a fucking snooze too, under a tree.

Just about the only sight I've seen is Tian'anmen. When I've made my money I'll buy myself a new outfit, have a good bath, and enjoy myself for a few days before going home. Then I'll be able to tell the folks back in the village. I'll sell the machine here. I'll get eighty for it – they don't make them in Beijing. People are always asking me if I'll sell it.

[6]

If you ask me, Beijing tax officials are a lot better than Hefei ones. They don't bother about us land-mine operators, and they don't make us pay tax. Anhui's no good: you've got to pay fifty cents tax a day. I ran into a tax man a couple of days ago. He asked me if I'd paid any tax. "I don't know about tax rules and all that," I told him. I was acting dumb. The tax man asked me where I was from and how old I was. Then he ended up by saying, "Forget it. You're from a disaster area. Go home and go back to school, and stop doing this. You're only thirteen." But I'm definitely not going back to school. I'm going to make money. I'm not going back till I've covered the cost of the machine and the fares and made another couple of hundred on top of that. That's what I agreed with my family before I came here. And there'll be no more school for me even when I do get home. I'll be farming and getting ahead. If the crops fail again I'll come back to Beijing and make a living here, with my land-mine. I've heard you can make even more collecting scrap-paper here than you can with a land-mine. I can believe it, but I'm not going to sink that low. I'm a skilled man.

It's none of your business what I'm called. It's on my letter of introduction, but the hostel's keeping it so I can't skip out on them. I'm staying there on credit. Of course we'll meet again. I'll be setting off my land-mine around town all day.

Ten Thousand Yuan

Tianjin. One of the best tables in the Dengyinglou Restaurant.

A young married couple. The woman is wearing a semi-transparent pink nylon blouse and a pair of standard black trousers. A Seagull twin-lens reflex camera lies on the table. They order six dishes and two jugs of beer, then hurried out to buy a fried chicken in the street. They tear it apart with their hands, spitting the bones on the floor.

A few minutes later we get into conversation with her. Her husband is extremely taciturn and only puts in the very occasional remark.

You're very observant. We're both peasants from Jinghai county. We came here early this morning, and we'll have to be going back tonight. We're very busy, but we can have a bit of time off for a day out in Tianjin before the wheat harvest. How much do you make a month? Huh. That's nothing. Just look how we eat: we're really pushing the boat out. Fish, king prawns – this spread's setting us back over thirty bucks. We're burning our money. Doesn't matter. We've got piles of banknotes. Honestly, we don't care. Making money's the way to glory now. *(Her husband discreetly shoots her an angry glare and denies what she has said, but she continues.)*

You're wrong. We haven't just got 10,000 flaming yuan – we've got 10,000 pounds of grain too. I rake money in with my minks, and he grows grain on the land we've contracted for. Last year we earned 11,000 yuan and harvested 13,000 pounds. So we've really made it. Townies are useless. We poor and lower-middle peasants are ahead: we've left the working class behind. They were stinking rich for thirty years, but now they're crawling along by oxcart. *("Never mind what she says," her husband puts in. "Once she starts talking she doesn't give a damn. The workers are the leading class.")* Leaders? Sure. But would you become a worker if anyone asked you? And why not? It'd be because you couldn't make any money, right? We two can pull in a thousand a month – more than workers see in a whole year.

We've only made it in the last few years. We were broke a few years back. My family and his come from the same commune, but from different villages. When I was nineteen he was chosen for the army, so I got engaged to him. That was because we were poor. When you're poor you can't afford ideals. Once I saw he was going to be a soldier I wanted him. Soldiers usually leave the forces after three years and get sent home to work in the fields, but there was just a tiny chance that he'd be commissioned. Then I'd have been able to move into army housing and eat government grain. Of course, the odds were ten thousand to one against, but it was better than marrying a peasant: they didn't even have that one chance. *("Just look at her," her husband interrupts. "That's the way she thinks, and she's shameless enough to tell everyone.")* What do you mean, shameless? Have I ever let you down?

Things were tough then. We were always having to "learn from Dazhai" and the other model communes. We never got any money – just slogans. After he joined up there was an earthquake. The house fell down, the well went dry and his dad was crushed to death. Some people say my father-in-law wasn't a bad sort, but everyone in his village hated him. He was the brigade leader, great at bawling people out but a shirker, not a worker. If his old man hadn't been the village's brigade leader he'd never have got into the army. *(Her husband denies this: "That's rubbish. Don't believe a word of it. We soldiers were chosen by the county armed forces office. There was no back-door deal.")* What's that you're saying? If he couldn't get in by the back door your dad would have made himself a back window. The people in the armed forces office knocked back enough of your family's booze, didn't they? Did your family slaughter your "revolutionary chickens" to feed to your dogs? You see, a family was only allowed to keep two chickens. Any more and it was what they called "spontaneous capitalism". That's why people in the village called their two chickens "revolution-ary chickens".

Anyhow, we two have always got on like a house on fire. He came out of the forces in 1980 and we got married. I didn't get many presents from his family: two outfits of clothes, a watch and a bike, only a Red

Flag – they couldn't get a good make. *("Well, now you've washed all our dirty linen in public," her husband puts in.)*

We invited some friends and relations for a meal, but there wasn't much meat – we had to stretch the food with beancurd and turnips for all we were worth. Even though it was four years since the fall of the Gang of Four our standard of living had only just started getting a little bit better. Two years before that there was still all that nonsense about learning from Dazhai. Things only got better after old Deng Xiaoping came to power. If you want to know who's popular, the ones the peasants most trust and respect are old Deng and Premier Zhao Ziyang.

My man's able and he's got guts. When he was in the forces he really figured out what the Centre wanted. He came home just when the land was being allocated to families. There were two ways it could be done. One was for it to be contracted out by head – so much land per head. The other way was for it to be contracted out by how much of it you were able to work. In their village – well, I suppose I ought to say our village now I've married into it – a lot of people had gone off as traders, so the land was contracted out by ability to work it. You didn't have to take any land if you didn't want to. *("She's talking through her hat," her husband says. "She's never got it into her head that when the land was contracted out by ability to work it you had to take some. If you didn't, nobody was going to provide you with grain to eat. Not taking land meant fixing on the quiet with someone to work it for you. You had to pay them to work it. It was only last year that you could buy grain and not take land.")*

He contracted for a hectare and started work. In 1981 we got over 5250 kilos to the hectare, just 6000 in 1982 and about the same last year. So we've been a 10,000-pound household three years running. The first year we got a prize of a hundred yuan, the second year it was a bike coupon,* and last year it was just a certificate. *("No," says her husband. "All she notices is the money. We were given chemical fertilizer too, and priority in buying pesticides. Besides, there were a lot more 10,000-pound and 10,000-yuan households last year. If we'd all been given prizes that would have been a hell of a lot. But it would have been great.")*

But he doesn't make any money! You've got to pay for the use of a

---

* Authorizing the holder to buy one of the better brands of bicycle.

tractor or a truck, for pumping water to irrigate your fields, and for fertilizers and insecticides. You've even got to pay to use a donkey now that they've all been contracted out. On top of that, we've put a lot of fertilizer into that land and levelled it too. If the big officials ever take the land back we'll have lost everything. All our investment will be down the drain. *("It won't happen," her husband says. "The Circular Number One put out by the Centre this year* says the contract system won't change for the next fifteen years. She's getting herself stewed up about nothing.")*

I go in for sideline production, because that's the way to make money. I raise mink. I buy the kittens from the state. They cost eighty yuan each. If you buy a pair and look after them for a year or so you can sell them for 300 yuan. They breed too, and when the kittens grow up they have more kittens. So in a few years you can have a whole lot of them. Me, I spend all my time with my "300 yuans", and I love it. I got someone to buy me my first pair of kittens down south in 1981. I borrowed the money from the bank and bought two pairs. It's bloody hard getting a loan from the bank. You've got to have official letters and official stamps. They investigated my credence. *("Not your credence, your credit," her husband says.)* Anyhow, they were worried I wouldn't pay the money back.

You wouldn't understand the technical stuff, so I won't go into it. Believe me, you need a lot of technique to raise mink. The vital thing is that you absolutely mustn't let one of the kittens die when you start raising them. They're your capital, and you need them to give you more little ones. They die on you ever so easily when you don't have any experience. But nobody can teach you that. I can't just write the dead ones off as experience like a state enterprise. Besides, when one of a pair of minks dies, the survivor won't mate again. They've got real feelings — not like people. When people get fed up with sleeping with one partner they go off and find another. *(Her husband opens his eyes wide in astonishment or anger.)* I've been lucky. None of my minks died. *("Shit! At least a dozen have died on her." Her husband has finally found a way to get his own back.)* They don't count. Once I'd got a whole lot of them, losing one or two didn't matter. When I'd got a bunch I started selling kittens. I couldn't raise that many. Minks eat

---

* A Communist Party policy directive on agriculture issued 1 January 1984.

meat, any meat, and when they get in a bad mood they bite. Look at how they've bitten my fingers.

Last year I did really well, made over 10,000 yuan. The state makes them into mink coats to sell to foreigners. It gets several times as much as I do. I've got a conscience and I won't cheat the state. Smugglers from the south have offered me a colour TV for my pelts, but nothing doing. Besides, we've got a colour television already. I won't cheat private customers either. There are some people about who'll put a widow mink and a male who's lost his old woman together as a pair to sell to folk from other parts. That's a terrible thing to do. When a mink of mine loses its mate I feed it up till I can sell the pelt. Of course, I lose out by raising one of those because it won't breed, but I'm not prepared to do anyone else down. If the first two pairs I was sold had been like that I'd have had to kiss all my money goodbye, and my credence at the bank would have been finished.

Sometimes my mink kittens die. It makes me cry. It really cuts you up – it's worse than losing your own father. That's good money dying on you. People are really great, I must say. They don't lift a finger to help you. All they're interested in is cash. The township head's just as bad as the old commune head.* One day he makes us pay some tax or other, and the next he's holding an on-the-spot meeting at our house with everyone feeding at our expense. I'm no fool. What I say is, "If you're going to tax us, do it openly, and make it a good big round number. I'll contribute 2000 for the primary school." Get it done once and for all, then they won't be going on at us all the time. What? It's not allowed under Central policy? They think they're the Centre. They don't understand what the Centre wants.

If we gave money to the primary school the teachers would bring the kids along to thank us, and they'd promise to teach our son properly if we have one. We've got no kids, yet. I've been to the hospital for a lot of check-ups and there's nothing wrong. It's just that I've never got pregnant. *("We're fine without a kid," her husband says. "Saves a lot of worry. Besides, births are planned now.")* Crap! Only a real idiot wouldn't want a son. Don't be taken in by the casual way he's talking – he's even more desperate than I am. I'm desperate too. I want to send a son to university. Money's one thing we aren't short of.

---

* In the early 1980s the township (*xiang*) was brought back, replacing the people's commune as the basic state administrative unit.

Goes without saying, everything you've got we've got too: colour TV, tape-recorder, bike, fridge and a house. Have you got your own house? *("But you haven't got education," her husband says.)* Education? Education's useless. The first three years of middle school is all you need to get rich. Education's not worth anything.

Go on, have some of this food. And have a drink. Go on, eat! We can afford it. No? Suit yourself: we won't force you.

All the clothes I'm wearing are from Hongkong. I got someone to buy them for me in Shenzhen. Cost me seventy. It's a big place — everyone's rich there. *("Anyone'd think she'd been there herself; she's talking nonsense," her husband says. And we tell her, "Those trousers aren't even medium quality. And the style doesn't suit you. For the same amount of money you'd have done a lot better to buy Chinese-made clothes. For seventy you could have got worsted.")* Cut it out. You're just trying to make a fool of me because I'm from the country. Of course Hongkong stuff's good. Why do small traders go all the way to Shenzhen to buy Hongkong stuff? I know all about it. When I can spare the time I'm going to Shenzhen to take a look round, and I'll go to Shanghai while I'm about it. I've been to Beijing five or six times. The Temple of Heaven, the Summer Palace, the Dongfeng Market — that's all there is to it. The roast duck's all right, but it's not worth all that queuing.

What are you laughing at? We really are rich. The Centre's policy is okay — everyone getting rich. What's the Communist Party for, if not to rescue the poor from their sufferings? *("That'll do. If you go on talking any longer you'll start singing opera," says her husband with a smile.)*

After three years as a 10,000-yuan household never mind Shenzhen, even a trip to the US wouldn't be such a big deal for us . . . To hell with passports. We're poor and lower-middle peasants, we've got tens of thousands of yuan, and we can go anywhere we like.

Dr Yang

A standard apartment. Washroom and bathroom next to each other in the middle, and a narrow corridor linking the two main rooms at each end. The total floorspace is thirty-seven square metres.

Dr Yang Wenzhi, the deputy head of the Urology Department, shares the bigger room with his wife; their two sons sleep in the smaller room.

The operating theatre is on the fourth floor. I don't use the lift: I run up and down several times a day, and I never stop for a breather on the way. It's no problem: I do a lot of running. The Academy of Medicine organizes a long-distance race. I've won the veterans' class two years in a row. Can't let myself get old. Once my hand starts shaking that will mean no more surgery. The blood vessels in the testicles are so fine. One tiny slip and a man's sex-life could be over for good. That's why I keep fit. I do exercises for my legs and back and anywhere else I feel stiff. A few days ago, I suddenly got cramp in my hand at the operating table, so now I've started exercises to keep my hands supple. I'm fifty-eight this year and I'd like to carry on until I'm sixty-five.

I do kidney stones, prostate operations and contraceptive jobs too, especially vasoligation, which is used a lot for male sterilization. Although we have a national family-planning policy, there's no family-planning department in this hospital: it's mostly up to Gynaecology or Urology. I like to keep the incisions very small when I operate, and I'm quick and accurate, so there are no post-op complications. My operating techniques were cited at a national meeting of specialists. Contraceptive surgery has moved ahead very fast in China and now lots of places use the injection method. That's more advanced than vasoligation. In fact, some even more advanced methods are being tried out.

But ligation is what's most common, and there's certainly nothing backward about it.

I've been to Xishuang Banna* with a medical team which was sent there to promote family planning. Of course the restrictions on numbers in national minority areas can't be too strict, but you still have to push family planning as far as possible or where would we be?

Down there each village seems to use a different method, but within each village everyone goes for the same thing. It's not that the area is being used for experiments, it's just once they see a particular method is all right, that's what they all trust. If the first person in the village to have an operation is a man, then they all believe in male sterilization. If a woman starts taking the pill, they'll all go for that.

When she realized how simple vasoligations were, the team's head gynaecologist wanted to learn the technique from me and switch to doing male sterilizations. "That won't work," I told her. "You might be happy enough, but the men just aren't going to accept a woman operating on them – especially on their privates! Sorry, but you'd better stick to your own line of business."

People are saying that you'll be allowed a second child the year after next. That's rubbish. There's no chance. The one-child family policy will go on. Last year's census figures give only one side of the story. In our profession we've got our own figures and they all lead to the same conclusion: China is overpopulated. Forty years ago Beijing had a population of just over a million. What is it now? Eight million? Nine? Ten? It's exploding. The government has been pushing the single-child family as policy for several years now – but look at how many women are still having a second one or even a fifth.

Apart from family planning I'm also involved in settling domestic disputes. A lot of couples are really troubled by sexual problems. If we produced a Chinese Kinsey Report like that one they brought out in the United States in the 1940s, people would be appalled. When divorce cases are heard in court, sometimes purely political grounds are cited and sometimes economic ones – but do you have any idea how many marriages really break down because of sex? Are quarrels between husband and wife really about grocery bills? Of course not. Lots of people fight the whole time but they don't have a clue why. It's because

* An area in southern Yunnan mainly inhabited by Dais, the same ethnic group as the Thais of Thailand.

they're completely ignorant about sex that they put the blame on other things. They don't know the first thing about it. Others do know but can't talk about it. They just carry on to keep the family together. Take one of my patients, for example. He and his wife had been married for years and never had a child. They'd had a check-up in Outpatients but nothing was wrong. The husband came to see me. When I started to question him, I found that after all those years he didn't know the most basic facts about sex. And he was a university graduate! I called the wife in, talked to them together, and went through it all in detail – practically an on-the-spot demonstration.

You get young people who are completely in the dark too. One couple started quarrelling the day after the wedding. After a couple of weeks of this, the wife demanded a divorce – said her husband had something wrong with him. The boy's father was most upset. A relation of his is a doctor here, so he got her to arrange a consultation. I had to take it very easy with my questions because he kept blushing and was terribly embarrassed talking about the problem. It turned out that when his wife cried out with pain he went limp. It was ignorance, not impotence. I had to explain what to do and how to take care of her.

Afterwards of course things went fine. They came to see me with their baby later. Another result was that the colleague who had brought the boy in – I must tell you this story, although of course I can't mention her department – well, she came to have a word with me herself. She told me she had always disliked that sort of business. At night when they went to bed it was a matter of, "Come on then . . . Have you finished?" I was really shocked. It wasn't that she didn't love her husband, but she'd always been that way. I'm afraid ignorance is often at the root of frigidity.

There's a real need for general sex education in this country. They introduce it too early abroad of course, and they overdo it. What with all the films, the television and the press, it gets too much exposure. Here there's none at all. You find young couples who think the girl may get pregnant if they so much as lie down together. They die of fright if her period is a few days late. And I'm talking about research students. How can this be right? Recently though, they've introduced classes in physiology and hygiene which start at the middle-school level. A few years ago, they reissued a little booklet called *Sex Knowledge* with a few cuts and a new section on family planning. When I bumped into the author, who's an old friend of mine, I told him we were all in his debt.

"Don't," he said, with a wave of his hand. "I've had a mountain of letters from the readers. I can't possibly reply to them all." Some of them had addressed him as their saviour or benefactor or even their father! The booklet sold out in no time. It fetches several times its cover price on the black market now.

There are kids who get pregnant through ignorance before they're married and kill themselves because they're so afraid of the punishment in store. That's dreadful too. And some people are just wicked. There was a man who didn't get on with his wife but went on living with her in one room. They didn't have sexual relations for years, but he wouldn't agree to a divorce. Imagine, he was a state cadre. That's inhuman. But what showed on the surface? What could people tell from the outside? In such cases I try to persuade people to get a divorce.

A while ago I spent three months in Japan on an academic exchange. By Chinese standards I live at quite a pace, don't I? But I had a real shock when I first arrived there. At pedestrian crossings everyone rushes across as soon as the light turns green. You'd think they all had trains to catch. A lot of women were wearing tight skirts and high heels and yet they still seemed to fly along. I tried to keep up with them – unobtrusively of course, I didn't want people to take me for a dirty old man chasing after skirts. Anyway, I couldn't keep up. Of course I was very impressed by Japan. I went to Tokyo and Osaka. I watched operations and heard lectures. It was like being a student again. We Chinese can put up with hardship and we're not stupid either. That trip made me realize there aren't many people as long-suffering as we are. Of course I'm a bit different. I do my long-distance running and keep my spirits up.

But I reckon that we're behind them because we don't have proper scientific management and accounting in a lot of areas. Take the price of vegetables in their supermarkets for example. It's appallingly high. People buy just half a cabbage or a couple of leeks. They wouldn't dream of doing that here. The difference is their vegetables are absolutely clean, all wrapped in plastic film. It's different here. We buy vegetables in huge quantities. That's supposed to save trouble and money. But we end up throwing most of it away – it goes bad before we finish it. Even if you get less for your money when it's been properly washed, I reckon it's a better bargain.

Of course none of this has anything to do with my job, but people should think about things like this. Take the transport system at our hospital. At one time although we had only two vehicles, they were available when needed. Now we've got lots more, and yet in emergencies we have to borrow ambulances from other hospitals. Our own drivers' demarcations are so strict. The vehicle may be in, but it's the driver's day off, or the driver's at work but the vehicle's being fixed. Can't he drive another one? No, only the one allocated to him. If he took someone else's and it went wrong, there'd be trouble between the drivers. Not even the director of the hospital can do anything about it. He introduced the "personal responsibility system", so he's caught in a trap of his own making.* We borrow ambulances from other hospitals which still work on general availability. They can do us a favour if it's been okayed by their hospital director or department head. In our hospital that wouldn't be on.

You have to think about the big issues sometimes. The one-child family policy we were talking about just now is a very effective measure. In theory it will reduce the population of China by 70 per cent within the next half-century. But it's not at all certain that the policy will last that long. In the space of these two generations there'll be enormous changes in the family system. No siblings, no cousins, no aunts, no uncles – they'll all be just history. In-laws, that's all there'll be. On those grounds alone I wouldn't give the policy fifty years. Mind, we shouldn't delude ourselves that even if there were no relatives in fifty years' time, we'd get rid of nepotism.

I like the jingle which promises that the next generation can have two children if this generation has only one. People have to be given a bit of hope for the future, and it's no good forgetting the importance we Chinese give to human relationships.

Other hospitals sometimes invite me to do especially difficult operations. But for real application, I'll never be my father's equal. He used to be the head of the Dalian Medical Institute and later he became director of the hospital at the Kailan Mines. He's retired now. He's in his eighties but he leads such a disciplined life. He spends every morning reading, takes a midday nap, writes in the afternoon and goes to bed early so that he can get back to his books first thing in the morning.

He's interested in medical theory but he also buys a lot of second-

---

* Presumably under this hospital's system each driver was responsible for a particular vehicle.

hand books in English and French on clinical medicine. He plods home with them and then he plods slowly through them. He's no utilitarian. Such disinterested commitment. I admire him for it, but he doesn't think much of me. His faith in himself is also hard to live up to.

I have a fair amount of self-confidence but it's not of the same order as my father's. I can't help losing it sometimes. When we were in Xishuang Banna, a lot of people in our medical team ran a fever. Mine was the highest of all. I had a check-up and a blood-test but nothing showed up. I simply had a fever. I suppose I hadn't acclimatized. The other members of the team were very concerned and wanted me to have an anti-pyretic injection but I took aspirin instead. We didn't have many of those shots; if we used them up ourselves there'd be none left for our patients. I couldn't let myself start getting scared that I had cancer or malaria.

(A young man enters.) This is my younger boy. He hasn't made it to university. He's determined to learn to drive a truck, but I don't approve. What if he has an accident? He says that's his worry. What nonsense. He's still a kid. I'm still responsible for him.

Bandit Turned Housewife

In a public telephone room where she is in charge.*

Well, you're a funny pair, aren't you, the way you keep turning up. Worse than folk trying to make their phone calls.

You've found out my name already. Think I don't know? I get wind of a lot more than you can hear on these phones. My name is Jin Shuyu and I'm sixty-seven, not a day less. I've been minding telephones a good twenty years. My home's back in Andong – Dandong, "Red East", they call it these days. Sounds more friendly than the old name, "Pacified East". We ethnic Koreans are really much the same as Han Chinese. They give us a special vote as an ethnic minority when it comes to electing the People's Representatives. But I'm no more Korean than you are. I became Han Chinese long ago.

Over the Yalu from Andong is Sinuiju – that's in Korea. But you didn't have all these formalities in those days – you could come and go as you chose. If meat was cheap on that side we'd get it there, and when rice was going dirt cheap on our side they'd come over and buy it up. The controls are much stricter now. You've got to have a passport and a Border Resident's Identity Card. It's two separate countries.

I joined the Anti-Japanese Resistance when I left middle school. It's the devil's own job getting into the army these days, but there was nothing to it then. Me and my classmates we just arranged to run away from home and head for the hills. We found the resistance and joined up. Seeing as we were girls, and educated too, they made us into nurses. But it wasn't really as cut and dried as all that; we nurses got in on the action as well. It was a real hotch-potch if ever there was one, that

---

* In most neighbourhoods a telephone is available for public use on payment to an attendant.

[20]

Anti-Japanese Army:* there were some communists in it, but the main leaders weren't communists. Our commander was the master of a spear society – a martial-arts teacher they'd call him nowadays. And our chief-of-staff was a village head – in class terms, an enemy. But he'd fallen out with the local officials: that's how he'd come to join. A village head then was like the secretary of a village government now, but I'm not too clear about all those old government posts. Anyway, I heard he joined the communists later, and died in action.

We didn't fight pitched battles with the Japanese then. We blew up their storehouses and truck convoys and raided shops run by traitors, all at night. Our commander was a popular man with enormous appeal, and he was no fool. But he couldn't fight and he was superstitious too – always had to consult the spirits before going into action. Of course we didn't know anything about united fronts or guerrilla tactics. The communists and nationalists were still fighting each other south of the Great Wall. Nobody was joining forces with anybody then. We all hated that bastard Zhang Xueliang.† What we liked best was fighting the Koreans from Korea. They'd gone under a lot earlier than us,‡ and they were even worse than the Japs.

It wasn't just the traitors we had against us. The poor didn't like us much either: if the Japanese caught us they got it in the neck too. And we didn't know the first thing about arousing the masses or doing propaganda. We lived off ransoms. I was actually in on kidnapping the head of the chamber of commerce. We took him off to the hills, and told his family how much they'd have to pay. If the families didn't pay up we really did kill the hostages. We'd have lost face if we hadn't. But most of those rich folks were in with the Japanese, so we weren't doing anything very wrong. Our commander once said my father was supporting the Japanese too, and we'd have to deal with him. I was terrified! But the chief-of-staff had his wits about him. My father was a doctor, so it didn't make sense to talk like that, he said. He'd support us if we had any wounded. Then he said we had to do right by me. How would it look if we messed my old man about? So that was the end of that. You see, we didn't play it by the book.

* The North-eastern Anti-Japanese Army was a resistance movement based among Koreans in what was then Japanese-occupied north-east China.

† Warlord of the north-east from 1928 until he took refuge from the Japanese with the nationalist government in Nanjing.

‡ Korea was annexed by Japan in 1910.

Come to think of it, the communists were always trying to win us over, and our commander was keen to get their advice. But I don't know if the Party was ever actually guiding us. I found out only a couple of years ago there were communists among us. But they weren't in command and didn't let on who they were then. Our commander was the only boss in those days.

A year or so later we got smashed by the Japanese and had to scatter. They came down on us so hard we had nowhere to hide, we couldn't give them the slip and the peasants didn't dare shelter us. The commander and a few others escaped to the north, and later they joined the Anti-Japanese United Army and the Communist Party. I escaped back to Andong, but my family said I was a known bandit now, so I couldn't hide there. They told me to go to Korea, and I did; I escaped to Sinuiju.

Korea was Japanese-controlled too, of course, but at any rate it wasn't the same country. So no one knew about me being a bandit and they didn't ask any questions. To begin with I went to Songjin – they call it Kimch'aek now – and I worked as a servant. I wanted to get myself settled there. What with Korea being occupied longer than China there really was quite a "New Order" by then and they were very tough about residence permits. But seeing as I was an ethnic Korean and had lots of connections, I managed to get one in the end by greasing some palms.

Once I had proper papers I went to Seoul. The Koreans weren't very well educated in those days, so someone like me could do okay in a big city. I started by teaching middle school. It wasn't easy for a woman getting a job there then, but they certainly respected you if you had one, especially if you were a teacher. They're not like us in Korea: they really think the world of their teachers. Later on I got married. My husband owned a restaurant – not any old joint, a fine big place. He was Chinese – Han Chinese in fact. He'd no idea I'd ever been a bandit. And anyway, once I was married and couldn't go out to work any more, my ideas changed: I stopped worrying about saving the country. I had enough to think about with the children. The bandit became an ordinary middle-class housewife. I was even mixing with Japanese.

The Japanese went berserk before they surrendered in 1945. They ransacked our restaurant, and we lost all our savings when the banks folded. We were flat broke. We had to pick ourselves up and start all over again. But he was a popular man, my husband, so with loans and gifts from everyone we managed to start up a new restaurant. It seemed so easy in those days – within a few years we were a big business again. In 1949, when the People's Republic was set up in China, I was all for going back. But not him: "So you can't wait to be off now your bandits are in power, eh?" Someone must have told him about my "revolutionary record" long before then. He reckoned that the Civil War was far from over so going back would be a bad idea, especially as we were bourgeois – just the sort the revolution was aimed against. And sure enough the UN forces did fight the Chinese Volunteers and the Korean People's Army. When the Chinese People's Volunteers went into Korea, my husband said, "They've asked for it now. The UN's bound to invade China." But I never believed it, and he turned out to be wrong.

Nowadays, all our books and films go on about driving the Americans back to the 38th Parallel, but actually there was more to it than that. At their peak the Volunteers drove the Americans back to Seoul – that's on the 37th Parallel – but we couldn't hold it, and they pushed us back to the 38th Parallel. I remember it as though it were yesterday: it was the end of 1950 when we reached Seoul, and we were still holding the city in the New Year. We came very close to taking it back again later. And we were actually there to see those big-noses take to their heels again. By the autumn of 1951 it was obvious that the war was going to drag on and on, so while we carried on trading, we started to think about going home. We were doing a roaring trade: the Americans, the French, the Belgians – they all liked Chinese food, and if they couldn't fight their way into China, they'd settle for eating Chinese in Seoul. Well, my husband still wouldn't leave, but he agreed to let me go north and size things up. If things looked okay I'd write and let him know.

So in 1953, when it was obvious that Kim Il Sung and Syngman Rhee were going to set up separate northern and southern states, I crossed the 38th Parallel, taking the children with me. We made our way slowly back to China. He and I have been apart for thirty years now. It's even worse than having a husband or wife in Taiwan. We're not just living under rival governments, we're in two different countries. Still, we've been able to write to each other all this time through his cousin in Japan. Last year I was allowed to visit him there. Did you ever hear such nonsense? All one family and we have to go to a foreign country to meet. There's nothing to stop him coming back, but he just won't hear of it. He'll wait until he's older, then see, he says. But I ask you – a seventy-eight-year-old! How much older has he got to get? The truth is he's scared of us. The propaganda they put out about us in South Korea is even worse than in Taiwan. My son's tried to persuade him as well: "Look, even North and South Korea have a dialogue going now," he says, "so why don't you come back?" But it's the same old tune: "Let's wait till we can compare things," he says. "From what I hear it's a bit of a mess up north." Once, when we were eating in a Korean restaurant in Japan, someone asked us if we were Korean. I said no, we were Chinese, but he said yes. Would you believe it? Me, a born Korean, saying no. And him, Han Chinese, and he says yes! I really do miss him, but I tell you, I hate the man too. I reckon he's gone and got married again. But he's never told me, and I haven't asked him.

In 1958 I started working for the street committee, and I've been running the telephone room ever since. I get twenty yuan a month, not counting the telephone charges. We split them. The truth is I don't really need the money now, with my son as an associate professor. But I want to work. It really tickles me watching these youngsters making their phone-calls: grinning from ear to ear or bowing and scraping as they talk into the phones.

You name it, we've got it at home: my son's bought everything, apart from the fridge and colour TV my husband gave me in Japan. But I don't get on with my daughter-in-law; she's too particular. She's always giving my son a bad time. If he wants to put up with her temper that's his headache, but I'm not letting her push me around. She even blames me because she couldn't go to Japan! She wanted to meet the old man, she said. A likely story! She'd got it all worked out, I could see that a mile off. It wasn't just to broaden her horizons a bit: she wanted an extra person's tax-free allowance.

Some of my comrades from the resistance days are still very much alive. They're top brass now. It took some searching but we managed to track each other down. I wanted them to testify I wasn't a "female bandit". That's what my son and his college lot called me a few years back in that "movement to purify class ranks".* Of course my comrades spoke up for me. They said I'd belonged to an unofficial Anti-Japanese force, and I'd distinguished myself, so the local government ought to give me some money. I'd have been very happy to have it,

* An attempt in late 1968 to deal with the chaos of the Cultural Revolution and clarify who was "friend" and who "foe".

but nothing came of it. The local government said I wasn't a hardship case; they would have considered it if I had been. It didn't bother me: I wasn't short of money. But it made quite a difference to my life: they classified me as an "Anti-Japanese Alliance Veteran", the Overseas Chinese Department called me a "Repatriated Overseas Chinese", and the Women's Federation had some other fancy title for me. What all that means is that at New Year and other public holidays I get invitations to receptions and conferences. I did even better this year: I actually got invitations from the Taiwan Office and the Taiwan Society to attend their mid-autumn Moon Festival. But none of my people are in Taiwan! My son reckoned having a father who lived in South Korea was as near as made no difference. So I stayed at home, and he and that wife of his had themselves a free meal.

2

LOOKING BACK

Ancient Footprints

In the modern world very few customs are completely dead and buried. Some things return in a more scientific, modern form, such as ear-piercing by laser. But foot-binding will never return, at least not in this century. A woman with bound feet willing and able to talk about it is now hard to find.

That's how it used to be: men took the imperial examinations and women had their feet bound. The best feet for a woman were "three-inch golden lotuses"; and the best thing a man could do was to pass the exams for the highest degrees. And aren't modern high-heeled shoes a kind of competition for feet?

I don't find bound feet inconvenient. They were very particular about foot-binding when I was a girl. Mine were done in 1911, the last year of the Manchu dynasty. After the Republic was founded, foot-binding was made illegal. It was all very well for the government to issue its orders: but whether the common people obeyed them or not was another story. In my home province of Fujian they went on binding feet till the Anti-Japanese War. During the May Fourth Movement of 1919 I was in Shanghai, agitating against foot-binding with the students, although my own feet were bound. As I see it, foot-binding is terrible, but unbinding bound feet is even worse.

Nowadays they would say my family were local tyrants, but my father was a very enlightened man, against Chiang Kaishek from the Great Revolution of the 1920s right until his death. He had his views on the communists, of course, but he was beginning to come round to them during the Anti-Japanese War. He died soon after that. He was an educated landowner who rented out land, quite different from the local landlords and always a bit apart. His views were close to Deng Yanda's and he supported the Third Party.* I often think that the reason he sent us away to be educated was that he was that sort of man. Then we children accepted the new ideas when we were away and influenced him in turn.

I still read the paper every day, although I need my glasses. I'm seventy-nine this year, my health is top-hole, and I've still got a few of my own teeth left.

Unbinding feet that have been properly bound is painful and doesn't work. When I tried it I used a kind of ointment that was supposed to soften the bones, but I reckon it was the same stuff they used when feet were first bound. I couldn't walk without the bandages: my feet splayed out all over the place. It was all right as long as I put no pressure on them, but if I walked on them they bled. Once the binding had shaped them like that, unbinding was impossible. All you could do was put the cotton bandages on more loosely. But actually, once the foot-binding process is complete the feet have to be kept tightly bound if you are to walk. Those so-called "liberated feet" – our name for them was sweet-potato feet – were freed before binding had reshaped the feet. Feet that had been bound for nine or ten years couldn't be freed. I tried it twice and it failed both times.

When my feet were first bound the pain was searing. After a fortnight or so it wasn't so bad. First they bound the four smaller toes under the sole, then they put tighter bandages on to make the foot smaller. Oh, I can't remember the details any more.

I was betrothed after that – to my children's father. My children have all done well. I live with my son now. He's a department head – joined the revolution before 1949.

My husband used to support me; now the children do. I never had a job. That's how feudalism hurt me. Eighty I may be, but I'm the one who does the shopping. Yes, feudalism did terrible things to people, but I'm still alive to tell the tale.

* Deng, once a leader of the Kuomintang's left wing, founded the Third Party, formally the Peasant and Worker Democratic Party, a small party of intellectuals that tried and failed to find a middle road between communists and Kuomintang.

Her Past

She didn't want us to publish her name. She is now a retired worker of sixty-four with a pension of fifty-two yuan a month. She shares a two-room flat with her daughter in a newly built housing block for workers.

I am from Fenghua county in Zhejiang province, like Chiang Kaishek. My father was a peasant. He rented his land from a landlord. When I was thirteen my father sold me as a maid. The landlord took me in lieu of rent. When I was fourteen, he raped me. That's what happened to most pretty servants.

I was very ignorant then. All I knew was that a girl who wasn't a virgin would never find a husband, or if she did, he would ill-treat her. I was ruined.

The landlord's house was near the town centre. One day I heard that a labour contractor had come from Shanghai, so I sneaked off to put my name down with him. It hadn't occurred to me that he would ask for a guarantor. I had no one to vouch for me so I went quietly back. I only wanted to become a worker to escape from the landlord's house, although I had heard that it was easy to earn a living in big cities like Shanghai, and that men there didn't mind about their wives being virgins as long as they could work and earn money. I knew that I was a hard worker. Of course I wanted to get married. In Fenghua, girls married at twelve and often had a baby by the time they were thirteen.

That autumn a girl who lived nearby told me that another labour contractor had come to look for girls to work in a silk mill. He wasn't asking for guarantors. I stole into town again. I was told I'd earn three silver dollars a month. I made my mark on a contract agreeing to go that very day.

When we reached Shanghai, the man took me with three other

girls to a two-storeyed house where a woman looked us over very thoroughly. I was the last. "I won't keep her if you've slept with her," said the woman. I thought as this factory was so strict, it was lucky they didn't know about the business with the landlord. I made my mark again and the labour contractor went off with the other girls.

"From now on I am your Mama and you are to behave yourself," the woman said.

I didn't know what this was about, so I just nodded. She took out a cheongsam and a pair of embroidered slippers and told me to put them on.

"I can't get dressed up like that," I said. "I've come to do factory work."

"I've bought you," answered the woman with a strange smile. "There's no factory work here."

I had been sold into a brothel in a well-known red-light district. It was 1933 and I was fourteen.

For the first three days I didn't have to receive any clients. They were waiting for someone who was prepared to pay a lot for the first time. My first client was a young gentleman and he gave me a terrible beating. He refused to pay a penny which meant the Mama went for me too. I had never claimed to be a virgin – it was the contractor who had tricked them. The gentleman simply hit me but the Mama jabbed my calves all over with a needle. Nothing showed afterwards and I had to receive more customers.

The brothel was a hell on earth. Every day I had between a dozen and twenty customers or even more. They paid according to how long they wanted. When their time was up the Mama used to bang on the door and shout, "Send him out."

We had to receive men just the same when we had periods, only then we took those who wanted to "penetrate the red" as it was called. I got pregnant twice. We had to start work again on the third day after the abortion. I don't know how many men I've been with altogether. There must have been tens of thousands of them between when I was fourteen and thirty.

No, there was never one who wanted to buy me out and marry me. That only happened in novels. In the brothel there was a saying, "The stream of men is like an endless river." I was riddled with disease. I had syphilis and I was a heroin addict. No one would have wanted me for a wife.

As I'd been sold to the brothel I had no right to refuse a client, unlike the girls who were working there on their own account. I should have got 30 per cent of my earnings, but I never did. After that first outfit which the Mama paid for, I had to buy everything for myself. Any man who caught the pox got what he deserved. Even when I had the sores I had to receive clients just the same. They had given me the pox and I gave it back to them. Of course it's curable, but we couldn't afford the treatment. After the Japanese left, the new American medicine came in, but we couldn't afford it.

There were about 30,000 prostitutes in Shanghai. Women took it up for the money. Many were from very poor backgrounds like mine, but some had mixed with the rich. There was a woman in a classy establishment not far from our place who'd been a film star. She'd gone from starlet to dance hostess, then she'd started to sell herself. She said she'd been cheated by men so now she was going to cheat them. You've got to have some idea in your head to keep you going. Otherwise you just couldn't take it, going with all those men. At first I just felt it was my fate and nothing could be done about it. Later I believed some of the things the other girls said. The craziest idea was it wasn't men having fun with us, but us having fun with them and they still had to pay good money.

It's true that men did sometimes give me tips but not jewellery like I once saw in a Japanese film.

When you ask me about going straight, you show you're not very well up on this sort of thing. We never used that expression. After all, we weren't thieves. We talked about "getting out", or "coming off the game". I finished with it on National Day in 1952. I was one of the last. *(The new municipal government began to close the remaining brothels on 25 February 1951. They rounded up over 500 prostitutes for rehabilitation. On 25 September 1952 another order was issued under which clandestine prostitutes were to be dealt with and the last group of nearly 1000 women was taken in. Finally, in July 1953, the Security Bureau banned bar girls, dance hostesses and the like.)*

I was hardly conscious of the setting up of New China. I'd seen so much already. The Kuomintang, then the Japanese, then the Kuomintang back again. Now it was the Communist Party, but I was still hustling. A lot of the girls were finishing with it. The government found jobs for those who left of their own accord. But I didn't follow them. I didn't believe they'd really be able to support themselves. I was

[33]

still waiting for a good man who would free me from that life by marrying me. People said the communists were good. All right. I would wait for a good communist to marry me. It never occurred to me that a communist wouldn't go to a brothel. I thought that all cats ate fish.

Then I heard a terrifying story: that the communists were going to close the brothels, force us to shave our heads and make us into communal wives. Just as life was getting a bit easier, here was trouble again.

Why do I say life had got easier? Well, in the campaign against counter-revolutionaries in 1950, the government executed a lot of the gangsters who ran girls. That meant there was much less pressure on us. What's more, the government didn't collect any tax on what we made. With the Kuomintang, we used to say, "Each of them wants our bodies, and together they want our money." So afterwards we did feel life had got easier and that we had the Communist Party to thank for it.

All the brothels in Shanghai were closed in the 1951 campaign. I carried on under cover, working from a coffee bar. I couldn't have gone to a dance hall. You need the skills to work as a dance hostess. All my earnings went on heroin, for my addiction was getting worse. Sometimes I got desperate because I couldn't find a customer. In September 1952, just as I was expecting a bit of extra business with the holiday, I was detained by the Security Bureau and ended up in a labour reform school.

Over a thousand of us were hauled in that night. We cried and yelled. People like me made especially hard cases. I'd been living that way so long and heard so much reactionary propaganda. Heroin was banned there. When the craving came on, I couldn't help crying. The cadres used to claim that they were helping us to escape from hell, but I felt they were pushing me into it.

In the first years after Liberation there was still trouble in Shanghai. About two weeks after National Day the school was surrounded by hundreds of gangsters. They wanted to get us out and we tried to force our way out to join them. We started to struggle with the cadres. Under the rules they weren't allowed to strike us or even swear at us. They just stood their ground, barring the door. Some of the girls who'd been there nearly a year helped them. They knew we might actually kill someone, so they tried to grab the kitchen knives we'd got hold of and a real fight broke out.

Lots of police arrived outside and arrested the gangsters. We saw there was no point in going on. However tough they are, prostitutes are always scared of the police. In the old society they'd given us a really bad time. We didn't take much notice of the cadres. In fact we rather despised them. Before Liberation it was the poor who were mocked, not the prostitutes. We thought the cadre women in their baggy trousers looked nothing like women, or men either. We felt superior to them. The governor was a spinster called Yang a couple of years older than me.

"Knows fuck-all about anything," we used to say in private. "How can they put her in charge of us?"

Actually she turned out to be a much better person than us.

When I was first there, nothing put me to shame. Nothing seemed too foul for me to stoop to. We were supposed to study for half the day and work the other half, but as I was an addict, I didn't. Some of the others just messed about instead of working. Half of our study period was devoted to politics and in the other half we had meetings to "remember the bitter past". The girls who had been there longest took the lead, then some of the others joined in. I thought it was all a lot of hot air. What was real bitterness anyway? Wasn't it waiting to be sent to an army barracks as a communal wife? The cadres kept telling us that the story about us being sent to the north-east to farm wasteland was only a rumour. The government just wanted us to start new lives.

Suddenly a new rumour sprang up: the army was being beaten in Korea, the wounded soldiers needed transfusions, and the government was going to take our blood. In those days I was so naive I believed everything I heard. A few days later people really did come to take blood. I made a great fuss and managed to break one of the flasks, but in the end I let the doctor draw out just a little. I said to myself that they must want to find out what group I was. I didn't realize that people with syphilis have infected blood, but I knew about blood groups from a film I'd seen.

After a while the doctor came back with the cadres. "The tests show that you have syphilis," said the doctor. "You must stay in the sick bay while you have treatment." I was struck dumb. What the girls said was true. The communists did want to save me.

So I moved into the sick bay. I weighed less than six stone before I was treated, now I am about eight and a half stone. You can see I'm not fat now, so you can imagine, I was just skin and bone.

When I was getting better, I started my new life. I learned to read: I can read newspapers now and I get the gist, although there are characters I can't recognize. We worked, too. Each of us learned a skill. I was taught to knit socks on a machine.

Actually, people like me were quite easy to reform, because our origins were humble. Once we saw the light, we knew what was right and what was wrong. The difficult ones were the "good-time girls". They claimed to have sold their smiles not their bodies. That was nonsense of course. Silly liars. Their heads were full of stupid notions. They were vicious too. One of them asked a cadre if she had ever been to Shanghai's theatreland, Bailemen, or eaten in one of the grand restaurants. "Why are you so proud of the very things you should be ashamed about?" asked the cadre. But in those days you just couldn't put that girl down. She started to curse and break things. The reform worked in the end though. She's a good worker today. She couldn't hold out against the People's Government. No way!

There were some things about the reform school I hated. The cadres treated us like members of their own families, but we did a lot of quarrelling among ourselves. The "good-time girls" bullied us. They thought they were clean and we were dirty and vulgar. Some of them didn't even want their beds to touch ours.

"You've slept with officials and yet you're so fucking clean," I used to yell at them. The reform school had a slogan about seeing who could be the first to wash off the filth of the old society and start afresh. It was quite catchy, but I can't remember it properly now. Have you seen the film *Stand Up Sisters*? It's all about prostitutes in Beijing before and after Liberation. It's a pity it hasn't been shown for twenty years. It tells our story just the way it was.

I wept when I got my first wages at the reform school. The first clean money I'd ever earned. I left in 1956. You had to satisfy certain conditions before you could go. Your political attitude had to be good, you had to be completely clear of syphilis and you had to have learned a trade.

The Labour Bureau found me a job in a clothing factory. The sock-making I'd learned was no use to me there, but it was still thanks to the reform school that I could support myself. If the government hadn't cured my disease and changed my outlook, I would never have lived to do that.

I have to fill in details about my life on forms sometimes. I used to hate answering questions about employment before Liberation. So I went to ask the factory director's advice and he said it would be all right to put "no regular employment". That was a great weight off my mind. I was ashamed to put down that I had been a prostitute, and yet it would have been untrue to claim I had been unemployed. Everyone needs to keep face. I never wore a red armband during the Cultural Revolution and I didn't join any rebel groups either. Why? Because I couldn't have attacked such a good director. One should have gratitude. As to filling in my class background on forms, it should be "lumpenproletariat", but during the socialist education movement in 1964, I was told that I could just put "urban poor".

I got married in 1958, the year of the Great Leap Forward. My husband was a pedicab driver. Our go-between had told him all about me and he said he would decide when he had seen me. I was quite straightforward with him at our first meeting. "Although the government has re-educated me, I have been woman to 10,000 men," I said. "That's something that can't be changed. If you'll have me that's fine, but I can't demand it of you." "That's all over and done with," he replied. "What matters is that things are all right now." Things were settled very quickly after that.

Just before we were married, I asked him if he minded about my past. "I'm lucky to find a wife at my age," he answered. "You must give me a son so that we'll have descendants." I told him that it couldn't be guaranteed because I'd had two abortions. "We'll get married anyway," he replied after a little thought. "We like each other and we're both from poor families." His attitudes were less progressive than mine – I had been through the reform school.

We had a good life together. He was a nice man, kind and honest. Very caring. He passed away last year, a month before our daughter graduated from university. He didn't live to see it.

"Was your life so clean in the old society?" I asked him once. He reddened and said nothing for a bit. "We pedicab drivers couldn't afford to marry," he replied at last. "If we had a bit of money we went off to a brothel." We never spoke of it again. No. You can't dwell on the past. We might even have been together before. The new society allowed us to be human beings for the first time.

I was never able to have a son. I got seriously ill when I was carrying my daughter in 1959 and had to spend three months in hospital. It was a difficult birth and afterwards they found a growth on my womb. They had to operate, and there were no more children.

I hardly met any discrimination at work. Most of my workmates were good to me and treated me like a sister. From time to time I still see a few girls from the reform school. Some of them became workers, some shop assistants, some nurses and some peasants. It closed in 1958. In all, it had saved several thousand women.

(Women who left the school also became cadres, kindergarten teachers and actresses. A small number went back to their old profession and had to be taken in again. Former officials from the school say that before 1953 women became prostitutes due to the historical circumstances. The women whom they had to take back again had broken the law and were treated differently.)

My daughter didn't know about my past until she had just started middle school. She quarrelled with a neighbour and the woman started screaming about my past. I explained to my girl that I had been forced into a living hell in the old society and the new society had released me. I had done my best to help build up New China. I was better than someone who had been an ignorant housewife all her life and didn't know how to work. Then I ran out and had a big fight with that woman. I didn't feel guilty. She was the one in the wrong.

In the old society I wasn't a high-class prostitute but I wasn't one of the lowest either. Of course we prostitutes were at the bottom of society anyway. In New China I've learned I'm equal with everyone else. Ex-prostitutes like me owe everything to the People's Government. The best of my sisters have joined the Communist Party and others have been chosen as model workers. I'm fairly well off – others haven't done as well – but we've all got our problems.

As I said, I didn't join any organizations during the Cultural Revolution. Once in those years I went to hospital and saw the doctor who had cured me. He was scrubbing the floor. A consultant dermatologist. I began to cry. He looked up. I suppose he thought I was very ill. He put his hand out and asked me what department I wanted. I told him my name but he didn't recognize it.

"Remember the reform school?" I prompted.

Only then did he nod his head slowly and walk off. There was no place for good people in those years.

Last of a Kind

Tianjin. A farmers' market within the city.

Shang Jinxi, fifty-eight, grasps a big copper kettle. He sells tea broth, a runny, sweetened porridge made with sorghum flour.

Don't stand on ceremony, drink. In this trade, I'm the last one left. Outside Beijing and here in Tianjin, nobody even knows what tea broth is. They call it "pasty porridge". I reckon I'm probably unique in China, even the world. Otherwise why would so many foreigners and reporters have come and photographed me? In Hongkong they made a movie about this big copper kettle! *("What a braggart he is!" his wife interjects.)* Who's exaggerating? It's a fact. Just take a look at these photos I've got inside my stall: they're genuine. *(The walls of his stall display several dozen photographs of him and his kettle, captioned at the bottom: "Taken by an international friend", "Taken by a friend from Taiwan", "Taken by a press agency reporter", and so on.)* I'm famous!

This is what I did before Liberation. When it came time to learn a craft, this is what I chose. In the old days there were a lot of people in this business. The competition was all over the street. At least there was some competition. A bowl like this cost just a few coppers. But not afterwards. This bowl of tea broth would have cost you tens of thousands of yuan.*

I gave it up after Liberation even before trades like this were put under joint state–private ownership. I went into a large-scale collective. A transport agency. Moving things was heavy work, but there was no worry to it; everybody ate out of the same pot. Life was

---

* Due to hyperinflation during the last years of the Kuomintang government.

still tough, but it never even occurred to me to go back to being a small pedlar. Anyway with welfare subsidies as well you could get by. Then again, you couldn't become a private pedlar even if you wanted to.

These last couple of years, while the nation's been trying to rev up the economy, I've retired. I thought about it a while, then dug out this big old kettle of mine. Rubbed the shine right back into it, so that I could take up my old trade again. I can make over a hundred yuan a month from it, on top of my pension. I've got it made.

TV? Cassette player? Not me. Kids! I got kids to raise. Sure, they've all got jobs, but I have to support 'em just the same. I got seven kids. Five boys. They all want to get married, and every one of 'em knows how to get money out of the old man. We haven't come to the point where they're supporting me, not by a long shot. Each one brings in several dozen bucks a month, then insists on a two or three thousand yuan wedding – that's where I come in! I'll be supporting them till I'm in my grave. But I'm willing. If my kids can get on all right, I'll have peace of mind.

There's a story about a father and a mother. When they got old, their son didn't want to support them, so he carried them up on his back into the hills to abandon them. His mother cried all the way, but as they went she broke branches off the trees and threw them on the ground. The son asked, "What are you up to?" The mother said, "I was so afraid you might not be able to find your way home." That's how old folks think, all right. Not that my children are that bad to me. Not yet anyway – I guess we'll find out later.

You can't do without us private pedlars. Society isn't that advanced yet; if you abolish all private buying and selling in one fell swoop, things grind to a halt. All these years of fuss about it – what good have they done? It's just like this tea broth of mine. You can talk up hot chocolate all you want, but not everybody can afford it, and not everybody even likes it, right?

Who's going to take on this big kettle of mine when I'm gone? Who wants it? Even if folks still want to drink this tea broth, there'll be no young people willing to sell it to them. They wouldn't know how, either. Seen any travelling barbers lately? No rickshaws, either. Now there's progress. But why should I worry? My old customers have a taste for this stuff. Young people are just curious to try it.

They don't come a second time, they're off to Kiessling's for a coffee.*

How about it, will you have a taste? If you like it, help me spread the word, will you. Tell 'em that here in Tianjin there's still somebody left selling tea broth.

* A Tianjin coffee and ice-cream parlour famous throughout China.

Banker

Mr Zhang is seventy-eight. He spent all his working life in a bank, with only changes in the bank's name and his promotions and demotions to vary the pattern.

He lives in two north-facing rooms inside a dark little doorway at the end of a cul-de-sac of an alley behind the Peking Hotel. On the wall hang various little packets of rationed foodstuffs labelled with a writing brush: day lily, tree-ear fungus, beanstarch vermicelli, and so on.

I don't go in for *taijiquan* exercises, I don't diet, I eat fat pork, and I don't bother at all with techniques for living longer. Every morning at about nine, I walk along East Chang'an Avenue to Dongdan to buy food. Throughout the year I get what's in season. I don't insist on eating hothouse chives and tomatoes in the middle of winter. Hothouse vegetables are expensive, and they aren't necessarily all that nutritious. Then I walk back. I cross the southern end of Wangfujing,* turn back in here when I see the traffic lights, and come straight home. I never go into the shops. Wangfujing is no place for us Beijing people to do our shopping. And when you get to my age there isn't much that you want to buy.

In the afternoon? I walk to Tian'anmen and stand under the gate tower watching the traffic. Then I come back. Those are my two daily walks.

I'm from Hebei. I left there when I was eighteen to be an apprentice. I started in the Salt Bank, which was a Chinese bank. When Xuantong, the last Qing emperor, pawned his treasures for silver, the Salt Bank was involved. Later on I worked in the Huifeng Bank and the Banque

* Beijing's best-known shopping street.

de l'Orient et d'Indochine. That was when I learned English. The Huifeng was called the Hongkong and Shanghai Banking Corporation, Peking Branch in English. I didn't work in the Banque d'Indochine for long, so I didn't master French. I never made a proper study of it. I never worked in official banks, like the Central Bank, the Bank of China, the Communications Bank and the Agricultural Bank, or in a bloody Japanese bank like the Shyokin Bank.

A bank's a good place to be. "Get in the railways, the post office or a bank and your worries are over." People always want to move things, send letters and spend money. That's why in the old society those three jobs were iron rice-bowls – really secure. Being an official wasn't. They were always getting kicked out by the next lot.

I spent my whole life in banks, from when I was an apprentice to when I was deputy manager of the credit department. But I never worked in a bank that had the right to issue currency notes. After Liberation I worked for the Bank of China. But the Bank of China didn't have the right to issue banknotes either. It was only after I retired that it livened up and started printing banknotes – foreign exchange certificates.* They've got the same face value as ordinary money, but they can buy things that ordinary money can't. Take that bean vermicelli on the wall, for example. You can only get it with ordinary money if it's written down in your ration book. But with foreign exchange certificates you can get as much as you like.

Of course I've got some foreign exchange certificates. I've got all the denominations. I got someone to buy them for me. I keep them to look at.

When I was an apprentice I earned just a few silver dollars each month. When I'd paid for my board and lodging and was free in the evening I used to go out. I went to the theatre and sometimes down the "alleys". That was outside Qianmen Gate – Yangmeizhu, Crooked Alley, Hanjiatan, and all those places. The "alleys" were the brothels. In those days nobody was bothered about going there for a bit of fun.

My parents arranged my marriage back at home. We'd never met. After I went home and married her I brought her back to Beijing. In those days there was plenty of housing and not many people. If you wanted to buy or rent a house you could take your pick. Nowadays,

---

* Notes used in exchange for foreign currency, with a higher purchasing power than the equivalent Chinese currency.

even with all the big blocks they've put up, there's still a housing shortage – too many people. All the people in the streets are young.

I bought this place fifty years ago. In those days it was easy to get a small courtyard house. It's near East Jiaomin Lane, and it's very quiet, being at the end of a little alley. In those days all the big banks were in East Jiaomin Lane or in Qianmenwai Street: you could be there in next to no time by rickshaw. This isn't such a good place to live now. The new part of the Peking Hotel blocks out the sunlight. The original Peking Hotel was just the grey building in the middle. The red west wing and the yellow east wing were built after Liberation. I don't think the yellow wing is right for the Peking Hotel: it's too foreign. I've heard it's all very splendid inside, but terribly expensive. Anyhow, it's no place for Beijing people to stay. It makes a lot of money out of foreigners.

As for prices, that depends on how you look at them. In the old days everything was cheap except calico, grain and paraffin. A one-way tram ticket cost three coppers and the circular round the city five. Now it costs five cents just to get on a bus. But in 1947 and 1948 money wasn't worth anything. A sack of banknotes wouldn't buy you a sack of grain. You didn't bother counting low-denomination notes: you just sorted them out into their different values and weighed them. Later on accounts were kept in millions and tens of millions of yuan – rows and rows of noughts. In those days a 100-yuan note was worth less than a sheet of toilet paper. Well, no: people didn't take banknotes to the toilet with them. That's just a figure of speech. That's where the communists are better than the Kuomintang. You have to admit it. There's no inflation. Old Chiang didn't care whether he had the gold and foreign currency reserves or not, he just printed banknotes like a madman and did for the man and woman in the street.

But when we revalued the currency in 1955* prices went on rising. Later they came down a bit. A few years back there were pay increases and the last couple of years they've been issuing exchequer bonds. Things really are more expensive than they were. But the standard of living has gone up in the last few years, and everyone's got things like televisions, refrigerators and electric fans. That's good. It gets money circulating faster and the state is deliberately encouraging people to buy things.

* The currency was revalued at the rate of 10,000 old yuan for one new yuan.

There's no other country in the world with inflation as low as China's. What does the reputation of our currency depend on? Stability. You can put your money in the bank and forget about it. It won't depreciate much, and it won't shoot up either. Foreign currency's hopeless. It's always changing in value. Look how the Hongkong dollar collapsed a few months ago.

I was in the credit department before Liberation. I didn't make the loans: I used to work out the value of assets. That meant checking up on a factory's ability to repay before the bank made a loan, to make sure that they wouldn't default. We had specialists to estimate what potential the factory had for development. You had to keep your wits about you. I depended on a very sharp eye.

I was in charge of estimating the value of assets when a factory we'd made a loan to went bust. I'd have to work out what their buildings, machinery, raw materials and so on were worth and apply for an indemnity. When the case came up the capitalists would try to get out of their obligations and talk all sorts of nonsense. Then I'd bring out our assessment of what it was all worth, and tell them what percentage was owed to the bank. I didn't appear in court: the bank had lawyers.

In the last years before Liberation the bank simply stopped making loans. Things were in such a mess that no factory stood a chance.

Chiang Kaishek couldn't get at us as we were a foreign bank. After Liberation we went in with the Bank of China, and I suppose you could say that I joined the revolution. I was treated as a senior official and kept a good salary. The Bank of China specializes in foreign exchange dealing and doesn't make loans. Later on it also went in for foreign currency credits, but there was never any bankruptcy work. All I had to do was supervise the removal of money from the vaults: it was very easy. Goes without saying – if the state's prepared to lend you money you can be sure it won't let you go bust. The factories and the bank both belong to the state.

I used to collect coins from every dynasty, and I had quite a collection. I started when I was a boy, and I loved it. During the Cultural Revolution I handed the whole lot in. Nobody told me to, but I was scared. Even the shop signs in Wangfujing were smashed up because they were supposed to be part of the "four olds".* The

* Old culture, old ideology, old customs and old habits – a formulation much used during the Cultural Revolution.

smashing-up reached this alley, Duke Xia's Palace – that was feudal, you see. The Red Guards had their Red Guard logic. My neighbour to the east was raided. He used to have a shop selling silks and cottons. He liked paintings and calligraphy, and his place was full of them. Nearly all of his stuff was fake, and there were virtually no genuine pieces. But he had one Ming dynasty painting by Qiu Ying that was the real thing. People from the city's Cultural Relics Bureau had wanted to buy it, but he wasn't selling. The old woman from the street committee brought a whole mob of Red Guards in to raid his place, and they burned all his pictures, including the Qiu Ying. It was torture for him. He kept saying, "Don't burn it, don't burn it, I'll give it to the state." But the Red Guards paid not a blind bit of notice. They just beat him up. "What would the state want with that 'four old' of yours?" the old woman from the street committee asked. That's why I took the initiative in giving my collection to the state. A few years ago when old wrongs were being righted they paid me some compensation.

But I didn't want the money: I want my old coins. I know what they'd fetch on the black market, but I'd never do that. I never once did any foreign-currency fiddles when I worked in a foreign-owned bank. Wouldn't it have been enough if I'd left them to the state on my death? But let me have them now. I do miss my old coins.

My wife died eleven years ago. I've got three children but no grandsons of our line. My eldest girl's a cadre – she and her husband are both quite high-ranking. She was a student when Beijing was first liberated, and she joined the underground Communist Party. None of us knew anything about it. Now she's the secretary of her Party committee. She can talk and she's capable – not much like one of our family. During the Cultural Revolution she got viciously beaten up. She always comes to see me at holidays and the New Year with her children and some presents: she's a good daughter.

My second child is a son, and he's very good to me too, but he's too far away. He graduated just when the Cultural Revolution came along, and he had to spend years and years on a state farm in Yunnan. The army had to be matchmaker for him – he married a painter's daughter. Both of them were well into their thirties when they had their child, a girl. He cares a lot about me. He says pork fat isn't good for old people, and often gets people to bring me big containers of Yunnan rapeseed oil. It's got a peculiar taste – I prefer peanut oil, but I only get 250 grammes of that a month.

My youngest, a daughter, graduated from senior middle school and then had to spend ten years in the countryside before she was allowed to come back because of our family difficulties. She married late. She and her husband are both primary-school teachers, and they haven't got a place of their own. They borrowed a room from a colleague to get married, and now she's had to come back to my place to live with the baby. It's a boy. But none of them gave me a grandson of my own name. I've only got granddaughters, and grandsons that belong to other families.

Apart from my little strolls every day I go out for a meal with some friends every Friday. We're all retired. When the bill comes we split it equally. There are so many restaurants and so many different styles of cooking in Beijing. This week we're going to the Laijinyu Pavilion in Zhongshan Park to have steamed buns with dried cabbage stuffing. The Laijinyu still looks the same, but the fillings aren't what they used to be. The dried cabbage isn't fresh enough, and they're too greasy.

Eating out's expensive these days, and you have to know the right people. I can't take queuing for an empty table. Last time we got someone to fix us up with a private room at the Hongbinlou, so we could take our time over the meal. It was very comfortable. We usually get someone to put in a word for us beforehand. If you do that you can usually get your meal a bit cheaper. There are some dishes you can only get by using contacts, like the hot bamboo shoots at Makai's and "Buddha jumping over the wall" at the Zhensuzhai vegetarian restaurant. They're perfectly ordinary, traditional dishes, but the restaurants can't be bothered to put them on the menu as they're too much trouble. A couple of years back restaurants were still really bureaucratic. Things have got a bit better now, but they're only interested in serving the dishes they make a big profit on.

We all got to know each other on our strolls. We used to do all sorts of jobs before – a doctor, a gardener, a professor, a worker. But we don't ask each other where we live. We get on all right. Even when we make friends we don't visit each other at home. We just meet every Friday for our meal. If someone fails to turn up and we think he might be sick we'll arrange for a message to be sent to him. Whoever sees him will tell him where we're eating the next week. If he still doesn't come the time after that we reckon he's probably passed on. But nobody says so in as many words.

Next week we're going to the Donglaishun to eat mutton hotpot. If we don't go now it won't be on the menu any longer: the weather's getting too hot. We're not like you, we have to have it now. We can't be sure we'll last out till next winter.

3

WAYS UP

Newly-weds

China's biggest industrial city, Shanghai.

A triangular street park where Huaihai, Fuxing and Urumchi Roads meet. This is in the former French Concession, what Shanghai people call the top quarter; the much larger and more crowded slums are called the bottom quarter.

Young Feng and his bride, who will not let us reveal her name. Today is the first day of their honeymoon trip. We start talking to her in a tourist coach that purports to be "air-conditioned". The air-conditioning has not been turned on.

How much folding money you going to make out of interviewing us? If we talk we'll be helping you earn more.

Why did you pick us out of all the couples getting married? I'll bet it was because we were laying on such a good meal. The better the spread the more people respect you. And we're from the top quarter, so we really had to do things in style.

I went to technical college, and after that I became a factory worker. Of course, we technical-school graduates are graded higher than other workers. He's a middle-school teacher in a very high-class school. Only good students can pass the exams to get into it. He was assigned to teaching after he graduated from senior middle and only went to normal college later. (*"It was an advanced training course for teachers run by the city district,"* her husband interjects.)

I went to an ordinary middle school, not a key one, but the best one around where we used to live. It was quite something for us to get into technical college – hardly anyone got to university. I graduated in 1982, so I've been working just two years and we've been going steady all that time. He's twenty-eight and I'm twenty-two.

I reckon that everything's possible in this world if you really set your mind to it. I was determined to find myself a capable husband with social standing, and I did. The top quarter is at the top of the social ladder. You can swap ten square metres of living space here for fifteen anywhere else. He picks everything up very quickly. The Czech-style furniture he's made himself is fantastic. He's a terrific cook, and he's got his own room.

Me? I didn't have any boyfriends before him. *(She looks at her husband.)* He didn't have any other girlfriends either. We've always seen eye to eye. If the person who introduced us hadn't made him sound okay I'd never have started going out with him.

We've spent over 4000 yuan on setting up house. We've got two complete sets – a complete set of furniture, and a complete set of electrical equipment. We haven't had to make do like other girls at work, borrowing a TV and an electric fan for the wedding and giving them back afterwards. We've got a wardrobe, a chest of drawers, a cabinet, armchairs, a desk, a spring bed that cost 435 yuan, a TV, a washing machine, a refrigerator, an electric fan, a radio cassette, a reading light with a dimmer switch and a crystal chandelier. We can fit it all in our room. It's big – nine and a half square metres. You could fit even more in there. We want to buy ourselves an extending dining table and a pair of chromium-plated tubular steel chairs but we haven't been able to find anything we really like yet. The money's put away ready for when we do.

The wedding banquet cost another thousand. Ten tables at ninety yuan a table – that's the best you can get, apart from 100 a table – and the drinks on top of that. We could never have done it all out of our earnings: both families had to help.

We'd got our own savings as well. I've only spent ten yuan a month on my food in all the time I've been in the factory. It's enough as long as I don't choose more expensive dishes with a lot of oil in them. I grab something for breakfast, have green vegetables and rice for lunch, and pickled vegetables with reboiled rice for supper. That's the way I've always eaten. It's the same for everyone – it's nothing. No, I don't mind talking about it. *(She looks at her husband.)*

Of course the wedding was an even split. My family invited fifty guests and so did his family. But only ninety-eight actually turned up. Some of my relations and my family's friends aren't respectable enough to be shown off in public, so we didn't invite them.

The best day to get married on is a double even – an even day of the month in the Chinese and the modern calendar. We had to get married on an odd day, but it still ought to be lucky. We couldn't get a restaurant for the 2nd or the 4th even though we booked three months in advance. So we got married on 1 October – National Day. It ought to be lucky anyway having both celebrations together.

The banquet didn't set us back all that much. Everyone gave us presents: fifty yuan each from members of our families and about thirty each from friends. People who didn't give us enough didn't get invited. A lot of the presents were no use at all. We got nine dolls and thirty-two quilt covers. Doesn't matter. We can give them to other friends when they get married. Some people gave us things they'd been given when they got married. All in all our ten tables made quite a few yuan for us. You can always make something with a banquet. That's why you invite them three months in advance.

We're only going to Suzhou for the day. That way people will say I'm a good housekeeper. Isn't that right? You can only save money by watching what you eat. Money doesn't fall out of the sky and you can't start picking people's pockets.

If it's for a really stylish wedding, you don't notice that you're doing without. Every time I went to see him I passed all the grand shops in the Huaihai Road and looked in the windows but I never bought anything. He's just the same. Everyone in my family likes him. He never came to visit us empty-handed.

Shanghai people can tell who's got class just by seeing them walk along the street. The ones we hate most are the people from north of the Yangtse. They all do low-class jobs, coolie labour, working in bath-houses, hairdressing and garbage disposal. Even if the kids don't have jobs like that, their parents do. That's why you can't marry a north-banker. Northbankers are disgusting – they're lazy, they're dirty and they're uneducated. The best thing is for northbankers to marry each other. And you can't have a Ningbo man as your boyfriend, but it's all right for a Ningbo woman to go steady with a man from our top quarter. It's because . . . because Ningbo mothers-in-law are all real terrors. (*"My family came from Ningbo originally," her husband interrupts.*) Yes, but his mother died a long time ago. His father worked in a bank from before Liberation and had a very high position, but he's passed on as well. He's got relations in the US too. They haven't come back yet, but it'll be good when they do because they can bring us presents and take us into the Friendship Store and to the supermarket in the Jinjiang Hotel. We Chinese can't get in there unless someone takes us. When my relations come back I don't just want a look round, I want to buy things. Of course his relations are mine too.

The fashion now is to have a honeymoon trip and a wedding banquet. If you only had one, it'd be a lousy, cheap wedding.

We invited our friends to see our place. We all like to have a look at each other's places so we can see who's doing things in most style. For the first few weeks we'll have to make up a bed on the floor and sleep there – that's what we did last night. That's because we've got sixteen quilts and four blankets on the bed, and it'd be too much trouble moving it all on and off the bed every day. Besides, if you're not careful you can mess them up. Then friends would say I can't run a home. *("In fact only four of the quilts have been made up: the others are just quilted fillings with the covers folded over them," her husband explains.)* That's what everyone does. What's the point in sewing them up when you're going to give them to your friends later?

All the girls I know got married like us. Still . . . there was something a bit . . . shall we tell them? *(When she consults her husband he nods and smiles.)* Yes, there is something a bit different about us. I used to live in Zhabei, which made me a bit common. You could say I came from the wrong side of the tracks. But now I'm from the best part of town. Not one in a hundred girls would be able to marry into a good neighbourhood like ours. People in the bad districts are dead jealous of the likes of us.

There's nothing wrong with doing things in style when you get married. It's the only moment of glory we'll have in our whole lives.

Makes no difference whether we have a girl or a boy. We people from the best part of town aren't too bothered about having a son. If we have a daughter she can marry into the best part of the best part of town, where the top people live . . .

In Suzhou her husband answered some of the questions we put to him.

My father was dead against our marriage. He didn't want me marrying a girl from the bad part of town. That's why we waited until after he passed away.

Her father is a worker in a transport co-operative. Or you can put it more bluntly and say he pedals a pedicab.

Because she's beautiful, and a bit shorter than I am.

Diploma

Li Xiaochang. Born in 1949 – the year of the establishment of the People's Republic of China.

I need a university qualification to be really secure in my job though I've been doing it for the last four years. Our posts are going to be graded, and without qualifications we'll be nowhere. There are several ways to get them: the television university, or a correspondence course, or, if your unit agrees, you can follow in-service training courses laid on by the university. I've been doing a course, then sitting an exam, then doing another course, then sitting another examination. I need to do nine courses to get a diploma equivalent to a university degree. So far I've done four. Really I'm too old for exams now. I have to learn the subject up and then sit the examination straight away, otherwise I'll forget it all.

In 1966 I was in the first year of senior middle school. I hadn't started thinking what university I'd try for or what I'd study. I played volleyball. I was in a special school for coaching amateur sportsmen and sportswomen. I never took it easy, in fact, I pushed myself really hard.

I was learning oil painting too. As far as I was concerned, volleyball was a sort of duty, but painting was my pleasure. I couldn't decide whether to take it up professionally. My family wanted me to go to art school, but I liked music and other things too. In fact, though I feel a bit embarrassed to say so now, dancing was what I liked best. But what everyone seemed to agree was that whatever I did in the end, I should get a university degree first.

It was early in the summer of that year that I first learned to swear. The first time I heard one of my girlfriends swear, I was astonished, it was so unlike her. The first time I swore, I felt a little faint, then I

[55]

thought my friend must have felt that way too, although she didn't show it. The day before I had been criticized by the "advanced elements" in my school for dressing in a weird bourgeois way – wearing a frock. Next day, I wore trousers and joined a Red Guard organization – the first one in the school. We just called it "the Red Guards", but later, to distinguish ourselves from other organizations, we had to add something to our name. I remember we met on the school playing field and spent a whole evening arguing whether we should call ourselves "The Red Guards of Mao Zedong Thought" or "Mao Zedongism Red Guards". Everybody went up to the microphone to put their point of view. I didn't say all that much, just listened to what the others said.

Of course I took part in the movement to search people's homes and confiscate things. Even today I don't know who some of our targets were. The call would come and we'd get together, stop a truck in the street, and scramble aboard. Off we'd go to ransack someone's house. Sometimes we didn't know what we were up to, or what we were confiscating, or even who we were with. We caught the members of street gangs too, like the "Nine Dragons and a Phoenix". They sounded frightening, but when we caught them, we beat them until they begged us "Red Guard ladies" for mercy. Of course I don't like talking about those things now. It's something I'm rather ashamed of. It's funny though, when I do talk about it, I remember all sorts of other things. I remember cutting off girls' plaits; giving out leaflets; confiscating leaflets from other groups; endless activities and meetings. I went on the great journeys to "exchange revolutionary experience" as well. That was the first chance I'd ever had to go a long way from home – it didn't seem far then. Trains would be full of people in khaki wearing red armbands. If all the seats were taken, they'd squeeze under the seats; if it was full there, they'd sit in luggage racks. Sometimes the luggage racks couldn't hold the weight and they'd fall down. You'd get a dozen or more people squatting in the little space between two carriages. You just can't imagine it. There was nothing to drink, and no way of going to the lavatory. Everyone would be playing the mouth-organ or singing.

After these mad, obsessive days, many of us began to drop out. We cooked at home and went out to buy vegetables. I'd never done any cooking before then. Then there was the business of making boy-friends. In 1968, the street fashion for young people in Beijing was a blue outfit, black slip-on shoes and a surgical mask hung around your neck with only the tape showing. The girls wore their hair in short bunches. If you went out looking like that, boys dressed in the same way would come over and chat with you. The street gangs called this "hunting the birds". The older Red Guards had begun to get on quite well with the street gangs. We found we could understand them now. Not long ago I met up with a classmate from middle school, and when we started talking about all that she asked me how many boys I'd slept with back then. I told her I hadn't slept with a single one. She was very surprised and told me that a lot of stories had gone around about me. When she thought about it a bit, she could see she'd jumped to conclusions because we had all been brought up so strictly. In fact, I didn't know the first thing about sex then. That was something I learned about later.

Although our school life had in fact finished earlier, it formally ended in the summer of 1968. A lot of us went down to the countryside. I was sent to Inner Mongolia to live among the herdsmen. We set off playing mouth-organs and singing, but I did feel it was a long way from home.

We educated youth had a Mongolian yurt to ourselves. At the start, life seemed very fresh and full. I learned to ride a horse and developed a good seat – much more difficult than just hanging on for dear life. At first, I felt rather sick and giddy, and chafed between the legs. I learned to drink tea with milk in it, to speak a bit of Mongolian and to milk. I began to appreciate the great outdoors. Riding slowly across the great grasslands was beautiful. If now I have a sense of wonder, or of powerful, indefinable nostalgia, if I have an understanding for melancholy and quietness, it all goes back to those days.

Then something happened. I got on very well with the herdsmen and their families. I often used to go to visit them and to help them out. They looked after us and used to ask us over. But one evening the son in a family I knew very well raped me. The whole family was there and they helped him. The same thing happened to several of the other girls from the city who went to Inner Mongolia. Some of them settled down there. Later, some educated youth asked me to do self-criticism. Yes, that's right, self-criticism! They said I'd deliberately seduced a young herdsman from a good class background, because my father hadn't yet been freed. There was no question of bringing a case against the boy. They were national minorities, and this was their custom. This is something I've never told my parents about.

Later when they started recruiting workers, I went to work in a small chemical factory. I worked there for five years and it was there I met my husband. He's from a worker's family in the countryside. He was very good to me – helped me to wash my clothes, gave me eggs, all that sort of thing. That's how we got together. Just before we got married, I told him about what had happened to me. He was very upset: to my surprise, it was almost too much for him. We nearly called it off. But I still felt his kindness was one of the best things that ever happened to me. I'd never known anything like it. I learned to make clothes and pickles, to curl my own hair and to cut my husband's, and to gossip with the other girls at work. I found out how to pull strings with people who worked in shops when we needed things that weren't easy to buy. I managed to get hold of some timber, and I cooked special things for a carpenter so that he'd make us furniture. In other words, I learned everything that a housewife should know, and I made a good job of it. We got together a cosy home, and then I had a little boy.

In 1977, the universities started to organize entrance examinations again. Lots of young people took up their studies once more, learning up maths, physics and chemistry. Everyone you met asked you, "Are you taking the exams? What subject are you going for?" I didn't take them. I wanted to go to university. I had my home and my child. And yet, at the same time, I did have a feeling that there must be something else. I had adjusted my life and I felt satisfied, but I was still able and ambitious, and I knew I couldn't go on living in that little town for ever. I wanted to get back to Beijing, the centre of politics and culture – the town I knew so well.

It seemed like a wild dream. First, getting my residence permit transferred to Beijing was really going to be tough. I didn't think that just sticking a little advertisement on one of the telegraph poles in Beijing could ever work. And, what's more, it wasn't just me, there was my husband. The residence permit of the child normally goes with the mother's. But at the same time, I knew by then it's no use worrying too much, you just have to take your chance wherever you see it.

To transfer your residence permit, you have to move on several fronts at once. There's the bureau that handles transfers to and from the city you're in, there's the unit in Beijing that you want to work for, and most difficult of all, the office in charge of entry to the city you want to go to. To start with you've got to find somebody who wants to exchange with you. Only a few people want to leave Beijing. I found some. They were working in the track-maintenance department of the Railway Ministry. Their household registration was with the Railway Ministry, which meant it counted as Beijing, but they were actually moving around all the time. There were two of them who'd originally come from the town I worked in. They'd reached an age when they felt they'd like to go home. They lived in workers' shacks in the suburbs. I went to see them on my bicycle. There was one of those big winds you get in spring in Beijing, and I had to pedal against it the whole way. When I got there and talked to them I found that a lot of them wanted to go home. I felt quite sorry for them, but I couldn't tell all of them about the advertisements by people who wanted to swap residence with them. If I had, there would be no one left to maintain the track. Anyway, there might have been a fight over who'd get to leave.

My two contacts made a couple of conditions. One of them wanted me to find him a job, a good job in his home town. The other one wanted somewhere to live. Their bargaining position was so strong because they were in Beijing. Even when I managed all this the transfer people wouldn't let them go. So I had to think up some way to get round this new problem. Straightforward presents might not have done the trick. It's no good just spending a lot of money, you've got to use your eyes and ask around to find out what they need. A son-in-law of this official was soon going to be demobbed from the army. He'd gone into the army from the countryside, but his wife was from the city. Naturally, he wanted to be transferred to the city. This wasn't at all easy to fix, and I had to use the influence of old friends of my parents to do it. It was no use going to my father or my mother, they could never have managed anything like that — they'd have been too scared to open their mouths. Anyway I set it all up and finally I succeeded. My residence permit was transferred to Beijing along with my husband's and my son's. It took me everything I'd learned in my ten tough years in the big world and it showed me just how competent I could be.

Now I'm working on archival materials about ancient buildings. It's a job I wanted and got myself. The educated youth of my generation who've come back to the cities have something in common. When we get a job we don't mind working hard, and we're good at getting along with our colleagues. We're easy-going and pretty flexible. At first the boss here didn't want a woman working under him, so I was always being sent off to do odd jobs, things which I wasn't really supposed to do. But in the end, he kept me on.

I'm very interested in my work, although I never expected to make a career out of anything like this. It needs imagination and a feeling for history, and it's pretty steady too. Just over a year ago, they began to talk about introducing grades. During the ten years of chaos,* lots of young people lost their opportunity to study, but now some of us have landed good jobs and worked so hard we've more or less made ourselves into specialists. Our country's got to develop. It needs standards, and it needs educated people. The scientific research institutes want people with university qualifications. So are we all done for? Well, there's no point in complaining that you've been thrown on the scrap heap and missed all your chances. I don't think it's quite like that. These days you need a junior middle-school certificate even to work in a factory. And to tell the truth, I'm not sure I could pass those exams now.

It is difficult to be disciplined about your time. Sometimes I get really fed up with studying. I go through things again and again and I still can't remember them after all these years. Goodness knows why: last time I took an English test, I didn't pass it. Only about 200 passed out of several thousand candidates. I'll take it again next year, and I'll finish with it when I pass it. Sometimes I lose confidence and feel very frustrated. Going back to the start over and over again makes the whole thing seem like an endless circle. And what practical value is this diploma going to have anyway? When they introduce grading and a new wage scale I don't think it will really count as a proper university degree. But we'll cross that bridge when we come to it. I despair about every single exam. Some of the courses are okay. Reading about Chinese history makes me think a lot and look at my own past. I particularly like contemporary history, but when it comes to the exam, you're supposed to reproduce a few pages and that's that. It doesn't matter how much you feel about it.

My younger brother got himself into university and graduated properly. He studied Chinese too. He often tells me that I'm working myself to death quite pointlessly. According to him, there's no need to work hard. You shouldn't put your feelings into your course-work. The textbooks are all old hat anyway, and you just have to learn them off by heart, pass the exams, then forget them. I can't be that frivolous and cynical about it all. I don't want to grumble to him about my

---

* 1966–76: the Cultural Revolution.

problems with my courses either. What's the use? We are not the same generation, he's eight years younger.

We do all grumble though. We moan about the classes and the exams, about our children being sick, about having to go to buy coal or to fetch milk. We're rushed off our feet all day long and yet we don't seem to get anything done. When I went to get the certificate for the first course, the room was full of my fellow students. They were all the same generation as I am, so they are all parents. Yet there they all were, sitting at their tables, crying. Yes, they were all in tears.

Second Try

In the last ten years the success rate of candidates taking the college and university entrance examinations in China has ranged from one in over 20 to one in 7.8. Millions of final-year high-school students have to face the fact that there aren't enough places in the colleges and universities.

Fu Yawen is a quiet, cultured girl of eighteen. She failed this year's college entrance exams. We met her on a day when the maple leaves were red.

I told my mother: paradise is full, and I'll never pass the entrance exams. I'll get a job, and that's that. But she wasn't having it. There was nothing I could do about it, nothing at all. They've laid down over a dozen rules for me. I've got to be on time for my revision classes. No novels, no TV, no movies. I told them that was making life impossible, but they just told me, "Stick out this rough spell because life'll be fine once you've got into college."

I reckon they've turned me into an old woman before my time. They're always going on about people who don't study being worse than dirt, worse than animals. That's what my old man says.

My marks were 52 below the minimum needed to get in, and I can't believe I've got a hope for next year either. But they've told me that even if I fail again next year I'll have to go on trying. "Don't worry," they say, "we can afford to keep you." They even go on about how taking the exams is for myself, not for them, because they've got pensions to look forward to and won't need me to support them. It all really gets me down.

With such lousy marks on my transcript I couldn't get into a good cramming class – only into one that's got kids with really hopeless scores in it. We're all pretty down about it. One of the boys complained in class, "What crimes have we committed? Why've we got to work even harder than adults?" "Your crime was failing the college entrance exams," the teacher said, "and that's serious. It isn't easy for your parents to find the money to send you to this class. You have to feel sorry for them." He had us all in tears. But who feels sorry for us?

I feel I'm in an impossible situation. My class is run by the Teachers' College Middle School. We're only allowed to borrow textbooks from the school library. But I'm crazy about literature and I'd love to be an author. My mother said that if I wrote a book she'd let me off taking the entrance exams. It's really getting me down – not being able to read any literature is murder, and I can only write in my dreams.

My father's such a snob. Whenever a visitor asks what I'm doing he says I'm still in senior middle school. He's horrible. Once he even brought home a booklet about the ferocious drive against criminals and made me read it as a lesson in what happens to people who won't study. Maybe there weren't any university students in it, but some students are terrible, aren't they? In this building alone a couple of girl students got pregnant and had to come home for abortions on the quiet. What a disgrace – and they'll never be able to get married. Well, I didn't like to say too much, so I just said to him, "Those girls downstairs are no better than they ought to be. They're both . . . you know, and they're still at university." My father gave me an earful, and he even said . . . he said he'd be quite happy for me to be like them just as long as I get to university. I don't feel like a human being any longer.

It wasn't all my fault that I failed this year. When I was taking the exams they were both waiting for me outside the examination hall, and that really panicked me. I hate Sundays now. Every Sunday they're both at home watching me study – it gives me the creeps. They even give me queen-bee jelly and then tell me they'll make me throw it all up if I fail this time. It makes the pressure even worse – it's driving me crazy.

That's why I really wish I were dead. If only I could kill myself. But I'm an only child, and I'd hate to hurt my parents that much. It would be great if some murderer bumped me off. The way I feel now I'd be happy to die in a road accident.

Young people age too fast. I used to think about my ideals, but I don't any more. When you've bashed your head against a brick wall till it's cut and bleeding you can't take any more.

I once read a story about how Beijing gets its mutton. It's not trucked in: the shepherds bring the sheep in on foot, carrying their own meat into Beijing. I've never been to Beijing, and my mother says I can go there for a visit if I get into university next year, but I'm not interested. I feel I'm a sheep carrying my own meat along the road, and I'm dead beat.

Hitting the Jackpot

Lotteries were introduced in September 1984 in a variety of forms and under many different names. A year earlier they had still been coming under attack in the press.

The China Martial Arts Fund Lottery gave out the biggest prizes. Most of the people in the long queue for tickets were young and middle-aged men, but there were also old people and children.

Zhou Tianxiao. Ex-soldier. Thirty-two.

You never can tell: I might hit lucky. The first prize is a full set of furniture, a fridge, a radio cassette, a colour television, a washing machine and a motorbike – everything except a wife, and I've got one of those already. I don't need the furniture: I'd sell it. Nobody's got room for all that, everything for the living room, bedroom and dining room. Oh yes, and there's a six-day trip to Shenzhen and Shataukok. That's in Hongkong – you know, step outside and you're in the bright lights. Only an idiot would defect after winning that lot. You'd have everything – you'd be more Hongkong than the Hongkongers.

I don't know what the odds really are either – probably hundreds of thousands to one. But who cares? If you ask me, everything depends on luck, except the guarantee you'll go on being flat broke. You don't even necessarily get topped for murder – some people get a death sentence with a two-year suspension, right?

If I won I'd ask all the guys I was with at school and in the army and all my other pals. I'd show them who'd made it. Never mind that they've got fancy titles or are in research institutes now – that won't do them any good then. But as of now I'm the only one who's still broke. I've got no diploma, I'm out of the forces, and I'm just a worker. But when I hit the jackpot, I'll show them.

I was lucky to start with. When the Cultural Revolution came along

[65]

my old man was a target. You'd have thought that'd be curtains for me, but some of his pals managed all right. One of them commanded a regiment in the army. My old man got me into the army in the spring of '69. I didn't care that I was sent away from Beijing and only getting six yuan a month – it beat being sent to the countryside hands down. None of the other guys did as well as me then – they were all packed off to the countryside. But hell, they're the ones who've got it made now.

I did seven years in the forces, and luck was against me. No promotion, and no military academy either. Of course there was a reason. My dad's old pal got me to Hubei, dumped me in a mountain valley in Dangyang, and made himself scarce. He went off to "support the left" as Party secretary in an arms factory. So there I was, the only soldier from Beijing in my whole company. There was nobody I could turn to. It was a bloody disaster. The company commander was one of your Shandong heavies, and did he hate me! He was going to reform us "petty bourgeois" if it was the last thing he did. We were just the infantry, with no fancy modern equipment. The only cushy jobs were in the company office and the cookhouse. You wouldn't know what it's like in a company. The CO was practically an emperor, so all the easy jobs went to his Shandongers. But when we had training marches of over fifty kilometres a day he put us in the cookhouse squad and gave his buddies a rest. I even had to dig the bloody field kitchens. Then when the exercises were over we were sent back to our own squads for fatigue duties.

I don't think he was trying to get at the regimental commander by giving me a bad time. A piddling little company commander couldn't have had any quarrel with a regimental commander. He just had it in for city boys. Funny place, the army. None of the guys from the country wanted out: they were crazy for promotion. But when they'd done their time they were told to go home and remake the world. It was just the opposite with me. I knew I was getting nowhere and I was dying to get back to Beijing, but they wouldn't let us go. They had to make us put in an extra period of service – "veterans helping the rookies" they called it. So in 1973 I got my promotion – they made me a damned "wolfer" – that's the number two in a squad. On parade you're right at the end of the line, what they call the wolf-hunter.

I didn't get out till 1976. In 1977 they brought back university entrance and all the kids I'd been at school with got in. I hadn't got a hope. I wouldn't even have passed middle-school entrance exams.

They'd had all the time in the world to study in factories or the countryside while I'd been slaving away in the mountains. I never so much as opened a book. I suppose I'm a bit to blame, too. I'm not cut out for studying on my own. So by pulling a few strings I got a job as a driver in a factory. I wasn't doing so badly in the first few years. I started as a grade-three worker as soon as I left the forces. But things got worse and worse. As soon as the others graduated from college they caught up with me, and from now on they'll get ahead of me, unless I hit the jackpot.

Our factory's working on a contract basis now. We drivers have targets for fuel consumption, quantity of goods moved and safety. But you don't get much money even if you bust a gut saving fuel and beating your quotas. The old saying's dead right: "Those who do mental work rule; those who do manual work are ruled."* The people in the office have got it all worked out. I want to earn more, but there's no way. People like me are too stupid to join the rulers – we can't see far ahead.

A few years back the factory was encouraging people to take exams and improve themselves. They wanted us truck-drivers to do the test for a car driver's licence, but I wouldn't. I reckoned I'd never get to drive a car even if I passed the tests because the factory only had a few cars. Was I wrong! All the new taxi companies in Beijing are recruiting drivers like crazy, but I've got no licence. If I'd got one I'd have gone ages ago. Driving a cab you can make six or seven hundred a month if you work hard. So I'd made two wrong moves in a row.

It doesn't matter whether fate's on your side or not. You've got to find the luck – you can't wait for luck to find you. When we were in the queue just now someone said, "Why do the men from the sticks always get the big prizes? They've got a secret: they don't sleep with their wives. If you sleep with your old woman your luck'll be out the next day. You'll lose at cards, and of course you won't hit the jackpot." I wasn't so sure about that. I hadn't had it off the night before, but I still got nothing, not even one of the smallest prizes. I'm not going to let my old woman touch the tickets I've bought today: women's hands stink. And I only buy lottery tickets from the windows where men are selling them: I won't buy them from women.

The best tickets to get are ones with a six or a five and a seven on them. You know the saying:

* A quotation from the fourth-century BC philosopher Mencius.

Double six will see you right;
Five and seven – out of sight.
But three will give your luck the blight.

Never, never buy a ticket with the number three in it. They won't let you pick and choose – you have to buy what they give you. So if I get a ticket with a three, I sell it to someone else.

They show the draw on TV, so everyone can see what's happening. The public notary's office sends someone along to supervise the draw. The big bronze bowl they use for it goes right back to the days of the Kuomintang. It had been stored away since 1949, and now it's back in use. It said in the papers that there've never been any quarrels about it since it was first used in 1929: it's completely fair.

Ever since buying my first batch of tickets I've tested my luck a whole lot of times, and every time it's proved I'm going to win a prize. Okay, I'll tell you how. Every day I pick a set of traffic lights – say the ones at the Xidan junction – and decide what colour they're going to be before I get there. The test is whether I guess it right. I've tried it several times. I pick red, they'll be red; and if I pick green they'll be green. That proves my luck's good. Once I guessed some lights would be red, but before I got to the intersection I saw they were green, so I drove slowly and gave them time to change. No, that wasn't cheating. I didn't turn the engine off. If my luck was out they wouldn't have changed – they'd have stayed green.

There's something wrong with the tickets for this lottery. Instead of saying "We hope you win," it says "Thank you for your contribution." That really turns me off. Nobody buys the tickets just to develop martial arts. If they did, they'd tear up their tickets the moment they bought them.

Yes, I'm a Party member. I joined when I was in the forces. There's nothing in the Party constitution banning lotteries, so stop trying to stir things up for us. I can't see anything much wrong with it.

No, I can't tell you my address. I'm being very kind telling you my name. If anyone came to see you to check up on me and accuse me of talking out of turn I'd have had it. But you can give me your address: when I win I'll ask you over to have a look. When I've won I won't care if they do check up on me, I just won't care.

4

STATES OF MARRIAGE

Virtuous Wife, Good Mother

When you open the front door with its placard reading FIVE-GOOD
FAMILY, *you see a certificate on the wall opposite bearing the
words in gold* VIRTUOUS WIFE, GOOD MOTHER. *That was why the
propaganda people took us to see her.*

It's been in all the papers. Why write any more about me?

I graduated from senior middle school in 1966, and the Cultural
Revolution came along before I'd finished. When those who'd left
school were sent to the countryside I didn't go with them because my
father was ill. Later on I was assigned to teach in a model primary
school – we were always getting foreign visitors. When I'd been there
for a year the Education Bureau transferred me to a junior middle
school because I'd been doing so well. I was the first in our group of
primary school teachers in the district to be promoted to junior middle
school.

Teaching's no problem – all you have to do is set your mind to it. I
was a class monitor all the time I was in middle school, and in senior
middle I got a gold award for excellent character and academic
achievement. If it hadn't been for the Cultural Revolution I'd have been
certain to go to university. There was a rule that if you had awards you
could get into university without having to take the exams.

My husband and I never did any courting – honestly! We registered
our marriage a week after we'd met. He was just out of the forces and a
worker in a building outfit. They'd been given a foreign-aid assignment
in Zambia, and he was selected. He wanted to get his private life fixed
up before he went, and someone introduced us. Seeing how he looked
really honest, I accepted him.

No, you can't say I didn't know anything about him. The person
who introduced us told me he was a Party member who'd been an

organization commissar. Any comrade who's good enough to be an organization cadre is politically reliable. Nothing special about our standard of living – it's what we've earned. He's still a worker, but we live all right, don't we?

He went off with the army as soon as we'd registered our marriage and been given the wedding certificates. He was away three years. We didn't have the wedding itself before he went because we hadn't got a room yet.

Those three years were a test for us. The main problem was that my family was against it. They thought I was still only a kid and I'd picked the wrong man. What did they have against him? His family was too poor. Of course I won in the end – we'd registered and got our wedding certificates. We were legally married whether we had the family ceremony or not.

We had our wedding after he came back in the winter of 1973. His leaders and mine all came to congratulate us and give us presents. The usual presents those days were busts of Chairman Mao. I was twenty-six and he was twenty-nine. We've never had a row.

I never really wanted to take the college entrance exams. Then in 1978 the school leadership got us all to put our names forward. They said they weren't going to hold us back: the more of us who passed, the better it would be for the school. So I put my name forward, crammed for six weeks, and passed. I already had two kids then.

Anybody over thirty was only allowed to take the exams for teacher-training colleges. As a Party member I was class monitor. In the third year I got ill and passed out in the classroom. It turned out to be a stomach tumour, and I had lost a lot of blood. I was taken straight to hospital for an emergency operation. A month later I forced myself to carry on with my studies.

I reckoned the chance for study was too good to miss. And my husband was looking after the kids all by himself. I usually only came back once a fortnight. So I couldn't let him down.

My instructors urged me to take the exams for graduate school, but I didn't. I was already thirty-four, so what was the point of more study? There was another reason too. I didn't want an even wider gap between us: he hadn't even finished junior middle school when he joined the army.

It's bad if the gap's too wide. For example, there's a definite difference in our tastes in music and art, I have to admit that. But what really matters? Now we've set up this family we have to preserve it. Besides, look at all the sacrifices he had to make to see me through college. Men comrades all like a game of cards and that, but he was stuck with looking after the kids. He still doesn't get any time for himself – it's all work for him.

We've got a duty to each other. Our differences? The less said about them the better. We've always treated each other with the greatest respect.

Of course some people have made suggestions, but my advice to him is to respect himself and respect me. I'm not going to be like those men who ditch their wives when they go up in the world.

I'm the head of our school now. With this change in my status I've got to show even more responsibility for the family. Besides, I know how much he's done to get me where I am today. I've also got some duties in the municipal Women's Federation and Political Consultative Conference. No, I'm not being modest. I haven't done anything worth talking about, only my duty.

We've got to do a lot more educating people. There have been two cases of divorce in our school this year.

Whirlpool

The editorial office of a literary journal. It is like many others all over the country: small, cramped and full of desks, chairs and heaps of manuscripts. The editor, a woman of thirty-six, is busily washing cups and making tea for the guests in this tiny space just as she might in her own kitchen. As she's about to go to the street committee office we agree to accompany her.

If you'd been any later you'd have found me gone.

The sooner I get this divorce business over with the better. Otherwise, I won't be able to settle down and do anything. This time, he's the one asking for the divorce. In the six months we've been separated I've suggested it many times but he's always refused. It almost drove me round the bend. I would go into these terrible rages but he wouldn't let me go. Not because he still wanted me. He's the head of his section and none of his colleagues is divorced. If he gets divorced he'll be different, and he's afraid of that. I know him. At one time he wouldn't let me go out to meetings, let alone to parties. He reckoned it was all wrong to mix in literary circles. But now he's started wearing a western suit and tie and going to the dance at his work unit every week.

We've agreed that the eldest child should go to him and the twins will stay with me. I don't want any of the furniture. It would remind me too much of the past. If I'm competent, I'll be able to earn more, but even if I can't, we'll manage. I'll stay with my parents. He'll keep our two rooms. Neither of us will ask the other for child support. There's no money to split up. We've only got fifty yuan in savings. Not surprising when you think we've got three children! Of course I'm getting a bad deal but I don't mind. My parents can still help me a bit. My mother's more or less bringing up the younger boys for me. I can bring in some extra money with my writing. Friends tell me that if I don't take anything it'll make him look very bad, so I'm going to take a small bed and the dining table. And I'll ask the street committee to hurry things along before he changes his mind again. He's wavering even now.

It's only with me that he's violent. He doesn't stop to think, his arm goes up and wham! He really does hit hard. The first time was before we left the countryside to move back to the city. I was standing in the doorway combing my hair when I said something which annoyed him. He slapped my face with such force that he knocked me into the courtyard.

The more I think about it the more bitter I feel. The last ten years have been terrible. I've gone without to give everything I could to him and the children. And what have I got to show for it?

When I started writing I couldn't spend the whole evening with him any more. He'd come and tear up what I'd been doing and then beat me up. To tell the truth, after I'd had the children, I changed. I lost interest in sex. Before that he'd use sex to patch things up after each beating. I was still fool enough to believe he really was sorry and that he'd change. In those days we still got on all right in that way, but not after we began to grow apart in spirit. When they'd just started to hold dances again a few years ago, I stood and watched one at my office before I went home. One of his colleagues saw me and mentioned it to him. When he got home from work next day, he didn't even bother to ask what had happened, he just began to beat me. I used to think that wife-beating was quite normal. When I came back to the city, I asked around a bit and discovered it happened to a lot of women, mostly workers.

I have analyzed him. He really took "learning from the poor and lower-middle peasants" to heart when we were sent to the countryside. He also accepted the idea that intellectuals were despicable and so he "reformed" himself completely.

When we met, I was still in senior middle school and he was a law student. I was going to all the universities to try to borrow dance costumes for a show we were putting on. No one would help us because they looked down on middle-school students. He was in charge of cultural activities at his university and he opened the wardrobe and let me choose. I met him again later during the Cultural Revolution, when I was going round various campuses with a gang of Red Guards from my school. He bought me lunch. At that time my mother was a target for criticism, and I couldn't understand why. She was such a good cadre, working long hours every day. Although my parents were both quite senior, we weren't terribly well off because there were so many of us kids. She kept house very frugally and looked after us well. I realize now that she had a great influence on me. When she was under fire I was a Red Guard "suitable for re-education". The parents of lots of other Red Guards were targets – we were all in the same boat. His family was in trouble as well. We were a bit puzzled about the Cultural Revolution. He said all we could do was to show our loyalty to Chairman Mao. He was good at drawing and did a woodcut of Chairman Mao in profile, wearing an army cap, against a background of green pines and a red sun. We made prints and put them up all over the place. Later we dropped out of the struggle. We got hold of a letter of introduction and a jeep and went all the way to Yunnan province, seeing the world and "promoting revolution". We were already together then. Later, when we were back in town, we had nothing to do, so getting married seemed a good idea. His father was an army officer but his grandfather was a real old peasant who longed for a great-grandson. Soon after the wedding, they started sending young city people to the villages or mountains. My husband graduated and was sent to a farm in Langfang, Hebei province. I followed him as a volunteer, but I couldn't get assigned to that farm so I went to teach at a primary school in a nearby village.

Politically he matured rather late, and he absorbed the ideas which were around at that time. I was too preoccupied with family life to bother about politics. I used to spend hours just gazing at our eldest son and was often late for work. I'm very fond of children so I never found them any trouble, and I got pregnant again. This time it was twins! I shared accommodation with some other young people from the city, but I had my own little room. After work we used to sing and chat and do embroidery together. I kept hens and gave him all the eggs to eat when he got leave to see me once a fortnight. Materially we had absolutely nothing, yet I didn't feel that life was hard. The peasants there couldn't even afford soy sauce. My mother sent me small parcels of lard or dried meat. What mattered was my own little family and the feeling between the two of us. That was when I got the urge to write. I had to rely on my mother to send me paper. I just wanted to record the good old days, the happy times when I was a child. He demanded to know why I was singing the praises of those seventeen black years before the Cultural Revolution.

I admired his brains then. Later he realized that, over big things at least, I was the one who got it right. If we'd done what he wanted, we might never have got back to Beijing. He admits that he was cut out to be an official. As soon as the new policy of treating educated people properly came in, he got a job with the Public Security Bureau in the county town. He was very well thought of there. No wonder! He was so careful about appearances. In our courting days in Beijing we used to go about arm in arm, but in the county town he wouldn't even walk down the street by my side. There was a plan afoot to make him deputy county head when suddenly they decided they wanted him in the prefectural Public Security Bureau. He didn't want to go but I urged him to. I thought the nearer we were to home, the better. Later on, after the fall of the Gang of Four, they completely reorganized the Bureau and wanted to move him to Beijing. At first he didn't want to go. He felt he fitted in well where he was and carried a lot of weight. In Beijing he'd be a small fish in a big pond. I told him that the only thing that mattered was going home. He's done all right out of it, hasn't he?

He started beating me when the eldest was four months old. There was no one I could appeal to. I did go to the head of the production team, but in the countryside wife-beating wasn't regarded as a serious issue. After he was transferred to the county town, his leadership did try to do something, but he didn't take any notice. No wonder. The man who told him off about it was a wife-beater himself.

Whenever the child had done the least little thing, my husband used to make him stand as a punishment. Once when I came home he was relaxing on the bed while my little boy – only eighteen months old – stood in the corner. He'd been there over an hour. When I rushed over, the child collapsed into my arms. My husband insisted that without strict discipline the child might grow up to be a criminal. He said I spoiled the boy, gave way to him. Well, what harm could it do? He was only a baby. I got hit whenever we quarrelled over the children.

After he was transferred to the prefecture, I moved out of education into the local Bureau for Creative Writing. Although he'd got me the job, he beat me because I had to travel about organizing writers' groups and talking to amateur writers. He does read a bit himself – seventeenth-century short stories. What notions they give him! He told me some tale about a woman whose husband was at death's door. She swore not to remarry before the earth over his grave was dry. Then as soon as he was buried, she began to fan the grave to dry it. He said that was the sort of wife I was. His head was full of feudal ideas! After the divorce I can put all this behind me and live in peace. He'll marry again very quickly. He couldn't live without a woman.

Sometimes when he beat me I wanted to walk out, but I didn't have anywhere to go. There were the children to think about, and my pupils, and I really wanted to get into the Party. If I'd left him, there would have been gossip, so I stayed. When we first came back to Beijing we had nowhere to live, so we stayed with my parents for a while. Once, he started hitting me in the middle of the night. I couldn't cry out because I didn't want my parents to hear. I went out into the street for a while, but I got frightened so I came back in. Working in the Security Bureau, my husband knew of a woman who'd rushed out at night after a row and been sexually assaulted. That's why he came out to look for me.

Over the past six months he's assumed that I'll come back sooner or later the way I always have. But I am absolutely determined to make a fresh start. He can't face this. He came to the office, forced me into a corner and started to stroke my face, asking if I was still serious. I was so furious, I shouted at him. What would my colleagues have thought if they'd seen?

We look at things so differently. He always follows the line in today's newspapers. But when it's changed tomorrow, that will be the only correct line. He doesn't think things out for himself. There's a reason why he started pushing for a divorce. He had to go on a business trip with his boss. The boss saw him moping all day long and advised him to get the divorce sorted out quickly so that it wouldn't interfere with his work. My husband sat down on the spot and wrote me a letter asking for a divorce. The next step was to get a reference from his office, but his boss was quite upset when he asked for it and refused it. "I didn't mean that you should split up," he explained. "I just wanted you to get your family problems sorted out and stop looking so miserable." My husband came round to tell me he'd changed his mind. But I still have that letter. I just want to make a clean break. He asked me if we might marry each other again one day if he agrees to the divorce now. I blew up. "We are meant to be talking about a divorce," I said. "How can we start talking about remarriage?" I was nearly out of my mind. "If you won't agree to an amicable arrangement, we'll fight it out in court. I'll bring out all the dirty linen piece by piece. I don't care what people think. I just want a divorce! A divorce! A divorce!" He said as I was so unbalanced it might be better to let me have my way. So at the moment he has reluctantly agreed, but if there's any delay he'll probably change his mind again.

He's quite pathetic really. When I went to Shanghai on a business trip I didn't buy anything for myself, just an expensive suit for him. It was such good material, but whenever he went out he covered it with a blue cotton jacket so as not to look conspicuous. I told him he was spoiling the nap doing that, but he took no notice. Then, the other day, he wore the suit without an overjacket to go to the neighbourhood office about the divorce. His colleagues joked that he was fixing up his divorce dressed like a bridegroom. He claimed that he was wearing it for sentimental reasons. Very caring all of a sudden, but what about the last ten years? I practically used to spoon-feed him. He might do his own laundry, but never mine or the children's. When I decided to get a qualification at night school, he never even made the evening meal, not once! He wouldn't help. He said one graduate in the family was enough. I gritted my teeth and stuck out four hard years. Only once, on the very last evening, when it was raining, did he go to meet me with an umbrella, and then he missed me! Just once in four years! I was already earning forty-nine yuan a month so the diploma won't mean an automatic rise. In fact it's no use at all. What's more I've still got the English exam to take this year. There's no way I'll pass, because I never get the time to learn vocabulary.

In the nursery my two little boys used to go to, all they taught them was the song about the good soldier Lei Feng.* I used my connections to get them into a proper kindergarten "through the back door". It was a long way so we had to deliver them each week using a little sidecar hooked up to a bicycle. But he wouldn't take them. He even said it served me right having to do it. I'd brought the trouble upon myself. So I didn't complain, however tired I felt. Do you know when I had the children he said that it was as easy for a woman to give birth as it is to fart!

He won't miss me. Once we're divorced his position should make it very easy for him to find a new wife. He doesn't have any close friends but he's always polite to his colleagues and they're on good terms. That's because they're outsiders. He's even pleasanter to me now because I've become an outsider.

* Lei Feng (1940–62) was a soldier in the People's Liberation Army held up as a model for people to follow.

When we decided to go to the street committee office, he cried. I couldn't look at him. I was beginning to waver. Afterwards I told a divorced woman writer how I'd felt. She said she'd felt sorry for her husband when they were getting divorced. But she warned if I gave up now all my earlier efforts would be wasted. She was right.

The civil affairs office of the street committee. In the little room, which is dark and narrow, the plump, middle-aged woman who is in charge takes two bright red marriage registration forms from the drawer and dusts them off as she speaks. "I think I've got to grips with your case now," she says. "But I must check that your husband does want the divorce and I've no time before the festival. There's so much to do and only me to do it. Afterwards . . ." She holds the registration forms out to a young couple standing together. "You can't take these away, you must fill them in here. Go home and fetch your household registration books. That's the proper procedure."

We move on to her parents' home, a single-storey house on one side of a large crowded courtyard. A small kitchen has been built on by the occupants themselves.

I write stories to tell people about the law. I've covered detection, smuggling, larceny and forensic medicine. All based on real cases. It's almost impossible for me to write. My parents sit in the next room watching television. My sons sleep right there beside me. They ask questions non-stop before they go off, they even want to know why I don't write faster. Some people say I'm not a proper writer but I don't care. I'm part of the security set-up after all, so writing this sort of thing is my job. In peacetime the Public Security Bureau is responsible for people's lives and for their safety. Of course there were flaws in our work during the leftist period, things it's hard to forgive. But nowadays members of our Bureau work very hard to protect people. Sometimes they give their lives for it. So whether it counts as good writing or not, I can only write about the world I know.

I have no self. There is the office, my sons, housework, my husband . . . *(Pavements, pedestrians, bicycles, cars, pedestrian crossings. A bus arrives at the stop. The people waiting for it crowd forward.)* Quickly, push, push harder. I'll give you a shove.

Staying a Widow

Xi'an. Textile design worker, aged forty-one.

It's seventeen years since my husband left us. Last night I saw him in a dream. He looked just as he always used to. He hadn't changed. I woke up in a sweat and I cried.

He was sent to Sichuan on business. We knew that there was fighting there,* but the design institute was still functioning so they sent him anyway. I had just recovered from the birth of my second baby. I was still on maternity leave. He said he'd come back as soon as he could. But he never did. He ran into fighting as soon as he got off the train and was hit by a stray bullet.

The telegram came first. Then his ID and his money were posted back. The Railway Bureau handled it because he'd been killed at the station. A year later I went to collect his ashes. "Is this my husband?" I asked. They showed me the spot where he died. Some time later, the leaders of the two rival factions were arrested, but no one knew who'd shot my husband. He had been killed by a stray bullet – no one would take responsibility. When I watched the trial of the Gang of Four on television, I cried all the time. If Jiang Qing had been executed ten times over it wouldn't have been enough for me.

So, I had to take the whole weight of the family – to be both mother and father. Tingting has started work now; Fanfan is at senior middle school. Her name used to be Weihong, "Defending the Red", but we changed it after my husband died; he had the character "fan" in his name. Things haven't been too difficult financially. We got a pension of thirty yuan a month after he died; it went down to fifteen yuan when

* In 1967 there were many armed clashes between rival factions in the Cultural Revolution in Sichuan.

[81]

Tingting started work. My husband was on business when he was killed. I don't know whether people got compensation for victims who'd actually been doing the fighting.

I always had the courage to carry on. There were the children, and I got a lot of sympathy. Everyone was sorry for me, from the Party secretary right down to the cleaning staff. And I had people to understand me . . . one man especially. I won't say his name. I don't want any gossip. He's a technician in my factory. When Fanfan was little, she got measles, and he carried her to the hospital in his arms. And yet, just a while ago, my daughters had a row with me about him. They said they'd leave home if I married him. But how could I marry him?

In those days I was always in tears. I went round in a daze. When he was sent to work in our factory we were in the same office. He was a designer and I was in charge of the pattern library. He was always telling me it was no use crying, that I should busy myself with something. He started to teach me design. There was no need to go to university to learn it, he said.

I began to feel better. After life settled down a bit, I started to learn to draw. In 1973 there was a fabric-design exhibition in Beijing. A pattern of ours was accepted for display. In those days, exhibits usually only carried the name of the workshop in which they had been designed, but as there were foreign businessmen at this exhibition, names were used this time. So the label for our pattern showed both our names.

Rumours about us started flying around the factory after that. Of course I was terribly hurt and upset. I felt I had done him a wrong. He hadn't done anything, but he'd got into trouble over me. I told him to stop coming to my house. He started yelling, loud enough for other people to hear, about how there's such a thing as friendship as well as love. Things like that. I knew that he really loved me then. He's so stubborn. He kept on visiting me as he had before.

So the rumours got worse and worse. I didn't know what to do. In the end, I told him his visits were making things difficult for me. He never came again. He even began to avoid me at the factory. But before he left that day he warned me not to think that if he stopped coming everything would be all right. It wasn't so simple.

I just wanted a quiet life, and gossip was the thing I most hated. Think how tough it was for me. I became the butt of people's jokes. The people who had been sorry for me now went on about me behind my back. If I wore anything new, people would say I was flighty or vain or worse.

He's never married. If he'd proposed to me a few years back I'd have married him. Now I'm too old to think of such things. I'm nearly at the change of life. How could I possibly marry now? And then my daughters are against it. After all I have been through to bring them up, I don't want to upset them now.

Yes, I have read Zhang Jie's story *Love Must Not Be Forgotten*. Writers are always writing about unattainable love. Why not write about a love like mine which I had, but then I lost? The younger generation have no experience, they don't understand. My tragedy is even sadder than the one in that story. I've had everything and lost everything – love and friendship. I brought trouble on him too.

Some things can't be explained. You wouldn't understand. Let me tell you a story I read somewhere. There was once a widow who used to scatter a hundred copper cash in her room each night. She would put out the light and grope around, picking them up one by one. In the end, she would go to bed exhausted. After her death, the hundred copper coins, shiny through so much handling, were the proof of her life of chastity. What age are we meant to be living in? Surely I can't do as she did? I can't make the People's Currency my "chastity money". When will these old prejudices die?

My life is quite full. I just have more worries than other people. I've brought up my children. I've worked hard for the country. There are probably foreigners somewhere wearing fabrics I designed.

He still hasn't mentioned marriage to me. Of course the person I loved most was my husband. How could it be otherwise? And next come my daughters.

I earn sixty yuan a month – with bonus about eighty-two yuan altogether. That's plenty. But we don't live as well as some people do. What husband earns only thirty yuan a month? If mine were still alive he would be an engineer. And he would have seniority. He graduated in 1963.

That colleague is the person who has moved me most, but something happened last year which I found very touching. In autumn a lot of us were sent to various places to find out about new developments in our industry. After the economic reforms, every unit became responsible for developing its own products. One afternoon I was told that I was to go to Sichuan. Then very early next morning the factory director came specially to my home to announce a change of plan. "You go to Shanghai and Suzhou," he said. "I'm new here. There are still things I don't know about." I began to cry so he added, "Don't cry, I changed the plan because I didn't want you to be upset."

Lots of people offered to introduce me to suitable men. They still do, but I've always refused. They say if I just take one more step everything will be all right. I don't believe it. Ever since I asked him to stop coming to my house, I've known that nothing in the world comes right easily.

5

REFORMERS

Builder

December 1984. Fang Yichun, thirty-four, manager of the Harbin New Sun Construction Company. In four years he has turned a maintenance and building team run by a street committee into a big construction company with fixed assets of 3,000,000 yuan, liquid assets of 7,000,000 and a work force of 2000.

I came back to the city from Heihe State Farm in 1971, and stayed at home waiting for a job like a lot of other educated kids who'd come back. We were waiting for the authorities to assign us to state-owned factories and mines, or to collectively run service enterprises. I reckoned the best thing would be to get into a state-run factory. But after learning carpentry from scratch as an apprentice I was fed up. When I'd waited over a year for a job I joined a maintenance and building team run by the New Sun Street Committee office. There were twenty or so unemployed kids and six married women in the team. We patched walls with heating flues in them, swept chimneys and went from house to house asking, "New Year's coming: do you want your walls painted?" When work was scarce the "social monkeys" who hung around the streets all day had their chance to make a pile. If one of them got us a job they could pad the worksheets for the job, take the extra wages and keep everything that was left after paying off the people who'd done the work. They didn't give a damn about building up our capital. After a few years I became a foreman because I could get us work too. Nearly all the fellows working for me were kids who'd come back to the city. We used our spare cash to buy equipment because we really wanted to make a go of it in the building trade. At the time I passed up chances for a regular job. At first, working for a street committee doesn't sound anywhere near as good as working for a big collective or some state enterprise, but in those outfits you're stuck in whatever job you've been assigned to. In 1976 at the street committee's request I gave a written undertaking not to complain if they stopped trying to find me a regular job. For one thing, I was interested in the building industry, and I liked the idea of making run-down places presentable. And for another, I was making a lot more money being paid by the job than I would have as a worker in a state factory. Later, when my father and mother retired I could have taken either of their places but I didn't.

By 1979 there were over 200 people in the maintenance and building team, and I was in charge of half of them. A building team is labour-intensive: you don't need much capital or technology. As a lot of other outfits were setting up their own building teams too, work was harder to come by. The "social monkeys" had all made their pile and cleared off. The street committee office was hopping mad, and we were on the point of going under.

Everyone was pushing me to take over, so when contracting out was starting in 1979, I asked to contract for the maintenance and building team. There wouldn't have been the slightest chance of making a go of it the old way. I wanted to run it as a business enterprise, with control over finance and personnel. Practically no one would give you the right to hire and fire then, and not enough places do now, but the street Party committee agreed. Their only condition was that I had to get the team into the black within two years. In the previous seven years we'd lost nearly 60,000 yuan. If I made a go of it they'd give me a black-and-white TV worth 520 yuan, and if I failed they were going to fine me 360 yuan. I told them they'd better dock my pay in advance by 30 yuan a month as we went along, because they'd never be able to get all that off me at the end. Well, after I'd been running the show for a year we'd made 56,000 yuan profit, just a few thousand short of what we needed to clear off the accumulated deficits. I got my TV. Of course I replaced it with a colour set ages ago. My foreman has got one too: he's on a contract with me.

We've got four iron rules. One, each level of the company works on a contract basis. Two, you get paid for work done according to the job. Three, cadres get paid according to their responsibilities. Four, managers and technicians get paid as much as or more than workers.

At first the maintenance and building team was scared of building anything big, and the city's construction committee wouldn't let us either. Our technique and equipment weren't up to it then. But if we were going to hold our own we had to learn how to put up big buildings.

We heard of an outfit that had offered the contract for an apartment block of 2400 square metres to the city's Third Construction Company. The Third wasn't co-operating at all – it was making a lot of demands, like transport and canteen facilities for the builders and cash on the nail for overtime. We moved in fast, made no demands at all, guaranteed we'd use good-quality materials, and put in a lower tender. We told them to look at the office building we'd put up for the street committee a couple of years earlier to see what we could do. The client agreed, but the city's construction committee blocked it. They didn't think much of us. So I went and told them that there was a new man in charge – me – who'd been a foreman before and put up big blocks. If we made a good job this time, we were going to carry on, and if we screwed it up we'd forget about building.

The construction committee was okay after that. They agreed to give us a chance. We got it up on time, and it was a quality job too. Now we'd won the right to put up big blocks we built a whole string of them. In 1981 the building industry all over China was taking its cues from the River Luo East Wind Construction Team. Their way of doing things had been approved by Deng Xiaoping and Hu Yaobang. I suppose East Wind was the first model of urban reform. We went along to find out about them, and it only took one look to tell me that everything they'd done we'd done already, like cadres being promoted and demoted, workers being hired and fired, and flexible wages. They were a building team under a street committee too, but there were only 300 of them. We were already up to 600. We were made a kind of guinea-pig to see if the East Wind methods would work in Harbin. This meant we got a lot of backing and grew even faster.

A year later we had become a company, which was a step up in the world. We were supposed to come under the district authorities, though in fact we insisted on staying under the direct control of the street committee. We liked them, but the main thing was we wanted to stay unofficial. We didn't want the district putting state cadres in, and we absolutely weren't going to guarantee anyone a job for life. The structure of our company is very simple. There's only one person in charge at each level: no deputies. The technicians and management get a standard wage of 98 yuan, which is doubled by the special responsibility supplement; and as we work Sundays and public holidays that brings their monthly pay up to 240 yuan. But if they're not up to it, they get demoted and their pay goes down straight away. Our workers get more than they would in state enterprises too, though they have to work harder and for longer hours. In the last few years we've had over a hundred people defecting to us from state and big collective enterprises.

In 1981 we became one of the "big four" in the Harbin construction industry, and in 1982 we won a provincial silver medal. In 1983 we completed a job that was graded an all-round high-quality one. All-round high-quality jobs take more time and material and involve much higher costs, but what it does for your company's reputation makes it worth it. State-run outfits used to push collective ones out, but now we're giving state enterprises the elbow. When we finished our first big apartment block we started putting up the exhibition hall beside the Songhua River, and after we'd been on the job for a month we were very politely given the boot. They said that it was a top-priority project, the mayor was taking a personal interest in it, and they weren't going to let a street-committee building and maintenance team make a mess of it.

But this year we very politely saw the city's First Construction Company off. It was for a big block at Harbin University. The First were so sure of themselves they moved in with all their gear before the contract had even been signed. But we showed that we could do a guaranteed top-quality job for 5 per cent less than the First, and in a year instead of their year and a half. The city's construction committee told our clients we could do it: they knew from experience. We'd give it top priority, but the First would only treat it as a routine job. Now the state-run outfits get scared when our name comes up. No harm a collective shaking things up a bit. We've got six site units and a transport team. We completed over 11 million yuan's worth of work in 1983. I went to Xi'an for a meeting and had another look at East Wind: they were still the same size.

Technically competent management is important. Every section has an engineer in charge. One engineer volunteered to leave a state outfit to join us. He used to be on 78 yuan a month: he gets 240 here. I've run eight technical management courses for foremen and technicians. I encourage people to study and improve themselves. We'll pay the study costs of anyone who has passed the exams for the civil engineering department of the spare-time university. There was one guy who passed the exams, but his site unit didn't want to release him for study in case it interfered with his work. On top of that when the authorities at the spare-time university heard he was only a temporary worker, they wouldn't admit him because they didn't want to be responsible for finding him a job after he graduated. As soon as I heard about this I called him to my office. He told me he'd come seventh out of four or five hundred in the exam. That was quite something. I decided there and then to put him on the permanent staff and let the company pay his fees. I didn't want it charged to his site unit, so I transferred him to the company's technical safety section. The kids were keener on studying than ever after that. I announced that they had to get the course diploma and we wouldn't let them leave the company for six years after they'd finished. It's got to be civil engineering. You can't study classical literature at the company's expense. I want everyone to study so that we'll build better and make the company even stronger.

I've only got a junior middle-school diploma. But not long ago I passed the national exam for managers. In non-state companies we don't choose and promote our cadres on their paper qualifications. In fact there's more flexibility about qualifications than there was a while back. As I see it, what the country's most short of now is managerial talent, not formal education.

I reckon I've got that talent. When I was a foreman I was always thinking about how to get my group to do a better job so we'd all benefit. I'd never been any sort of cadre before then, apart from detachment leader in the Young Pioneers at primary school.

We pay insurance premiums for all our regular staff, 50 to 100 yuan a month depending on their wages. When they retire they get about 110 yuan a month. Our fringe benefits are no worse than in state outfits. But the company only pays two-thirds. One third comes from the workers themselves. That stops them running off to other units in mid-career. If you go the company loses most, but you're out of pocket too. Our sickness benefits can compare with state ones too. Everyone gets three yuan a month for medical expenses, and if there's anything left over you keep two-thirds of the surplus. Hospital bills are met in full by the company, but you don't get a penny in sick pay. We'll cover medical bills, however heavy, but we won't have people abusing sick leave. We issue western clothing, heating allowances and food subsidies. We help our workers to build their own houses too. There's no store that sells building materials retail in the city, so people either have to ask their units for it or else pinch it. My rule is that if you steal anything you're fined ten times its value. But if our people are building their own houses we let them have the stuff cheap: two cents for a brick that usually costs five cents plus two cents for transport.

Last year there was a big fire in Harbin. Hundreds of families lost their homes, including two of our workers. I went to the scene with our Party secretary. The next day the company vacated some office space for them to stay in, and we all chipped in to buy them a new set of kitchen things. One of them was on our permanent staff, and he lost 2000 yuan's worth of stuff in the fire. We gave him 2500. The other was a temporary, and he got 1500 yuan. It brought tears to their eyes. State factory workers didn't get rehoused for ages.

In the last few years dozens of our people have been given jobs in state outfits but have come back here, including our Party secretary. Everyone says they'd rather spend the rest of their working lives in our company. We're very choosy about who we take now. Most of the men in the original maintenance and building team are still here and they're nearly all in the key jobs on the sites at 246 yuan a month.

I've already shelled out 400,000 on housing for our staff. We've built twenty-two apartments so far. You don't get one on seniority or because you haven't got enough living space. It's a reward for good work, and you're allowed to keep your old place too. We make an open assessment to decide who deserves them. I got given this place first because I'd done more for the company than anyone else. Nobody seemed to object – give the first one to the boss, they said. Two workers got apartments too, legmen who found us a lot of work. Nearly all the worksite cadres have now been given places to live.

As company manager I have a lot of power. People are hired or fired on my say-so. We don't have any personnel problems within the company, but I still find things very complicated outside, even after all these years. The trickiest stuff has to do with getting the building jobs. There are so many construction outfits now and the competition is ruthless. The clients used to ask us out to a meal and plead with us to put up a decent building. But now it's up to us to take them out. On top of that, the middlemen want hair-raising commissions: a yuan per square metre. So on a 10,000-square-metre project they get 10,000 yuan for doing nothing. But I'm not going to get mixed up in anything too shady. As I always say to the workers, "You may think that I've got a lot of power, but if anything goes wrong I'm the one who goes to jail." The only way we can beat the competition is through high-quality work at lower prices, and that's how we do it.

Another headache is the way everyone wants hand-outs these days. Anyone who's starting a magazine or an advertising paper always asks you for a grant. It's two or three thousand every time. A couple of days ago a film company turned up and said they wanted to make a TV play about us. They came straight out with a demand for 60,000 yuan. Who the hell do they think they are?

My wage is 115 yuan a month, the same as a grade-fourteen state cadre. The responsibility supplement and other things I get on top of that bring it up to 290. The joke is that I get more than the mayor. Of course some people object. "We've been making revolution all these years, and this is all we get, you so-and-so." But how many of them would it take to do my job? Last year I got 4000 in bonuses. I gave 2000 to the canteen manager for entertaining: it came out of my pocket, not company funds. This year policies are even more flexible and the company can pay for it – I can't go on shelling out that sort of money for ever.

Just keeping one business going isn't enough for me. I have to make them grow. I've invested a million yuan in importing Japanese equipment for printing colour photographs so I can compete with the state in that too. There's only one state place in Harbin that does colour prints. They take two weeks to process a film and charge 1.50 for a standard print. Private traders in Guangzhou can do that for only thirty-eight cents. I want to get into the travel business, and build a hotel to compete with state hotels. And I'm interested in trade too.

That's the way I operate. What it comes down to is, never give up.

As I was an only child I didn't have to go to the countryside or the mountains when I left school, but during the Cultural Revolution my father was branded an active counter-revolutionary just because of a remark he'd made about Jiang Qing's being in films in the thirties. He was sent back to his old home in Shandong. He took his appeal as far as the State Council, and it drove him crazy. Even when he was rehabilitated he had a black mark against his name for a long time. The company of the army's Construction Corps I was sent to was on the frontier, so most people had rifles. As I'd told my political instructor about my shady background he didn't discriminate against me, so I had one too. When I saw other people going places and getting into university or the Party I was grateful enough just to be holding my gun. But of all the kids I knew at school I've probably gone the furthest.

Joining Forces

December 1984 in Heilongjiang. We'd been asking about this restaurant for a couple of days. Everybody knew that a few years earlier this place, owned and run by two sisters, had been in all the papers and on television as the first of its kind, but now no one knew where it was or even if it still existed. Some people even insisted that it had gone out of business and closed down.

I guess we should start with how we opened the restaurant. I was jobless and my sister had come back in 1979 from working in the countryside with an army land-reclamation team. There was only my dad working then. My mum was a housewife. So what with an extra mouth to feed and me with no job, times were hard. The family blamed me because I hadn't done much of anything in school, and the state didn't assign me to a job.

My sister got a bit of piecework from the neighbourhood committee embroidery workshop, but she made less than a yuan a day. She couldn't work too late in the evenings because it used too much electricity.

So when we heard about the government policy relaxing a bit on private enterprise, the two of us sat up half the night working out how we could open up a restaurant. We did a rough financial estimate and figured it could make money. We didn't calculate everything down to the last penny; we just thought we'd give it a go. After all, the state places were doing well enough. If we'd known then that they were subsidized up to the eyeballs we probably wouldn't have gone ahead.

We went to the neighbourhood committee – urban commune it still was then – to get their agreement. At first they thought the new policy was just a rumour. When we went back a couple of days later they told us to write out an application, then they added on the bottom, "The signatories insist on making this application; please handle as you see fit." The Bureau of Commerce passed the buck and sent us to the Office for Educated Youth. They wouldn't touch it either, but at least they were friendly. Anyhow, after we'd really been given the run-around we were issued with private restaurant licence no. 001. After that we went to the Cereals Bureau, the Aquatic Foodstuffs Company, the Public Health and Sanitation Bureau, the Commercial Bureau again and so on to arrange for our supplies of oil, grains and fish; then we got a health inspection certificate and finally we were in business.

We set up in our own place; we originally had thirteen square metres for commercial use, and that got upped to fifty-four in 1982. The day we opened, the Educated Youth Office got the press here; then Xinhua News Agency came and the television and radio people got in on the act and made a big fuss about us. When we opened they said we were the first private place in the whole city – that was true enough, we had the first licence. Afterwards it turned out we were the first in the whole country.

In those days you didn't have to pay taxes for your first three years. The first year we made over 2000, an average of over 100 a month each. The second year we expanded a bit and took on more staff. One was my brother-in-law-to-be. Our average individual income stayed the same as it was the first year. But then a lot more private places opened up. Some had retired professional chefs who cooked much better than we did. On top of that the cost of seafood kept going up all the time. Even ending up with a few thousand was quite something. What more could we ask?

At the end of the second year, the neighbourhood committee asked us if we wanted to go in with their restaurant, the Hulan. Their reasoning was that with two restaurants in the same street neither of us was making that much. We'd be better off joining forces and edging out all the small street vendors around. My sister wanted to do it, but I wasn't keen on losing our freedom by joining a big collectively owned outfit. Finally she talked me into it. She said we'd be better off in a big collective even though it might not be quite up to a state-owned enterprise. It would still give us a pension, she said, and labour insurance, sick pay and work disability benefits. Take mixing dough, for instance. Within three months of buying our dough-mixer my brother-in-law caught his fingers in it and I had my thumbnail taken off. If I'd been disabled, we'd have had to close down. But if I injured my hand at the Hulan they'd have to support me for the rest of my life. You're better off in a collective. Besides, you don't have to worry about your basic supplies, or whether or not you're making money.

The first condition we put to the neighbourhood committee was that they had to take my brother-in-law as well as my sister and me. They agreed, and even made my sister deputy manager. The second condition was that they should purchase our equipment, and they came right out with an offer of 950 for the lot. Our third thing was that we had to keep our old premises, including the extra forty square metres, to live in ourselves. We got a bit of flak on this because the restaurant premises were classified as temporary commercial premises and couldn't be converted to residential space. Anyway we've managed to keep our forty square metres up to now, but when the state wants them back we'll have to hand them over dutifully. But when do you think they're going to get round to putting up high rises on this street? We'll face that one when it happens.

So everything got settled, and on 1 January 1983 we officially merged.

The Hulan has over forty workers now, plus several people on long-term contract. Today everyone in collective and state places is on contract; we were ahead of our time and it turned out to be the right thing to do. We're open for breakfast, lunch and supper, nine hours in all. We work in two shifts and get one day off a week. That never happens in your own place! You've got to slog your guts out from morning till night to keep afloat. In summer you have to take a cart out and sell snacks by the river, and in winter wander round the streets selling stuff – it's no joke.

My sister gets just over seventy a month. I'm in charge of the rice and cereals section and get a little more than she does. Just over eighty. It's only a few yuan less than we got on our own, and it's a lot less wear and tear. Some people say we've taken a step backwards, but I don't see it that way. We were the pioneers in opening up a privately owned place, and we're the first into a joint venture, which is the trend now.

The benefits are good. When we had our own business we didn't see a film for over a year. Now the state gives us free tickets and even time off to go.

We've got a higher social status too. We're official employees now. My sister's a cadre and she's in the Party. That would never happen if we were still self-employed. Everything's taken care of.

Why bother with a contract system with forty to fifty people? You'd have to knock yourself out the same as if you were self-employed and there'd be no guarantee you'd succeed. The Hulan is edging into profit now; we handed over more than 9000 last year, which was not bad going. If you work it out carefully, we don't make as much as we did with our own place. There are too many restaurants around these days, but that's not our headache any more.

We used to have a fourth partner, and we had a lot of trouble over him. We wanted to bring him into the Hulan with us but the neighbourhood committee refused because his residence rights weren't here. He said we were dumping him to look after ourselves. We'd only been at the Hulan a couple of days when he chucked a brick through the glass in the main doors. The manager called the police and they made him fork out thirty-six yuan in damages. That shows you how the system works. Would the police have jumped to it like that for a private restaurant? He's all right now – he's got a permanent job as a factory worker.

To be honest, I wouldn't eat here if I were you. They're not such good cooks. If it's somebody we know, we can give them bigger portions, but if it still tastes awful, what good is that?

Bridges and Rabbits

The two-storeyed Yang Mansion is unique among the thatched and grey-tiled cottages scattered among the dense bamboo forests of this part of western Sichuan.

Yang Sixian, the master rabbit-breeder, is forty-four and has the pallor of a bookworm. Not long ago the Guangming Daily *ran a front-page lead story on this ten-thousander from Guanxian county and a seminar for some local writers and editors was held at his home.*

Let me tell you about my life.

My class origin is landlord. We had four hectares of land at Liberation, and all three branches of the family were classified as landlords. My father was the eldest son, and when he was twenty-four they classified him as a landlord element. From then on he never dared go to market or shoot the breeze with anyone. He didn't drink and he didn't gamble. After work he just stayed in and kept his head down. Whenever anything happened he was called out for voluntary labour. He died in his forties.

In 1957 I passed the exams for middle school, but after a year or two there was a shortage of teachers and I was told to teach in a primary school. After a couple of years there the famine began, and there was a big cutback in the number of people allowed to live in cities and towns. There were no rations for us, and we were sent home.

There was terrible starvation among the peasants during the famine years. Seeing how I was a strapping boy my dad and my kid sister saved their grain for me and ate husks behind my back. When he'd been working in the fields for a while Dad used to say he had a stomach-ache and rush back home, clutching his belly. At meal-times he'd say he was feeling too bad to eat. One day I followed him home and I found out he was eating cooked husks. You grind them up into a very fine powder, then shape them into things like steamed buns and cook them. They'll fall apart in your fingers, so you've got to cup them with both hands to eat them. Can you imagine what they taste like? I cried my eyes out. That made my mind up for me: I was going to be a man and support the family.

If we were going to get through I'd have to go off and make some money some other way. A few of us went cutting bamboo deep in the mountains: the bamboo on the plain is all privately owned. We sliced it up into strips and hauled them down to market.

It was hard. There weren't any tracks deep in the mountains – you had to use your hands and feet to climb. And the rockfaces were so bare there was nothing you could get hold of. You had to wedge yourself into cracks with water running down them, stick your big toe into a crack and move along a step at a time. One foot wrong and you were dead. One of my pals missed his footing. He couldn't pull himself back up and he couldn't go down. There he was hanging on the cliff with a load of split bamboo on his back. He couldn't move and none of us could give him any help: all we could do was cling to the rock and watch. He finally got down from the mountains but when he was safe his legs started shaking and he couldn't get out of bed. All the 200 yuan he'd earned actually went in medicine.

But it was beautiful there, deep in the mountains among the tall, straight trees. When we were taking our load down the mountains we slid it down over the tops of the bamboos still standing. With all that light and the wonderful air you forgot how depressing it was indoors. But for being hungry I'd cheerfully have spent the rest of my life up there. No signs of people, only wild animals. Once a panda came to finish off our gruel, and staggered around with its head stuck in our cooking pot. He nearly bashed our faces in while trying to free his own! From then on we had a roaring fire of bamboo ends every night, and that kept the animals away.

I remember our last trip best. We were getting ready to leave the mountains when there was a sudden cloudburst. The water rose in the river, then with a great roar the flood was upon us. The river had been fifteen or twenty metres away, but suddenly it was rising all around us. The pile of split bamboo we were sitting on had turned into an island. Everyone was silent, dead silent and then we started crying. We were looking death in the face, and we knew very well that if we died there, nobody would know. My Sixth Uncle was a cheerful old bachelor and nobody's fool. He wasn't cracking any jokes now. He took a good look round, undid the rope from a bundle of split bamboo, put a running loop on it, and tried to lasso a tree stump on an overhanging cliff. He kept on trying and missing till finally he got the noose over the tree trunk. One by one we climbed the cliff by hanging on to the rope. There was just enough room on the top to squat there, clinging to the rock and watching in wide-eyed horror while the waters covered the split bamboo that represented all those months of work and our food. That set us all howling again.

We slowly made our way down the mountain. It took us hours to cover a few kilometres till we got to a house in the middle of the night. It was a family of loners who hadn't joined a people's commune but had fled to the mountains to clear a bit of land and raise some crops by themselves. When our host opened the door with a lantern in his hand we were a terrible sight. After the flood subsided we went back into the mountains. Our grain had been washed away, but the split bamboo was still there, stuck in the mud. We hauled it out, washed it, and sold it for next to nothing. That was the last time I went into the mountains.

Then my family urged me to learn carpentry from my uncle, so I'd be able to start earning right away to support us. I learned the trade in seven days. We didn't build foreign-style houses in the Sichuan countryside. We did it the Chinese way, putting up a wooden frame first and building the walls afterwards. They used to be made of split bamboo and clay; the new way is with bricks. Carpentry's hard to learn. It usually takes up to a year to master all the routines – getting the timber ready, setting the uprights, dovetailing. I'd only been learning for a week when my aunt wanted an extension to her house, so I slung my tools on my back, went there and spun her a yarn about how my uncle would soon turn up. I marked out the timber and set to, sawing, planing and chiselling. My aunt smelled a rat, but she couldn't really swear at me, seeing as I was her nephew. By the time my uncle arrived I'd done it all, and when we put the framework together it all fitted – admittedly, it was a bit loose – so off went the firecrackers to celebrate raising the house. My aunt gave me twenty yuan, I bought myself a saw and a plane, and from then I was a builder ready to go anywhere.

I always had a book in my pocket to read after work. I had to have something like *Outlaws of the Marsh*, *The Seven Heroes and Five Just Ones*, *Anna Karenina* or *The Ershov Brothers* to read. To this day I still ask myself why there can't be something like *The Ershov Brothers* in our literature. I don't suppose you'd expect a peasant to read books like that. But peasants do want to read.

Building Chinese-style houses doesn't take real technical know-how. If you can't read drawings there are a lot of jobs you can't do, so I taught myself to read three-dimensional drawings. I worked as a temporary factory hand by day and made furniture at night. Instead of taking wages I learned algebra from them and did equations in my spare time.

I became foreman of a team of contract builders. They all called me Site Engineer Yang. In the Cultural Revolution the unofficial building industry developed very fast, mainly putting up big halls, because everyone was crazy about meetings. The provinces and counties were building them so communes were damn well going to build themselves one too. The more the central authorities said we couldn't afford it and forbade unauthorized building, the harder everyone tried to find the money to do it. Later we switched to putting up housing. By then old-fashioned builders like my uncle were useless. All they can make are the doors and windows. Now we build in reinforced concrete.

What I really like talking about is the bridge I designed and built on the upper reaches of the Min River in Heishui county, Aba prefecture, where Tibetans live. In those days peasants weren't allowed to go off to earn money – that was "capitalism" – but building teams were still needed everywhere. The teams were always trying to outdo each other, and several were competing for the bridge contract. Another team had already got it with a bid of 80,000 yuan. I submitted an enormous pile of drawings and papers to the Aba Prefectural Bridge-building Office. I'd costed everything item by item, several times over, but it only came to something over 30,000 yuan. I was sure I'd got it wrong – how come the other team's bid was so much higher? Even adding a little extra to be on the safe side my total was still only 40,000. That was where my troubles started. The government limits on what could be spent on building projects were too low – you had to go over them. The old hands always faked up extra items, and that's where they made their money. But I didn't have a clue about any of that in those days.

Anyhow, I'd done these designs on the strength of only a year's schooling but they were all passed. My bridge was over fifty metres long altogether, with a thirty-metre span and a hyperbolic arch: that made for a light bridge. It had plenty of inherent stress, and needed only small piers. Our 40,000-yuan bid knocked out the competition, and so we took our team of nearly a hundred to Heishui county, over 700 kilometres away. We started work in October 1973.

The team boss was the head of our commune's revolutionary committee, but I was really in charge. We started with the cofferdam and the foundations. As soon as we started digging I had a shock: underground water coming up at the rate of twenty cubic metres an hour, so that the men were working in mud and water. I'd reckoned on them shifting a cubic metre a day each, but they could only dig a tenth of that. So I kept adding more and more pumps till I had up to twenty diesel pumps going non-stop day and night, and fifty men working round the clock in shifts. We gave them stiff drinks and endless commendations on the p.a. system, which brought a lot of complaints from local residents.

Just digging the two main foundation pits took over three months and more than 10,000 man-days above my estimate. When our boss saw that things were going badly he went home with several thousand yuan that he said he was going to spend on grain for us at above-quota prices. That cash was intended to refund the travel expenses that several of us had run up getting the contract. Our accountant chickened out too. I was really scared, but I couldn't show it. I had to wear a smile all day and try to reassure everyone that this had all been allowed for beforehand. I also had to win over the four key workers. They weren't foremen or anything, but they carried a lot of weight among the men and were the biggest potential trouble-makers. If I could steady them I'd be able to hold all the workers. All I'd got to pay the men's wages with was the part of our earnings we were meant to hand over to the commune and the brigade. I got into trouble for that too later on. I submitted a request for extra funds but nobody authorized payment.

From late 1973, we suffered two years of pure chaos. There were a lot of injuries on the site. One boy nearly died when something fell on him. There was blood everywhere. I went straight to the county Party committee and told them, "If this boy dies I can't go home," and started crying. It worked: with the best treatment and drugs the boy was saved, and so was I. If we'd failed the men would have made big trouble.

When the pressure was at its worst the people at a mine where I'd built some housing lent me a truck to haul sand. There was only one driver, and we had to shift the sand round the clock, so I learned to drive in three days.

I was so tired I often didn't know whether I was coming or going. To stay awake I'd have a man beside me lighting cigarettes or feeding me sour apples. I'd drive all night, grab a couple of hours' sleep around dawn, and be Site Engineer Yang again when the sun came up. My hair turned completely white. It's dyed now.

Well, we stuck it out till it was time to raise the arch. There wasn't a single crane in that part of the world. All we had on the site was a little electric winch that could only raise a ton and a half. The two halves of the arch weighed two and a half tons each. All the builders stood next to each other, lifted a half arch and slowly moved it into place, like an enormous centipede. I'd already put rails and a flatcar on the bridge structure, and we slowly moved the half arch till it was on one side of the bridge, then gradually raised it with timber to its intended height. Then we did the same thing with the other half. The day we joined the two parts together the whole county turned out, and both banks of the river were packed. The Tibetans were in their reds and greens, their holiday best, to witness the amazing spectacle of Han peasants putting up a big bridge.

The bridge is still spanning that river. It looks great.

When I went home after building the bridge, two militiamen carrying rifles marched me to the commune headquarters and locked me up in the study class. Mine was one of three big corruption cases that the commune, the Industrial and Commercial Bureau, the Tax Bureau and the Public Security Bureau were handling together. There was a craze for big economic cases all over China then. I'd been in study classes before. Because I was a landlord's son they'd come down on me for some "new tendency in the class struggle" whatever I did. In the Cultural Revolution there was often a big rush to set up study classes in response to whatever wind was blowing. Everyone in the commune and the production brigade who'd been a secret-society member, a bandit, an opium smoker, a local layabout or a member of a landlord family would get thrown into one every time. Whenever we had to hand in written self-criticisms I wrote the life histories for the illiterates among them. They didn't need to tell me: by then I knew all their stories off by heart.

The reason for running me in that time was that I hadn't brought any money back for the commune. I hadn't known enough to steal from the state. If I'd bid 80,000 yuan like the other team we'd have cleared a net profit of 20,000 on top of the wage bill and what we'd have to hand over to the state. But I was 16,000 yuan in the red, and it was the commune and the production brigade's money that was missing. That was unforgivable. It was a tough investigation. They spent months going through all my account books one by one. All they found was a discrepancy of sixty-three yuan. It was quite okay for the head of the revolutionary committee to be several thousand yuan out on his travel expenses, but I was expected to make up the whole deficit out of my own pocket. My house was turned completely upside down, and they took my bike and my watch and my wife's clothes, but they were worth only 300 yuan altogether. There was no light at the end of the tunnel. Later on a lot of other things happened and in 1978 the case was dropped.

I wasn't interested in working after that, so I drifted around taking it easy for a year. Then with the policy changes a lot of very capable people emerged, and that set me thinking about my successes and failures in building that bridge. Where I'd done well was technically and in choosing the right people. When I was being struggled against in the study class none of the contract labourers I'd employed gave me a really bad time.

One person I'd hired was a peasant woman called Big Sister Zhou, a real good-looker, with the gift of the gab. She knew her way around. Of course, a woman like that doesn't have the best of reputations but she had real talent, especially for social dealings. She could get on with everyone, including the county's Party secretary. She saved me a lot of trouble. The news that I'd given her a job on the site created a sensation in Guanxian town. The rumours about us went wild. Her husband and my wife got suspicious too, and there were rows. She and I got on very well, but it was strictly on the level. I did think about it, but it wasn't on. I couldn't be inside that woman's skirts, or she might have started giving me orders. I'll be honest with you: when a man and a woman spend a lot of time alone together you do start getting ideas, but I put them out of my mind. She was always good to me – she sent me cigarettes when I was locked up in the study class.

I had to put in a lot of effort making sure my wife saw things my way. People call her Big Brother Wang because she's such a good farmer, better than a man at threshing and at transplanting rice seedlings. She does all the fieldwork in our family. I lend a hand only in the busy season. She is from a landlord family too. In those days landlords' children had to marry each other: we couldn't aspire to the children of poor and lower-middle peasants. Big Brother Wang trusted me. If anyone teased her that a concubine was soon going to be moving in she said, "Good for him if he can fix it. Let's see if you're up to getting yourself one."

As it happened there was a simple way out of my trouble. I got us a big contract for the Wenchuan mines that Aba and Wenjiang prefectures were developing together. I kept all the financial power in my own hands. I could pay out ten or twenty thousand yuan just on my signature. The numbers were padded so we'd get some extra money, and the amounts of work involved were all settled on my say-so. So after eight months' work I handed over 110,000 yuan in net profit to the commune and brought back eight tons of steel too. The commune used the money to put up a distillery and a workshop and to buy tractors.

In 1980 I suddenly realized what a fool I'd been, all that sweat and only trouble as my reward. Other people were put in charge of the distillery and of the tractor team, and the steel was taken home for private use. I might be today's hero, but sooner or later the tide would turn, and that would be the end of me and my whole family. I made up my mind to wash my hands of the construction team. I'd ditch the skills I'd taught myself over all these years, go home, look after my kids and raise some animals.

I've got three kids. My eldest was studying in senior middle school, but I told him to drop out and come home. Rural education's a big problem here. What chance do ordinary peasants have of getting into university? We've only had a couple of dozen college students from this commune in over thirty years. He knew he'd have to come back home to farm when his schooling was over, so instead of studying properly he was learning how to smoke and play cards. He got too high and mighty to carry muck or sell vegetables in case his classmates saw him. Besides, the teachers get only twenty or thirty yuan a month: could they really care about teaching or feel settled in their jobs? My second boy's just started senior middle school and I've let him stay, but he's been warned: one step out of line and he'll be straight back home. My third's a daughter, and she may get somewhere in her studies. She's at primary school now.

I did some research before I decided to breed angora rabbits. I thought of fish, but the water's too cold to breed them in our paddy-fields here. Chickens don't pay. The papers have been urging peasants to get rich raising quails or earthworms, but there aren't the markets for them. I liked the idea of rabbits. They eat grass and that's every-where just for the gathering – and labour's dirt cheap in China. Ninety-five per cent of the angora-rabbit wool in world markets comes from China, and the demand can't be satisfied for the time being.

My idea in 1981 wasn't to be a specialized producer by myself, but to organize a dozen or so households raising rabbits, get some experience, then expand. I built my hutches to show everyone. A foreign business-man who came that year wanted to sign a contract with the county, and he sent for me to have a talk. Once he saw I knew what I was about, he started talking about a 7,000,000-yuan investment and asked us to do a feasibility study. The officials were all over the guesthouse floor with their calculators for a couple of nights till they'd calculated all 7,000,000 away. They were really going to do it in style with a processing factory and a machinery-repair shop.

The province happened to be arguing with some Japanese over an investment project, so our deal fell through. Just then the province's Yangtse Enterprise Company showed up, and they were taken with our plan. They lent the Guanxian county government 250,000 yuan to develop angora-rabbit breeding. That made me even more set on the idea. In Jiading county, Shanghai, they breed angora rabbits almost everywhere, so I paid my own way there and spent a month doing a house-to-house investigation. I got their set-up all figured out.

There was trouble at home as soon as my back was turned. The county authorities started talking about the rabbit shed I'd built and saying I was going to be a rich man any time now. So they got hordes of visitors coming to see my empty rabbit shed and ruining the paddy-field in front of our house. It was like market day. The county officials had set up an angora-rabbit company, with a board and a chairman, fixed their kids up with jobs in the company, and brought in a couple of university graduates. I wasn't on the board: I was head of the com-mune's angora-rabbit station. When I came back I was asked to give classes, so I wrote up some lecture notes and taught for a couple of weeks. Straightaway they were calling me a genius. I understood genetics and I knew five foreign languages as well! The county Party secretary called me by my first name and held me up as a model at a county education conference. They took a lot of pictures of me and displayed them for months. I was made the top angora-rabbit breeder in the county before I'd got a single animal.

I wanted the rabbits assigned to households to feed up, but under centralized control. To keep the stock pure and ensure scientific breeding I wasn't going to let just anyone breed them. The only sure way was to put quality before quantity.

But the county wouldn't agree. They wanted to get rich fast: quality could wait. They went on all day and every day about how angora rabbits had eight litters of five every year, and every baby was worth three yuan. It was bloody nonsense. You can make money selling rabbits, but when you're breeding angoras the whole thing's got to be completely controlled. They undertook to the Yangtse Enterprise Company that we'd have 10,000 rabbits in the county in 1981, and 100,000 in 1982. The 250,000 yuan were lent out to people to buy rabbits, and everyone in the county was scrambling for a share of the action. I went to Shanghai to get myself some rabbits and made money selling their litters that year. That's how I made my 10,000.

A year or so later the whole thing collapsed. Rabbits died of the cold, or got eaten by rats, or were mated wrong. Now I'm the only one with fifty or sixty rabbits left in the whole county, and there can't be five families with more than a dozen. The 250,000 yuan vanished into thin air, and all there was to show for it a year later were two and a half kilos of rabbit hair. Peasants with a few tufts of rabbit hair in a handkerchief came to ask me where to sell it. I bought it off them and sold it later with mine.

I felt terrible about it. Despite all the publicity, I'd failed. The peasants hadn't got rich by raising angora rabbits.

You city people imagine that we peasants are rolling in money. No such luck. Mind you, peasants haven't gone hungry the last few years, and we've been building ourselves new houses. Mouldy old thatched roofs have been replaced with tiles. But there isn't much money about. There are only a couple of ten-thousanders in our brigade, and I'm one of them. The other one's got a cassette recorder and he rides about on a motorbike, but he's got nothing at home. He's always got a lot more to say for himself at meetings than I have. When they were urging the peasants to get rich by breeding fish in their paddy-fields they got him to sell fish fry. They supported him and made him a ten-thousander. Everyone bought fry, but when they put chemical fertilizer on the paddy-fields the fish all died. What a farce!

The way we work out who's a ten-thousander here is to take your pigs and chickens and everything into account – it's not based on your net income. We've got a rattan craftsman in our brigade. His family's been making rattan chairs for generations and they've got pots of money. They really are ten-thousanders, but they keep quiet about it. If you stick to farming you might raise a pig so you can buy oil and cloth, but you won't get really rich. I've actually been pulling in only six or seven thousand the last couple of years. I've got a little shop that brings in over a thousand, and there's over 2000 yuan from sideline production, but I get only six or seven hundred yuan from selling angora hair, and I don't sell baby rabbits.

It was easy to make some money when the reforms started a couple of years ago, but if you wanted to make it really big you had to bend the rules. They say it doesn't do the country any harm, but who are they kidding? I've done things that way too, and I know. We've got Sichuan peasants running electric-cable factories, mica-processing works, plastics factories and so on, making tens of thousands a year. But government factories make all that stuff too. So how come only the peasants are making money? They give the official buyers a 20 or 30 per cent kickback for buying their lousy, expensive stuff. State-owned factories can't do that. So peasants make a pile and the state factories lose their markets. Traditional values, socialist morality – they all get buried in commercial competition.

It's hard to make money now when you're on your own against the province, the prefecture, the county and the township, who are all after it too; it's all hot air. People are always using buzz words – "third wave", "information", "main trend". But what I say is, there's no way of making money that hasn't been tried before. That's the main trend.

People have got to be able to make money out of production, not just out of wheeling and dealing. If we wheel and deal but don't increase output, does the country get any richer? When the *Guangming Daily* ran a lead story on us, a lot of ordinary people wrote to me wanting to buy rabbits and asking me about how to get rich. What was I to say? Was I to tell them that angora-rabbit breeding in our county has been a fiasco, and that with only sixty rabbits I was the county's greatest rabbit breeder?

Now I've had another opportunity, but it's given me a hell of a problem too. A Hongkong company wants to put up the money for me to breed angora rabbits for direct export. I've submitted a feasibility proposal to the county, but they've sat on it for over two months. If they won't back me I won't be a legal entity, I won't be able to go to negotiate with the Hongkong businessmen, and the investment money won't come through. I suppose the county can't be too happy about me starting another company when the 250,000 yuan they owe the province's Yangtse Enterprise Company have vanished without trace. If they neither support nor oppose me, they've covered themselves, but where does that leave me? Maybe I'll go in with the provincial company, or else simply take my plan to another county and supervise the breeding of angora rabbits there. I'm not in love with them, but I'm determined to have another go at it. I still think rabbit farming is a way we can all get rich.

Postscript: A month later we had a letter from Yang Sixian telling us that the county had set up its own company to breed rabbits: "I used to believe in relying on my own efforts, but I now understand that my own willpower is not enough: you need a lot of help and support from social forces. . . ."

Twenty-seven Days and Three Days

It's midday in the Shenzhen Dental Clinic, the first clinic in the country to offer a twenty-four-hour service. Some patients are waiting for attention. A cheerful young secretary in a white coat and cap greeted us: "You don't want to meet the director? You don't mind which one you talk to? Well, here's Dr Zeng Xiucong. She's not seeing a patient at the moment."

I came to this clinic when it opened in February 1983. The Guangzhou Dental Hospital provided all the staff. When they began recruiting, lots of people were afraid to put their names down. They thought it was going to be like the medical teams sent out during the Cultural Revolution. Nobody wanted to repeat that experience. I volunteered just the same. I spent six months in the countryside with a medical team in 1976. I looked after the peasants' oral health, teaching preventive methods and treating disorders, but I had to do a lot else besides. We grew Chinese herbal medicine, and showed the peasants how to construct latrines, to avoid unboiled water and to cook fish thoroughly. It was very tough.

My wages are still paid by the provincial hospital but my bonuses come from this hospital at Shenzhen. My basic wage is about 50 yuan a month, but I get about 150 yuan in my "red package", as they call bonus payments here. One month's bonus here is about equal to a year's bonus in Guangzhou. They're still on the old system there. Doctors, nurses and cleaners all get a ten-yuan bonus a month. That's the limit. Of course a lot of people are sorry now that they didn't volunteer to come at the beginning, but we can't take on any more staff. There are more than thirty of us, from the director to the handyman, each with specific duties. We only treat outpatients. We don't have facilities for patients to stay: we might lose money that way. Our

[111]

bonuses are on the low side of average by local standards according to the bank. I've heard that the singers at places like Silver Lake and the Ocean World get over 600 yuan a month and free board and lodging on top of that. They come from Guangzhou too.

The clinic gives good bonuses but not as much as we pull in for it. It's not publicly funded, it's a joint venture with a Hongkong company. As our standards are high and our service is quick, we get a lot of people who would be entitled to free medical care in a public hospital. They come from all over the province and from further afield, even though they have to pay. Peasants come too. Well, they've got more money than we have.

I know dentists abroad earn a lot of money. But this is still China, isn't it? We charge much more than they do in Guangzhou, but very little compared to Hongkong. Our director went there to check and found that our charges are between a fifth and a tenth of theirs. That's why so many people come across just to attend our clinic – in fact 70 per cent of our patients are from over there. The more patients you treat, the higher your bonus. The bonus is confidential, and we're not supposed to ask our colleagues how much they get. They are paid by the director himself.

Our director is wonderful. His professional standing in the province is very high. He always wanted to set up a hospital offering efficient, high-quality service and he's been able to do this here. He still practises, and sees patients just like the rest of us. If he goes back to the provincial hospital for a conference, it's in his own free time. The patients here can choose their dentist, but the dentists can't choose their patients. Otherwise each dentist would try to corner the cases paying the highest fees.

We don't have Sundays off. We work twenty-seven days at a stretch, then we go home for three days. It's a convenient two-hour bus journey. The hospital pays the fares. I can't take it easy when I get home. I have to do all the accumulated housework. Of course I'm married. I'm thirty-three. Don't I look it? We're still crowded in with my parents and my brothers. Housing in Guangzhou is very tight, but the hospital has got some staff accommodation under construction so I'm sure our turn will come one day. So we've no money and no place of our own. We haven't had a child yet. We get on very well. It's just nothing's happened yet. Apart from the director, everyone working here is under the age of forty-five. Most of us are women not too tied down at home. Our hostel is just behind the hospital. If a lot of patients arrive at night or during the lunch-hour, the receptionist can page anyone by name to go over. You get a good bonus for that. If anyone shirks or doesn't work properly they get sent back. There are plenty of others eager to come here. The profits from this hospital are ploughed back into building up the provincial hospital.

My own feelings? It's all the same, whether I'm here or in Guangzhou. I stand beside my dental chair and look after teeth. Oh, there is one difference. The equipment here is really up-to-date Japanese stuff from the 1970s. We have two first-class treatment rooms with the very latest American equipment. The equipment in the provincial hospital dates from the 1950s and their drills are much slower.

I'm not usually lonely. After work I knit or play table-tennis. Sometimes I take in a show or watch television. The twenty-seven days pass like that. I eat in the canteen for about thirty yuan a month. I couldn't afford to eat out. I go window-shopping but there's nothing for me to buy. You need foreign exchange certificates or Hongkong dollars for the good things. We don't have any. We just have more ordinary money than people in Guangzhou.

I wasn't outstanding at school. Some of my classmates were very bright. I started junior middle school in 1966. Later I was sent to Hainan where I worked in a rubber plantation. I passed the entry exam for the Guangzhou Dental Hospital in 1973.

The auxiliaries are allowed to treat patients here, the same as the dentists. That's one difference between Shenzhen and Guangzhou, the attitude to qualifications. Here the only thing that matters is whether you can do the work. Yes, it's a big difference.

There's another thing too. All our orders come from the director. What he says goes. That's because we have the system of managerial responsibility here so there aren't layers of administration. When we first came we were surprised that there weren't people to supervise things at each level. We weren't used to it. Later a few colleagues who'd just come made some quiet enquiries about their bonuses. They thought they were too low, and they wanted a system of democratic centralism here, but everyone else was against it. People wanted to go on taking orders straight from the director. He's full of ideas and really knows his stuff. This is a good place. We have clearly defined responsibilities, and we're straightforward with each other. I like it.

We really do work twenty-seven days at a stretch. We don't have

Sundays off and we don't have political study or vocational study either. To begin with it felt strange, though I couldn't really say why. With the old system we called it a six-day week, but with Wednesday afternoon for professional study and Saturday afternoon for political study, you could say it was like the western system of a five-day week. Here, we do our professional study by ourselves in our own time. Occasionally we have seminars to exchange information, but we don't have political study at all. That's another big difference.

The leadership of the Party? Yes, we have that. This year we've enrolled two new members in the Young Communist League. The Party secretary? I'm the Party secretary.

6

PEASANTS

Land

A village three or four kilometres from the railway line in Xuecheng county, Shandong. There are a number of new grey-brick houses with roofs fully covered in golden tiles. There are also a few houses with reinforced concrete roofs and some old cottages built with sun-dried bricks. This family lives in a thatched stone house with five rooms all in a row.

The head of the household, Zhang Yuxi, fifty-four.

Has Chairman Mao's body been kept? Are people allowed to see it?

Life has been better the last couple of years. I'm still hoping to get the money together for a trip to Beijing to have a look round. Before I die I want to see what Chairman Mao really looked like. I know about the mistakes in his last years. But they weren't his mistakes. Sitting there in his dragon palace, he couldn't possibly have known what was happening to us peasants. It was the people under him who were bad. They kept him in the dark and did all sorts of terrible things in his name. Chairman Mao had wealth and greatness written all over his face. He had the look of a real emperor, but he was better than an emperor. No emperor ever saved the poor. Chairman Mao was the saviour of the poor from the moment he was born. If he hadn't been, would we be missing him now?

I've got three sons and four daughters. The girls are all married off now, and two of the boys are married too. The other one's set up home by himself.

Zhangs are the top clan in this part of the world, but we're the only Zhangs in this village. The big families in this village are the Zhaos and the Songs. We came here in my dad's day because there was a terrible famine in our home village, eleven kilometres from here. That was before my time, but I heard my old man talk about it. Two baskets on a carrying pole he had, my big brother in one, and our raggedy bedding and cooking pots in the other, with my mam following behind leading my big sister by the hand. My sister died later, before she married. When they got to this village they turned for help to my dad's first wife's people. She had died of some disease a few days after she married my dad, but her family still counted as our relations.

When we first got here they put us up in their old lime-kiln and rented us some of their land. By Liberation we'd bought over two hectares, an ox, a donkey, and this house. There used to be four jujube trees and three pomegranate trees in the yard. One of the jujubes gave a real heavy yield, and one of the pomegranates gave very sweet fruit. When we first bought the place we kids ran round and round the trees, we were so happy. But a few days after we moved in the good jujube and the good pomegranate tree both died. They said the woman of the family who sold the house was so upset about losing it she fetched the bellows home, and boiled up a big pot of water, and poured it all on the good trees' roots. When Liberation came we'd just bought the house, so we were classified as middle peasants.

My dad was clever. First of all he relied on the Wangs, his first wife's people. The head of the Wang family was the village headman, and Dad was always running errands for him. When Wang got too old to carry on he let Dad do it. There he was, an outsider, running everything in the village. My dad had a gift for getting along with people. But he wouldn't be headman under the puppet government,* nor when the little Japs came either. There was plenty of folks did that. When the Japs left I took down their barbed wire and made it into wire sieves and ox halters to sell round the markets. Dad was already dead by then.

It wasn't easy for our mother, bringing three boys up and buying a home for us. A few years after Liberation the old lady started choking on her food. She couldn't get anything down. My big brother had gone off to join the Eighth Route Army† many years before that, and he was stationed in the Nanjing Military Region then, so he took her there for treatment, then brought her back again a while later. She was dressed up in new clothes and chattering happily about how she'd gone to Nanjing town and seen the world. But my brother called me outside, squatted down and said, "Brother, what Mam's got is cancer, and it's

---

* Set up under Japanese auspices during the occupation.
† The communist-led force in north China during the Japanese occupation.

hopeless." I didn't know what cancer was then, but when I saw him crying his eyes out I could tell Mam was done for. She lived another six months. She had her wits about her all the time, but she couldn't eat anything and was moaning in agony night and day. One day she called us to her bedside and took her leave of us. I knew she didn't want to go then, just as things were starting to get better at last, but that disease was living hell for her. I was a cadre in the co-op then, so I had to go to a meeting every evening. When I came back that night I found she'd hanged herself. She was wearing her best clothes.

In those days you were still allowed to bury people. My kid brother had gone to the Great Northern Waste. He throws his money about and he's always on the move. Well, he came back and looked after Mam's funeral. We built her a proper tomb with a good, solid, concrete tomb-mound. It was one of the best tombs in the village. My big brother didn't dare come back — he was scared that giving her a send-off like that would be committing a political mistake – but he sent money. That was thirty years ago. He came home a few days back, asked where she was buried, and went off there himself.

My big brother's been the clever one ever since he was tiny, and he was my parents' favourite. He started off in the village school, then went to a mission school in town. After that he came back to teach in the village for a while. My kid brother was the baby of the family, so he got spoiled. When he didn't learn his school lessons properly Big Brother hit him on the palm of his hand same as anyone else, because he was the teacher. I was stuck in the middle, but I never had a single day's schooling.

Yes, I've stayed here on the land all my life, and things have only really gone well the last couple of years since the land was shared out. That's a fact.

When we had advanced co-ops* I was the head of one. Quite the little activist I was in those days. When the call went out to form co-ops I put everything my parents had bought – the land, the ox, the donkey and all – into the co-op. At night I was grieving over losing them, but during the day I was taking the lead, trying to talk other people into joining – and trying to talk myself into it too. My big brother was away

* Nearly all China's peasant households were swept into Advanced Agricultural Producers' Co-operatives, in which land, draught animals and large items of equipment were collectivized, in the winter of 1955–6.

from the village as a revolutionary cadre, so I just had to do right by him and go along with the high-ups. To be honest with you, when he first ran away to join the Eighth Route Army my mam almost cried herself blind, she was so upset. But in the end the Eighth Route Army were the ones who conquered the country, weren't they? Well, I was a cadre back at home, and I didn't dare help myself to anything. Nobody did anything like that then. It's different nowadays.

If the co-op needed anything we had at home I told them to come and take it. You see, I take after my parents, and I'd fixed us up with all the farm tools and made sure we had everything, so we wouldn't be caught short and have to go begging.

Later on I got the feeling that things were going wrong. You couldn't fool the crops in the fields. The taller they grew the worse they were. Where we'd got four tons a hectare before Liberation it was down to half of that. People wouldn't put their backs into collecting and spreading muck. The land was being worked right out. That year my big brother stopped over while he was making an official visit. I showed him around the fields and explained what was happening. He asked me what ought to be done about it. Divide the land up, I told him, and let everyone work their own plot, then they'll care because they'll be working for themselves. My brother didn't answer. He just told me to watch my tongue, to keep my mouth shut. I couldn't say I saw the light then.

Remember that big movement for making iron and steel?* Village cadres were supposed to play the main role. I was in charge of the group from our village. We made a lot of steel. That was when we cut down all the trees on the hills. Learning how to make steel wasn't hard – it's not hard to learn anything. I just saw how they did it and copied them. As for the steel we made, well, of course there was no use for it. Later on the family sent me a message: they were all well nigh starved to death. That was during the famine. So I forgot about the steelmaking and got home as fast as I could to feed all those mouths. The first people who starved to death in those days were buried in thin coffins, then bodies were put in a couple of vats joined rim to rim. Later on, when everyone was so weak with hunger they couldn't move, whole families died and were just left where they lay. That's when I stopped being a cadre.

I really wanted out. I wanted to go down a big pit near here as a

* In 1958, during the Great Leap Forward.

miner. I wasn't bothered about getting killed in a cave-in as long as I could get the money for off-ration grain, and that cost plenty. But they wouldn't take me. They wouldn't let anyone with a rural registration become a worker.* I was a farmer so I was stuck scraping a living out of the soil.

We had our little orchard – 160 square metres to the east of the village. That's where we've built my eldest son's house. I planted vines and grafted peaches on them – May Fresh. In three years they were cropping – real darlings, all red and with a little twist at the end. When everyone else in the market was getting thirty cents a pound for theirs, I had people scrambling for mine at sixty. But when the "four clean-ups"† business came along in 1964 I had to cut them all down – every single one. I cried my eyes out and couldn't go near that end of the village for two weeks – even seeing that little orchard from a distance had me in tears.

Life got harder and harder after that. Later on we only got about eight hundred kilos of wheat to the hectare. Each of us only got five or ten kilos of unhusked wheat a year. Making noodles for visiting relations or a few griddle cakes for New Year cleaned you out. There wasn't any money to be had. When we harvested the peanuts I couldn't afford to let the kids try them. I cooked them by lamplight in the middle of the night and sneaked off before dawn to a market a long way away. If you slipped up they arrested you and confiscated the whole lot – and you didn't dare so much as moan about it when you got home. It was so hard to get by those days that . . . I can't find the words. The production brigade sent me off with a team to fence off the hills over there and plant a whole lot of new trees where we'd cut them all down in the iron and steel campaign. A few years after that I was put in charge of another team burning lime. You had to use any skills you'd got, but you never got a penny. And you weren't allowed to go and earn money anywhere else.

We couldn't have built this house without my big brother's help. It cost us over a thousand yuan even then. I had to keep writing to him asking for money. I suppose he hasn't treated me badly, all right, but I still reckon he's getting off lightly. When he ran off to join the Eighth

* And thus eligible to buy rationed grain from the state, unlike peasants.
† A campaign in 1964–5 supposedly intended to purge the villages politically, economically, organizationally and ideologically that curbed such "capitalist" activities as growing for the private market.

Route Army the Japs came to search the house. They stuck their guns in my face and asked me where he was. After the Japs were done for the Kuomintang came, and they searched the place too. They found a picture of him as a student. They tried to scare me. They said they could arrest him straightaway with it. We're peasants, and we were too stupid to realize they'd never be able to find him. Mam and me, we were so scared we were crying and wishing we'd hidden it properly. While he was away fighting the Japs and the Kuomintang I was rushing all over the place with our ox, trying to hide from the Japs and the Kuomintang. That's why I was fed up with him – he owed it to me to see me right. Two of my boys wanted to get married, but no girl was going to have them if they hadn't got houses. And my girls couldn't stay at home unwed for ever. At the very least they had to have a clothes press to take with them. It was death, being stuck on the land, but I couldn't even die.

It's been better everywhere the last couple of years, since the land was divided, but only this last couple of years.

We did manage to get our hands on some money pretty quickly. My youngest daughter and me worked in a lime kiln for one yuan twenty a day each. My youngest boy got into the commune dye factory, and he went off to Shanghai to learn the trade for six months. He's a skilled man now, pulling in sixty or seventy yuan a month all told with his wages and bonuses. Everyone earns his own and keeps it. When my eldest was demobbed he went down the pit – he's on his own now. All the ones who wanted to be are married. I can afford a cigarette and a drink now – but it's only been in these last couple of years.

If you figure it all together my sons and me have got two hectares between us – less than we had before Liberation. Of course, it's only contracted for from the production brigade. It's in about a dozen different lots. We grow a bit of everything – wheat, sweet potatoes, sorghum, millet, peanuts, sesame, the lot. Anyone can see whether the land's being worked properly or not. You can't hide the crops: they're like the farmer's face. Some families will only marry their girls to men whose land is choked with weeds, because that shows they've gone off trading or carrying. I'm no good at any of that: it's too complicated. If you contract for a tractor you've got to be able to get on with people who want goods moved. All that business was grabbed by the people with power.

I haven't contracted for hillsides. No. Even if I could work them, I'd never be able to get my hands on any.

You townies don't know the first thing about the countryside – it's a lot more complicated than you think. Take this place: the land here was divided up only last year, but it's been redivided again this year. Why? Because the brigade cadres could see other people's crops doing well and were jealous of their land. That's why they had another share-out and got their hands on the best land. They were bound to get it. We drew lots, but they fixed it. Everyone had to draw, but what we all got were the bad plots. They kept the other slips back for themselves. Nobody's going to have the law on them. That's village life for you.

My skills get me nowhere. A skilled man's no match for a brazen thief. I'm not going to make dirty money. Anyhow, these policies have been set for fifteen years. They won't keep changing like they used to before. Maybe we old peasants will do all right if we put our backs into it.

Deep in the Mountains

The Taihang Mountains in Shanxi province. A mountain village without water or electricity or a paved "government" road. Even on a 1/100,000 map, this place is marked only by a figure showing the elevation.

Old Lady Zhao who married into the Yang family. Sixty-eight years old.

People are like grass. They grow where the seed drops and that is where they belong. If the seed falls in these mountains, that's where it belongs. We're right out of the way here. Almost nothing reaches us. We heard about the terrible things the Japanese and the Kuomintang people did in other places, but they didn't get here. We only saw soldiers in the village once: some of General Feng Yuxiang's troops running for their lives after the Japanese had beaten them. There's another village, Wanquanzhuang — they're much better off than us. They've got water, they have troops garrisoned with them and a chance to see more of life. For the last couple of years the young folks have been saying Wanquanzhuang is doing better than ever, they've even got a government road. Well, let them. What use is it anyway? I hear they've got a new sort of moneybags there called a "10,000-yuan household". You'd think people like that would be afraid of a land reform!

Young folk here moan about their fate because they weren't born somewhere better. But is the big city so wonderful? Say you were born as a donkey there? I listen to the radio when I've nothing to do. I know all the new words. I don't want to be backward. If you're backward they take you to the commune headquarters to be criticized. During the Cultural a call went out on the radio for our team leader to go and face criticism. I heard his confession when it was broadcast. But a few years back, the Central had some meeting and they said it was our team leader who'd been right, and the Cultural was wrong. He was accused of "backsliding". They said he was secretly against the social and was pushing that freedom business forward. They say Chairman Mao and Chairman Liu were quarrelling in the Cultural about whether to go in for social or freedom but that's plain silly. The way I see it, Chairman Mao was wonderful and freedom is good too.

Our village is the biggest you'll find in these mountains. There are two households on the eastern side. Each household looks after its own slope. This is the team headquarters here, where people had to listen to all those meetings in the Cultural. We had two co-ops here to start with: a poor one and a rich one. They were joined up as a higher co-op. Then we became a production team under the commune. Our team leader's in charge of this village and the mountains round here for about five kilometres.

I married into this village from Beiwa. It was a swap. His younger sister married my elder brother and I married him. I lost out. They cheated my mum and dad by pretending his family was descended from the famous Yang family of generals. It was all fixed by the grown-ups. We young ones weren't consulted. That was feudalism. These days they marry the new way. They have a choice. In our day we wouldn't have dared. It would have been immoral. I don't hold with this freedom – they get up to no good.

We never had different classes here. We're all poor – the comrades from the Central settled that. We had no rich peasants and no landlords. Even the chieftains – that's the bandits – didn't set foot here. There was nobody for them to live off. Anyway, the richest man here was a middle peasant. He headed the rich co-op. He's gone now, dead many a year. His son's hopeless, can't run anything – he's just poor like the rest of us.

Times are better now. Deng Xiaoping knows what he's doing. Chairman Mao's government was good too when it started. There was no grain levy and we made a good living out of selling mountain products. When the "four clean-ups" started things got bad. Officials came to investigate us and wrote a report about how we were selling persimmons to buy our food instead of making fields on the mountainsides. They said we needed socialist education. Before they'd got that started, the Cultural came along. Even the old society wasn't as bad as that. At least there was no one to push us around in those days. They weren't going to risk their necks coming up here after us and even the grain levy only got as far as Wanquanzhuang.

When the Cultural started we were told to cut the trees down. With no fruit to sell we went hungry. They even accused us of taking the capitalist road, then made us pay a grain levy like Dazhai. The team leader cried like a baby. The workteam was in charge of everything. After Deng Xiaoping's big meeting a few years ago, they seemed to trust us again. But trees need time before they'll bear fruit. Damn fools! It'll take ten years to recover. Luckily they sent us a science man. He knows about trees so things are looking up. Not all these scientists are good, mind you. The ones in that team who only let you have two babies are science people. They give young women the pill. They even claim they're being especially generous to us. I've heard that beyond the mountains you're only allowed one. That can't be good. If you're unlucky and it's a girl, she still counts. How can people carry on their family lines? Are they to leave everything to an outsider?

Of course we've got the electric. We buy those tubes of it you use in radios. Everyone's been buying radios in the last few years. They cost a fortune: 100 kilos of persimmons each. Of course if we had a government road they'd be cheaper. What we need is a government road we can use to go down the mountain, but other folks can't take to come up here. They're a bad lot, the folk beyond the mountains. Even the youngsters steal. The pedlars who come up here are worse still. They take our savings for watches that don't even work. We can't get them mended in town, either. They just say we've been tricked by private traders. In the old days they used to smuggle salt, now it's watches. Just goes to show, city people are a thieving lot.

I've seen all the Beijing sights. They send us a film every month with a thingummy you pedal to make it work. Everyone was in tears when we watched the Chairman's funeral. We were all afraid of what it would be like without him. But now we've found out that things go all right even though he's dead. We were scared there'd be a change of dynasty. Afraid that the bourgeoisie would take power. I've heard on the radio that Chairman Mao himself made some mistakes. Jiang Qing was a bad lot. The news said she's not to be executed. Our Central is being very good, sparing her life. Still, however wicked she is, she used to be Chairman Mao's wife, didn't she? As I see it, a woman can't govern a country. It's a bad thing for women to be too free. You mustn't take liberation too far. There ought to be a rule against women being big officials.

Stay a few more days, it's a hard journey to get here. Things may not be too good but we're not so poor as we used to be, we can feed you! Write about the mountain scenery so that foreigners start taking trips here. The youngsters say that when foreigners take a fancy to a place, they throw their money about.

Boring But Glorious

Jiang Guoliang, male, twenty-two. Sentry at a radar station in the distant outskirts of Beijing.

I wonder where to start. I'm a farm boy and when I leave the forces I want to go home and be a peasant again. Our company commander told me just now I could answer any questions you asked, otherwise I wouldn't go shooting my mouth off about myself. Yes, sometimes our life stories have to be kept secret. You can't have loose talk. Fortresses are often taken from the inside. We're disciplined, and we know when to keep our mouths shut.

When I was a rookie I didn't know anything about anything. I'd never been on a train till our ride to Beijing. When the train announcer said, "With the co-operation of the broad masses of the passengers we have completed our glorious assignment of carrying the defenders and builders of socialism," it was a big thrill. I was so dumb then: I thought the announcement was especially in honour of us new recruits. Then the old comrades who met us said, "They've been making that announcement for years." When I went home on leave last year there was light music instead. There's only one thing hasn't changed: the fighter's responsibility.

I'm from Shangrao district in Jiangxi province. I've always regarded it as an honour to be a soldier protecting the nation's capital. I went back home to farm after I finished junior middle school, and I volunteered to be conscripted. Who says nobody wants to join up now that life's better in the countryside? Maybe the sons of the 10,000-yuan households don't want to join, but how many of them are there? Not many. There weren't any when I joined up in 1979. Jiangxi is one of the places where our revolution began, and the broad masses of the people know that defending the country is our duty. I often think we country people love our country and the Party more than city folk do. I guess cities are all mixed up.

I reckon inequality's the most serious problem. Not between officers and men, other kinds of inequality. City folk all call us "squaddies" or "soldier boys". They're not just cold – they look down their noses at us. But we're defending them and their peaceful lives. When our boys were dying on the Vietnamese border they were still going to the theatre and dancing. Even within the army the radar specialists look down on us guards, although it's them we're guarding. Inside the company men from the same part of the country stick together, but the city lads look down on the country boys, specially us Jiangxiers – they say we're tight-fisted. Just because we don't waste money on cold cream like them. What does a soldier want that muck on his face for?

In combat, we'd all stick together. Last year there was a fire in the generator room in our compound, and even guys who are always at each other's throats fought it out together. I've never seen real combat. As the saying goes, soldiers spend a thousand times longer in training than in battle.

I'll be going home soon. I've been on sentry duty four hours a day in all weathers for over four years now. The radar here is part of Beijing's early-warning system. It turns around up there over our heads day and night, year in, year out, and it never stops. What our job comes down to is protecting it while it turns. It's boring, but glorious too.

In my free time I like basketball and literature.

True, our monthly allowance is even less than an apprentice gets paid, but we carry a heavy responsibility. That's what makes the job glorious. I still think it's better in the army. The regimental top brass comes and spends the Spring Festival with us. Would you get that in civvy street?

It's hard to get into Beijing from one year's end to the next. I've only been into town three times and once to Tianjin – and that was on duty. In peacetime we protect you from afar, but if there were a real war we'd be the first to bleed and die.

What would we like? Well, we like it if one in ten or even one in a hundred of the people who walk past our sentry posts give us a smile. We can't greet them because we're on duty. But we thank them in our hearts.

Planning Her Family

A peasant household in the mountains of eastern Sichuan. Of the five daughters, three are sitting on the threshold, one is leaning against the doorframe and the fifth is in her mother's lap. They are all grinning as they listen to their mother talking. A three-year-old boy is snuggling up to his mother's breast and suckling.

Big Sister Zheng, forty-six years old.

I've borne nine children. The first was a boy but he died. Then I had seven girls, the sixth of them died. Only the ninth time did heaven send another son.

Once you've got one on the way you just carry it until your time comes. I worked and cooked right up to the birth, so some were born out there in the fields and some at the stove. I don't send for the herbal doctor or call for any help. I can manage everything myself. You just boil up a pan of water and scorch a pair of scissors over the fire so that you can cut the cord. My mum helped me with my first. My husband never does. He works with bamboo, so he's out going from job to job all day carrying his tools on his back. Anyway, he can't bear the sight of blood. It scares him. Go on, laugh, but if that first boy hadn't died maybe there wouldn't be so many of them today. I only had them because I wanted to have a son.

Girls are no use. They can't inherit your house or your property. You struggle all your life, but who gets your house in the end? Your daughters all marry out and belong to someone else. They get fourteen outfits from the groom's side. In the old days they'd all be cotton, maybe machine-made, maybe homespun. Here in the mountains you never even saw soft, smooth silks and satins. Later, at best you might have got gabardine but now there's wool, dacron and nylon. But you have to match each outfit by giving the bride a piece of furniture and

[130]

that means at least a dozen people, even a small bridal procession, to carry it. You've got to provide six or seven loads of furniture, each carried by a pair of men, at the very least, and someone to play the reed-pipe. Women do that here. That's the way I came here from the other side of the mountain, and that's how my eldest lass went back over there. She'd already had a daughter by the time I had my son. I don't know why her first was a girl. You take after your own mother in what you have first – a girl or a boy. And yet, my first was a boy and so was my mother's.

Of course my elder brother will inherit everything in my old home. We haven't even given it a thought. You can't rely on a son-in-law. Have you ever heard our saying, "A man will no more support his mother-in-law than a pot will make its own beancurd"? A son-in-law isn't family – you can only depend on your own son. In all those years before I had one, I had to watch my tongue. When I quarrelled with the woman down the hill she would call me names. "Barren old hag," she'd mock, meaning that I had a husband but no son. She had two daughters and three sons. I'd sit at home weeping with fury. I blamed myself for not being able to produce sons the way she could. It's fine now.

Bringing up a family hasn't ever stopped me from working. I've got 150 chickens and four pigs – one sow and three young porkers. I used to keep bees too, but not any more. It wasn't that I couldn't manage it, the price of honey went down from one yuan a pound to only forty cents. Besides, the honey wasn't any good. Pesticides ruin the pollen. I'm raising ducks now and still working in the fields. I plant wheat and potatoes in early spring, rice, corn and sweet potatoes in late spring, and winter roots and rapeseed in the autumn. When there's a rush on my man comes home to give a hand. We women can do everything men can, and some things they can't, like pickling vegetables, curing pork, preserving mustard root, having babies . . .

Of course, they don't let you have many babies any more. You're supposed to get a coil or have your tubes tied. The wives all troop off together to be done. If you have another without permission you get fined. The bigger your family, the bigger the fine. The fines here are 400 yuan for the third, 600 for the fourth, 750 for the fifth, 900 for the sixth, and 1300 for the seventh. Two of mine had died, so this boy of mine worked out at 1300. I checked up on that in advance. I paid cash on the nail. If I hadn't they'd have taken the furniture – and if that wasn't enough to cover the fine, the tiles on the roof too. I knew about the fine but I still wanted to go ahead and have the kid. There was always the chance it'd be a boy. What else could I do?

Once I was expecting, I couldn't keep it quiet. When word got out tongues began to wag and it reached the big ears of the district government. They sent people here to work on me. Not just one, a whole crowd of them, cadres from the district. They sat around in a big circle, and went on and on at me, one after another. I never said a thing, I just listened and kept on listening till they got fed up talking and went away. They came again, the whole lot of them, several times. In the end I went into hiding. I hid out at my mother's, but after I'd been there a bit I started to miss the kids and the chickens and the pigs so I'd pop back to see them. I'd stay a while and then go back into hiding.

I didn't argue with the township cadres. I didn't say anything at all to them. They were just doing their job. I know they've got their problems too. I hear the township fines the district Party secretary and the family planning commissioner a lot of money if even one baby more than they're allowed gets born in the district. It has to come out of their own pockets! When they get fined at the end of each year they're in tears. It's terrible. But it'd have been terrible for me as a barren woman. So I went back into hiding and gave birth to my son.

My sister-in-law had six daughters too before she finally had her boy. When the family planning people came to question her she didn't go into hiding: she drank pesticide! And she did it twice. That gave them such a fright that they never came back again.

I know I did wrong. I won't have any more. I went with the other women to the commune clinic to have another coil put in.

They fined me the 1300 yuan. We had to borrow 900 of it. Took us two years to pay it back. Having sons is what women come into the world for. What's the point of it all if you don't have a son? It's what we live for.

Hey, that bite hurt. Just you dare treat your mother that badly when you're grown up!

7

WORKERS

Mr Average

We stopped a young man at the Xidan Market in Beijing. We'd guessed right: he was a worker.

Zhao Pingguang is a twenty-two-year-old stoker in a steel mill. It's heavy work; only men do the job.

Sure, I'll talk to you, but let's get one thing straight right from the start: I never read papers or magazines. I'm so wiped out by the end of the day that all I'm good for is falling asleep in front of the TV.

My dad's a worker, so is Mum, and so are my two brothers. My sister married a fella from right out of town and she works in a bookshop.

Suppose I've got the most education of anyone in the family. At least I finished senior middle school. My brothers only made it through junior middle. My parents are both illiterate. They have to use a seal to sign for their wages every month. For their generation it didn't matter; they could live off their skills. Things are different now. For example, my senior middle-school diploma makes life easier for me than it is for my brothers. They'll have to pass the senior middle-school exams if they want to be grade-three workers; I don't need to. But I'm only a grade two. It all depends on how long you've been in the job. Once you've been around long enough if you aren't a complete disaster you'll get your upgrading and a few more bucks.

I started at Jinshifang Primary in 1969. We were all street kids. You wouldn't find anyone from a "good family" in a dump like that. You couldn't really call it a school — we just fooled around all day. My dad was in the Workers' Propaganda Team that occupied Qinghua University. The old man can't read a word, but there he was giving all those university people shit. The Cultural Revolution screwed me up from when I was a kid, but that's just how it was: "All power to the proletariat".

"Studying to become an official" was criticized, and everyone was talking about studying being useless. You should have seen all us little seven-year-old farts running around criticizing this stuff. Were we full of crap! But what use is studying? My teacher only made fifty yuan a month, half what my dad got, and he was much older than Dad.

I started studying seriously at junior middle school. By then everything had changed, and as I've always gone along with the crowd I started working. I went to Number Eight. We were the last year to get there just because we lived nearby. After that it became a key school – you had to pass an exam to get in. Kids in the lower forms looked down on us and said we were all duds. It was really weird – we didn't get to study the stuff they were doing in first year until we were in third year.

I finished my three years of junior middle school in 1979. By then you could only go on by passing an exam. I wanted to go straight out to work. I figured that's where I'd end up anyway. But they wouldn't allocate you a job if you'd only finished junior middle school, and I wasn't going to hang around selling bowls of tea on the street like all those other guys who were "waiting for work". I had no choice but to take the exams. Of course it would have been great to go to a college or a tech, and get myself a meal-ticket for life; but I blew it. The only places you can get in with low marks like mine are cooking schools and the Parks Department schools. Me, a cook? You must be joking. The Parks Department schools just teach gardening – they're even worse. You slave your guts out studying and graduate as a hick. Screw that! My senior middle school was an ordinary one: Number Thirty-five.

After school I started at the steel mill. I was lucky because I could take over my dad's place in the regular workforce. If it hadn't been for that I'd probably still be waiting for work.

He got out of the propaganda team ages ago. You know the saying, "Cadres back to your offices, workers back to the factories. The Cultural Revolution was one big mistake." You can forget about him being retired and all that: he's still at the mill going strong. All he did was give up his regular place to me. He's a Party member, and didn't want to end up drawing his pension and getting hired by other factories as an old expert. They'll pay for expertise these days and he could be rolling in dough if he wanted.

On my first day in the new job they sent me out roadsweeping. All the new workers have to do a spell in the "factory beautification brigade", and it was six weeks before they gave me any real work. Some guys ended up with good jobs, but I got stuck with a real lousy one. If I'd known they watch your attitude even when you're sweeping the fucking roads I'd have damn well done better. But I was a bit slow on the uptake, and I was sloppy. I really screwed myself. Those six weeks have decided the rest of my life. My dad didn't have a clue about all that. When he started out as an apprentice he had to clean the chamber-pot for his foreman. There were some guys even slacker than me, but they had connections – you won't see a section head's son doing what I do.

My job is feeding the furnace. It's unskilled work: you just keep on shovelling coal in. You're sweating from the moment you start. It's 50° to 60° centigrade in there all year round. There's this character who came in the same time as me. They put him in the repair shop and he spends all day fooling around. The reason you have it so good, you bastard, is that you took that sweeping seriously – that's what I think every time I see him.

It's an hour by bus each way from where I live. I give the mill ten hours of my life every day. I lived in a factory dorm for a while – six to a room, and incredibly noisy. But I kept losing things: meal tickets, money, clothes, everything. I finally gave up and moved back home. They eventually found out who was swiping my stuff and the bastard was given the boot. He's opened up a small restaurant and now he's doing better than any of us. I hear he's already made six or seven thousand. It's a rip-off joint too, if you ask me. I went there once and had a beer. It cost fifty or sixty cents a litre like anywhere else. "Call this beer?" I said. "Do you water it down or something?" "Yeah? And what are you going to do about it? You haven't got any proof. Go on back to your lousy forty-buck job where you belong." I was so pissed off I split his head open with my bowl. The fucker had stolen my meal tickets and never paid me back. He didn't dare make a complaint to the mill himself, but his old man had the nerve to call the factory and report me. The head of security hauled me in but I told him, "You can forget about that complaint. The man who spoke to you was Little Landlord's old man." We all called that guy "Little Landlord". His dad's been working in the commercial administration office for twenty or thirty years, but no one had any time for him before. Lately he's doing well for himself as the guy who gives out permits for new businesses, so of course he's very popular. Life's like that: you never know which cloud's going to piss on you.

I'm not in the Youth League or the Party. What would they want with me? I'm no progressive – not that I'm a reactionary either. I love my country, but there's plenty of no-good Party members. There was this one guy who lived near us. He got permission to visit his mother in Japan, and that was the last we saw of him. Hear he's started up a business over there. Makes you want to throw up. I wouldn't go even if I did have relatives overseas, not that I do, mind you. Don't even have any relations outside Beijing; we've always lived here.

Just look at our mill. They haven't got a clue about what to do with the foreign machinery they've bought. They finally got this technical expert from some company in Hongkong. Couldn't see the management for all the arse-licking that was going on. The man could do no wrong. If the truth be told none of them have the faintest idea about the technical side. They spend all their time swilling tea in their offices. People blather on about China going to the dogs if people like me had a say in the running of things; but we'd all be in the shit if everyone was like them, believe you me. They buy their technical expertise with our money. Who needs them? It'd be a different matter if they knew their jobs. Screw 'em. The high and mighty section head pointed at a crane one day and asked what the "1OT" painted on the side of it meant. It's a disgrace. A few months back they gave 'em all the boot and put in a bunch of specialists. But all the old penpushers are still doing okay for themselves organizing gardening brigades, canteen committees and that factory beautification office – screw 'em. They're all supposed to accept any position, to be ordinary workers if that is what is needed – but none of them would.

My biggest headache is finding a wife. My job's nothing great. Even with bonuses and extras the best is a little over seventy yuan a month and I'm no looker. My family's no help, and the girls I go for wouldn't give me a second glance. I'd never go to a marriage agency. All they do is scribble down a few details and match you up with someone. I don't have anything going for me; it'd be a lost cause. If I had 3000 yuan I could buy a colour TV, a sofa and a fridge, and they'd all be after me. But what am I supposed to do, steal the money?

If you ask me love's a load of crap. It's a material world, believe me. All the skilled men have married women with factory jobs. Let's face it, workers look down on peasants and cadres on workers. I'm just the same – there's no way I'd ever marry a hayseed. I don't care what they say about the villages being rich nowadays. Marry a peasant and you end up with one foot in the sticks. Then if you have a son his residence permit stays with his mother in the countryside; he'd still be a peasant.

I like playing cards. I go skating in the winter and swim in the summer. Never read, but I like the movies. Reading sends me to sleep; it's the same when I watch TV. That's what it's like for us workers.

I'm doing my bit for society so I guess I haven't wasted my life. I've got a stake in socialism. As I said, I just go along with the mob, so I guess I feel the same as everyone else: the country has a future. We're all in it together. I'm not touting any Party line, it's what I really think. Give me a bit of credit. You shouldn't take all that badmouthing I do too seriously – deep down I know what's what. Only the Communist Party can pull things round. *Real* Communists are okay.

I can't make any comparisons. There's tons of other young workers like me about. Some are more political than me, others worse. I'm just Mr Average.

Streetcorner PhD

A crowd of men with a sprinkling of women have formed a semi-circle outside a public toilet. He stands inside that semi-circle pointing at a big chart hanging on the wall and expounding his "Eleven Short Cuts in Calculation".

Someone squeezes in, then squeezes out again. "Huh! A charlatan!" This meets with a glare and a retort of, "Shut up – he's a mathematician," from another member of the crowd. A youngster giggles: "He's hooked on the sound of his own voice. He's a streetcorner PhD, the genius outside the lavatory. He comes here every day to talk about his short cuts in calculation."

Hey, no photographs! No interviews here. What the hell do you want? *(We assure him that we're not going to steal his patent, nor do we want to accuse him of disturbing public order.)*

My mistake, sorry. You get all sorts here, you see. Some of those swine are out to drive me out of business. One jerk sent a newspaper a photo of me teaching with pictures of people selling oil-stain removers and rat poison, showmen with performing monkeys and people putting up posters about swapping housing. Said we should all be cleaned off the streets. But I'm not like them. I'm popularizing quick calculation – that's science. Wait while I pack up, then we'll find somewhere quiet to talk. *(He addresses the crowd.)* "Well, comrades, something's cropped up, so that's all for today. If you've any problems they'll keep till tomorrow. See you then."

My name's Zhao Shipu. I'm forty-one. I'm a worker but mathematics is my hobby. It's fascinating. I know eleven short-cuts in calculation for all the fundamental operations: addition, subtraction, multiplication, division. I can do it faster than an abacus! If you memorize my formulas and use an abacus too, that's even faster.

Calculators? I can't beat them, but how many people have them? My formulas are for accountants, students and shop assistants who don't have calculators.

Actually these methods aren't my own invention. I've just put them together. In principle it's just complementary functions, logarithms, and all that. But I get a kick out of passing them on.

My parents are dead. I had a wife but we got divorced. She took the kid. We got on each other's nerves. I couldn't stand her.

I finished junior middle school in 1963. As I couldn't get into senior middle I waited to be assigned a job. In those days they didn't call us "young people waiting for jobs" the way they do now; we were "social youth". There was no private enterprise either, so all you could do was drift. Things weren't so free and easy in those days. Never mind American films, you hardly ever got a chance to see a Hongkong one. I remember clearly standing in line one night to see the Hongkong version of *A Dream of Red Mansions*.* It wasn't till I got in that I discovered they were all mainland opera singers singing in Shanghai dialect, which I couldn't understand! I left in less than ten minutes, got the stub back, and resold my ticket. I'd paid fifty cents for the ticket, watched a bit of the film and got one yuan for it! I realized I was on to a good thing. So I found out which films were popular, then started queuing at the box office at 3 or 4 a.m. to buy tickets. I hadn't much money, so I'd only buy a dozen tickets or so and sell them at higher prices. When I'd doubled my capital I bought more, and did pretty well out of it. In one month I made about fifty yuan. That was real money in those days, when a portion of roast duck cost only eighty cents – or one yuan six cents with pancakes, scallions and soup. Nowadays a meal like that will set you back ten yuan.

But I got caught. A cop nabbed me at a cinema entrance, and I was held for questioning for a week. In those days being arrested was a terrible disgrace – your family felt they'd never live it down. I couldn't face people after that. It's different nowadays, those little bastards don't give a damn about a few weeks in the slammer. They think they're a cut above people who haven't been in, and they go on swilling beer, dancing and swearing at everybody.

It wasn't too hard to find work then. You were encouraged to go to the countryside, but that was up to you. I started in an electrical-

* Also known as *The Dream of the Red Chamber*.

appliances factory. It was a collective, and not as good as a state-owned one. I could perfectly well have gone on waiting, but a state-run works mightn't have suited me either. Besides, this place was near home, so I signed on for a two-year apprenticeship. I'd learned the job in a couple of weeks, and I was qualified in less than six months. But I got paid much less than a craftsman doing the same job. The woman in charge was really foul. She'd started the place in 1958 with a dozen other housewives. She was always going on and on about how tough it had been then. Anyone would have thought she deserved a medal. But she never did a stroke, just kept finding excuses to run to the Party secretary to inform against people. It was only much later, when I saw her pay her dues, I realized the bitch was a Party member! Later still I heard she'd used her Party card to get herself transferred into the town from the country when she got married, so I'd even less use for her.

In the Cultural Revolution I organized a rebel group of nine of us called the "Revolt-to-the-End Brigade". We went after that woman and joined in the attack on Liu Shaoqi.* Looking back now, it was all wrong. But the whole country had gone red. Not many people kept their heads. Nearly all of us were taken in. We made complete fools of ourselves. Later a rival group got me. My crime was profiteering during the hard years, the evidence being the self-criticism I'd written during detention. They'd broken into the factory's personnel records.

That was the first time I knew it was in my file. Of course, the economic crisis was in 1961, and I was reselling film tickets in 1964; but if they were going to lump the two things together there was nothing I could do about it. They got me, and that was the end of our Revolt-to-the-End Brigade.

That was why my wife divorced me. She sells vegetables, the gutless bitch! I send her a ten-yuan postal order every month for the kid, but we don't meet.

After my rivals seized power, they locked me up in a small dark room with some other "bad elements" in our factory. And there we were stuck all day, never seeing the sun except at struggle meetings. We weren't even allowed to read the works of Chairman Mao: they were scared we'd use some quote to get at them. All we could study were the

* The Chairman of the People's Republic who was the leading target of attacks in 1967.

three old favourites* and later not even those, because "Serve the People" said, "These battalions of ours are wholly dedicated to the liberation of the people." What battalion did we belong to? A battalion of reactionaries! So we couldn't read it aloud, only to ourselves.

A technician in that small dark room asked me if I knew about optimization. Of course I did. He went on to tell me all sorts of fascinating ways of doing rapid calculations. I was eager to learn. By the time I got out I was hooked. I'd learned that society is so cramped, you'll get sworn at if you elbow or knock into someone. But maths gives you plenty of scope. I studied a little higher mathematics until I'd mastered integral equations. That was enough, I found, for quick calculation.

That's what I'm hooked on. I've summarized other people's findings into eleven rules. They really work. It's no real use to me, but for a laugh with my mates I can give them the answer to a division or multiplication sum with numbers in the thousands by the time they've finished telling me the sum. One of them suggested I should take up a pitch on the street to talk about my rules. I thought that was a good idea, so I went ahead.

Afterwards I discovered I could actually make a little money. It costs me seven cents to produce each of these booklets, and I can get them printed without any formalities. Printers have to have letters of introduction for works of literature or politics, and they'll only print them for organizations. It's easier with scientific or technical works: all you need is the money. I sell these for ten cents each, making thirty cents on ten copies. After work I can pick up about a yuan this way and have a bit of fun into the bargain: no problem. Besides, you learn a lot. There's nothing phoney about quick calculation. I'm not selling anything under false pretences. I'm fed up with the factory. That woman is still our boss, and though she and I were "classmates" – like all of us who were shut up in that small dark room – she thinks what happened served me right because I'd organized that Revolt-to-the-End Brigade. To hell with her. Women and crooks are all trouble. Anyway, she can't dock my pay.

No one's found me a girlfriend. Who'd have me?

Yes, I take a fairly dim view of things. But I enjoy this, and objectively

---

* Three very short and simple pieces in Mao's *Selected Works*: "How the Foolish Old Man Moved the Mountain", "In Memory of Norman Bethune" and "Serve the People".

it helps modernization, so the government won't stop me. The police don't interfere either: they know me, I come here so often. One man who said he was from a publishing house asked for a copy of my booklet so that he could give it some publicity. Later he came back and said my stuff was worthless – it had all been discovered already. True, but why shouldn't I spread other people's discoveries if I want to? I didn't ask him to publish me!

Some people think I'm crazy. Lots of people try to talk me out of this. Some praise me for doing something for the country in my time off; others say nasty things about what they call my hocus-pocus. Let them talk.

Before you go let me give you a copy of "Eleven Short Cuts in Calculation".

Gold Miners

*There is a hill by the hamlet of Wanzhuang in Pinggu county near
Beijing where people can mine freely for gold. Tens of thousands
of workers, peasants, unemployed youngsters, ex-soldiers and
cadres who have left their jobs have come here in the last few years
to pan for gold. When they leave the hillside scarred with
thousands of workings some take gold, some golden dreams and
some wounds and despair. Others never leave, and relatives have
to come to collect their possessions.*

*When we arrived at Wanzhuang we found nearly a thousand
people digging in abandoned, unlit and unventilated workings
without props or any other protection. They almost lay in their
diggings, hacking ore out with pickaxes, then crawled out drag-
ging it behind them in sacks, holding torches in their mouths all
the time. After that the ore had to be pulverized, sifted and refined.*

Lang Ping, male, thirty-one.

In a good month I find a hundred grammes of gold – that's over a
thousand yuan, and it's worth going for with all you've got. My lousy
life is so cheap it's fucking worth putting it on the line for more than a
thousand bucks. All I can make in a whole bloody lifetime of risking my
fucking neck is what the other Lang Ping, the volleyball star, gets in a
few games. She earns 10,000 yuan for a single win.

Of course I want to do it, and there's no pulling out for me.

The cards were stacked against me. The Cultural Revolution came
along while I was in middle school. When there was an order from high
to "make revolution by going back to classes" we all trooped back to
school, happy as dirt – and the school packed us all off to the Great
Northern Waste. They said we were responding to the Old Man's call,
but I got wiser during my years out there. All the kids whose fathers

were cadres who'd made revolution with the Old Man fixed it to get back to Beijing in droves as workers, cadres or university students. We sons and daughters of the working class that was supposed to lead everything were still fucking "building the Great Northern Granary". Even when there was no work to be done in midwinter they wouldn't let us all come back to Beijing to visit our families. The excuse was that people had to stay at the "anti-revisionist outpost" to garrison the frontier. The real reason was that if we'd all come charging back to Beijing together the Beijing market would have collapsed under the shock, but they only told that to the bureaucrats in the farm head-quarters. We were only allowed to leave for home on New Year's Day.

It was in the Great Northern Waste that I saw the light: you've got to make money. Everything else is phoney. The big boys need power, and us small fry need money. I had to make money.

Well, I hadn't got a clue then – I hadn't even seen any serious money. As a farmhand pulling in thirty or so bucks a month I thought that a man with a thousand was something fantastic. But now I'm worth tens of thousands it doesn't feel like anything much. I want to make more, and I've got to make more.

I came back to Beijing from the frontier in 1979. I was twenty fucking six and completely unskilled. I hadn't even learned how to farm. On the farm we worked blindly. We sowed and harvested when the bosses told us. Season, weather – that was all crap. The only thing that wasn't crap were the bosses' orders. They treated us like dirt – we didn't have the right to make a sound.

I had no skills, no connections and no money to give anyone presents. My old folks were hoping I'd do something for them, so they couldn't help. I had to wait for the street committee to sort something out for me, and what they fucking gave me was street cleaning.

We had to sweep all night till 5.30, then have political study after that, and all for fifty-four yuan a month. You didn't even get that till after you'd been there a year. I got married when I was a street sweeper. She was a shop assistant selling cabbages. In those days a cabbage-seller wasn't an easy find. Because I worked hard and my bosses liked me they made me a garbage truck driver – that was why I could get a wife. So I've got something to thank the sanitation brigade for.

With a wife and then a kid I was still only earning that fucking fifty-four a month in 1983. You can work it out for yourself – the three of us weren't going to have much of a life on our combined income of

120 yuan. Besides, I was on the night shift. The only night I spent at home was Sunday night, so I didn't even have time for a bit of the other. So when I heard you could mine for gold in Pinggu county I came here and started.

At first I came on the quiet, taking sick leave, to see how it went. Once I saw I could make a go of it I just stopped going to work. If they fucking want to fire me they can go ahead. As far as I'm concerned, it's me that's fired them. If I hadn't split up with them I'd still be on fifty-four a month. The brigade's really uptight about it. They're hanging on to my dossier instead of handing it over to the street committee the way they ought to by the regulations. They're trying to make sure that some regular work unit can't take me on as a driver: no unit could employ me without my dossier. What a load of crap! I'm never going to be a driver again unless it's behind the wheel of my own car.

I teamed up with another bloke for about six months. He cut the ore and I ground it up. We hadn't got any machinery – we just used this stone roller mill and panned it till all that was left was a speck or two of gold dust. We refined it together because he was scared I'd swipe some of his. Mining's quite a fucking art. One man brings ten sacks of ore out of the workings and gets not a whiff of the stuff, and another bloke gets fifty grammes out of a single sack.

It's no good working with a partner. You've got to go it alone. You know how it is with us Chinese: you can only trust family. When you team up with a guy he can be a real pal as long as you're poor, but once he smells money he'll fucking do you out of yours. We'd agreed at the beginning to go fifty–fifty, but when it came to settling up the bastard wanted 20,000 yuan for himself and was only going to leave 5000 for me. "That's not very big of you, pal," I said to him. "I did more work than you." Then the little bastard said he'd been the one to risk his fucking neck in the pit, and that I'd have got nothing at all but for him. So I agreed that time, but I told him I'd be risking my own neck from then on.

I found myself a gallery in an abandoned state-run mine. Lots of people know it's a good one – it's got the stuff – but they won't go in there because there were a couple of accidents there when men got killed. But I'm a materialist, and it don't scare me. You just use your pick, and if that won't work you bang a drill rod in. When it comes to shifting rock, I'm the man.

It's fucking tiring. I get so shattered I can only just drag myself out of there.

Well, after a few days mining ore I ground it and panned it, and that was fine, because I could see the stuff. When I wanted to use the crucible, I found the bastard I'd been teamed up with before using it. He'd got a fucking pile of gold, and he told me he'd got a lot more to come. When I thought about it it was obvious that the little shit had stashed all the good ore away. That's what people are like.

The old-timers say that in those days the panners were real mates. Anyone who found a "dogshead" nugget bought enough liquor to get everyone along that stretch of the river lying dead drunk in the snow. Now you'd take it straight back home to show your old woman. Nobody cares about anyone else now.

Anyhow, in a couple of years here I've made tens of thousands of yuan, and I've done it all legal and sold it all to the government. Dealing with smugglers is illegal, and I'm chicken.

The trouble with money is that the more you've got, the more you want. You get hooked on it, like opium. Sometimes you want to chuck it in, like when you've got fuck all from a dozen sacks of ore. But then you think you might hit a vein tomorrow and you carry on. And when you're on a good streak that makes you even keener.

I rent a cottage from a peasant for eighty yuan a month. Worth it? Eighty ought to be enough to buy a shack like that outright. But even though I have to pay through the nose for my rent, I don't stint myself on food – I eat *well*.

My ambition is to see my boy through college. If I could send him abroad, better still. I'm not going to let him have a hard and dangerous life like mine. Everything's for sale these days, and I can pay for him to go to college even if he doesn't pass the entrance exams.

Wu Naiqiang, male, twenty.

I'm off. I'm going back to Beijing to decide on my next move. It's not that I can't take the hardship, and of course I want to make a go of it now I've come here. But I'm never lucky when it comes to getting rich. I've been here over a month, and I still don't even know what gold looks like. There are lots of people as unlucky as me.

I had to come here. After flunking the university entrance exams I started a trading company, but it folded – bad management and bad information. The competition was too tough. I still owe over 9000 yuan. I wanted to find some gold to pay the debts back, but it didn't happen.

I can't say it's been such a big disappointment. Finding no gold shows my information was inaccurate. I thought that anyone could find gold. A few days ago I heard on the radio about diamonds being found near Dalian, and I've been wondering about how to use this information. I might go there, but I'm still thinking about it.

I'm not out to make a lot of money. I didn't start that company up to get rich. I've set myself a limit: once I've got 20,000 I'm going to stop making money and shut myself up in my room to write film scripts.

Male peasant from Wanzhuang village, about fifty.

Don't write my name down.

It's not everyone in the village that's mining. Some are, some have even made seventy or eighty thousand yuan. But there's others that aren't doing it. It's not basic. The basic thing is the soil. Mind you, there's less of us think that way now that we've had the "campaign".

All the mines were kept closed before. They all came under the Pinggu county mine security office. The year the land was divided among households the government said we could mine freely, and some people started digging like crazy. Some people had already started mining on the quiet before that. They'd made their pile, but they'd kept it secret before because they were scared of getting arrested. Once we were told we could mine they brought their money out. They built new houses, and bought TV sets, even cars. They're really rolling in it.

Nobody gets killed farming, but some do mining for gold. It's not worth it, getting killed for money. It's even crazier when outsiders and townies come here to mine.

I'm happy enough farming. Besides, who's going to get rich in derelict mines the government has no more use for?

Cyclist

Bicycles are the main form of transport in Beijing, which has 3,600,000 of them.

It is 6.40 a.m. on one of the capital's main thoroughfares, West Chang'an Boulevard. Zhao Shulan is a woman worker of twenty-nine.

I've never heard of anyone being stopped to ask how she feels about cycling. Riding a bike's so common, almost everybody cycles to work in Beijing. Hardly anybody goes by bus. I've cycled to the factory ever since I started there in 1971. My dad rode a bike for thirty years.

My pay is forty-seven yuan a month, plus ten yuan or more bonus and food subsidy. We started getting a food subsidy two years ago when the prices went up – five yuan a month it is. I'm a Hui,* so I get another four yuan diet subsidy. Not all Huis get that, only those whose units have no canteen for Muslims. Then there's two yuan to help with travelling expenses, which all regular workers get, and I get two extra because I ride my own bike to work. It's not bad when you add it all up.

I look after the statistics at work, so I need to ride about all over the plant: that two-yuan allowance isn't ripping the government off. I was transferred from the shop floor to the head office, but I still rank as a grade-three worker.

I don't mind wind or rain, but I don't use my bike in the snow. The buses get more packed than ever when it snows, because lots of people stop using their bikes. You can get killed when the roads are slippery. As soon as the snow melts I'm back on my bike. The stench of toothpaste, dirty socks and greasy hair in those buses is revolting. And everyone's packed in like sardines.

* A member of a Chinese-speaking Muslim ethnic group.

I live in Yongding Road and the factory is at Dabeiyao. That means crossing from the western to the eastern outskirts – two hours there and back every day. Some have much farther to go. You get used to it. It's too difficult to get a transfer. Two years ago they gave us forms to fill up, asking where we lived and how far we had to travel each day. That raised my hopes. But it turned out to be for a graduation project for some college student, giving the number of people who lived in the east and went to work in the west, and the number who did the opposite, and proposing that they should swap jobs. It's not so easy! How could a textile worker swap jobs with a steel worker?

I used to be Youth League secretary in our shop, so I know a few basic principles of politics, but not much. Not many of us put other people first. If we did we'd all be Lei Fengs. But I still think we ought to put the country's interests first.

Buying a bike isn't easy. It's not just the money – it's getting a bicycle coupon that's the headache. I had to wait three years for this one. When I started work I rode Dad's bike, but it was so old it was always breaking down. There are lots of bikes you don't need coupons for; the shops are full of them. But no one wants to buy Unicorns, Butterflies and rubbish like that. I wouldn't take three of them for one Flying Pigeon or Phoenix. They fall apart in a couple of months. The ones from Taiwan are worst. I don't know how they get in. They look all right but they break down in no time and you can't get them repaired because you can't get the spare parts. They're not smuggled, they're sold in state shops. At first people grabbed them, but nobody will buy one now.

You're taxed just the once, then you get your licence and bicycle plate. It's eighty cents. That's the only tax we pay in China. (*In fact, monthly incomes of over 800 yuan are taxed, but that obviously doesn't affect a worker.*) The parking charges soon add up. Two cents a time may not seem much, but it all adds up. Parking a bike once a day comes to seven yuan a year, that's seventy yuan in ten years. By then this bike won't be worth that. Besides, you have to park it more than once a day. Once when I was looking for a pair of trousers I tried a dozen shops without finding any that would do. So I spent twenty-eight cents on parking without buying a thing.

I do think about all sorts of things when I'm riding my bike. The kid . . . my husband . . . squabbles at work. Doesn't stop me from keeping my eyes on the road.

I've had accidents. Usually it's men brushing against me as they rush along like demons. Sometimes they knock me right off my bike and don't so much as look back, the louts. They don't necessarily have any reason to hurry, that's just their way, always tearing along as if someone's life were at stake. My husband's just as bad. He dawdles at home when he gets up and then makes up for it by speeding.

Not many collisions are deliberate – only hooligans bump into you on purpose. And as I don't get dolled up and I'm not good-looking, no one bothers me. Except sometimes silly kids will shout at me, "Hey! Your back wheel is catching up with your front wheel!"

I had over a dozen stitches after my worst accident, and was in bed for ten days. It wasn't a crash: it was a manhole. The streets are badly lit at night and the men repairing the sewer hadn't put back the manhole cover. My front wheel went in and I was thrown off and stunned. I had to have nine stitches in my arm and seven on my head – you can see the scar. I couldn't claim damages. They'd only ask if I had eyes in my head. Of course it was their fault, but I didn't go to complain: it wouldn't have been any use. Anyway, with free medical treatment it didn't cost me anything. The bike wasn't damaged, apart from a few broken spokes and this dent in the mudguard. Another time my bike got smashed up it was all the fault of a man who crashed into me. He gave me ten yuan on the spot. I didn't call the police. Cyclists have got no time for cops.

Sure, they all salute when they fine you. But that salute costs you at least fifty cents. They fine you for jumping the lights, not carrying your licence, giving people rides – all sorts of things. If they don't like your attitude, it's a bigger fine. They have the right to fine you. We do resent it.

The volunteer traffic wardens are even worse. They're all little so-and-sos who don't do their own jobs properly. If they did their units wouldn't choose them to go out to police the streets. They've never had any power before, so they make the most of it. They won't listen to reason. Last month there was a city-wide check-up on traffic, with inspectors at every crossroad, and the wardens had nothing to do except watch. Each time the police stopped someone they yelled, "Fifty cents fine!" Swine! Of course there are only a few like that, and the police do have their job to do. The traffic would be all snarled up without them, wouldn't it? They mean well and it's their duty, but they should be a bit nicer about it. Why turn everyone against you?

In Beijing your bike's got to have a bell, brakes and a lock, not that a bell's any use: no one gets out of your way when you ring it. A lock's useful, or your bike may just disappear. Brakes are the most useful of all – they can save your life! Women often ride men's bikes. It's awkward getting on and off when you wear a skirt in summer. When you swing your leg over, your panties show. But women's bikes are too difficult to come by. Periods make no difference to riding a bike. Why should they?

None of us riders know each other, we don't talk to each other, we all ride our different ways. I think all cyclists are the same, workers, students and ordinary cadres going to work or back. I once had the idea that someone should make a film of us and show it to our children and grandchildren in twenty or thirty years' time. They should see how we raised them, cycling like this, taking our licences, ration books, grain coupons and oil coupons with us . . . From morning till night, for the sake of the country and our families, we weave in and out of the traffic on our bikes to help modernize China. This makes me very proud. Naive I may be, but that's honestly how it is.

I'd never have stayed all this time chatting if I'd been going to work. I'm on my way home. I worked an extra shift last night to finish up the accounts. Can't you see I'm heading west, going home?

The Human Factor

A second-class compartment. Wheat fields, shelter belts of trees and advertisements flash past amid the shouts of card-players.

Qiao, an operative in a chemical factory, sits opposite us holding a copy of The Ills of Western Society. *There are scores of his colleagues in the same carriage with him.*

We're all going on a ten-day trip to the coast, to Beidaihe. We'll buy crabs. Go back empty-handed and your mother-in-law will give you hell.

The factory organized it, and everything's free – food, fares, the hotel. Our factory's well run – it's got money. We never used to have tours. They gave us towels, notebooks, fountain pens. I had over a dozen notebooks, all sizes. What use are they to a working man? Then it was umbrellas, mugs and bowls, till people started complaining they'd got enough to last their great-grandchildren's lives out. Then they started spending the money on touring instead.

They began with the older workers who'd already got fifteen years behind them, then there was a queue, except that some guys started jumping it and taking their trips years in advance.

The only snag is you have to take what's organized. You can't ask for a week or two off just to hang around at home. Some of the older workers go to the union boss and say, "If there's money going, buy a couple of pounds of good tea. I don't want to go sea bathing." But the kids would want to see the ocean. The fringe benefits at our factory are okay.

My wife's a typist with the city government. She gets so tired her head's splitting and she can't see straight any more, but she hasn't even had a day trip to the Great Wall. That's fair enough. Our factory makes money for the state, unlike her place. But her office ID cuts a lot more ice than mine.

Me, I'd sooner read a book than go to the coast. I reckon it's books, not dogs, that are your best friend. I've got a lot at home. My father left them to me. He killed himself in the Cultural Revolution. I sympathize with him, but I can't respect him. He was too weak.

In my grandad's time we were poor. He was an ordinary farmer in Hanzhong, in southern Shaanxi, but it was a prosperous area and he did all right. My father was an only son, like his dad before him, so the family could afford to send him off to school. Later he joined the Kuomintang's Youth Army and went to Burma. He taught Chinese in middle school after Liberation, but he never got picked on in political movements because even though his record wasn't spotless it was in the open. But come the Cultural Revolution they gave him a terrible time for it, even though he never joined the Kuomintang, only the Youth Army. Things got better again for a while and he went back to teaching. Then he got another beating up during the campaign to "purify class ranks". And he caught it again after Lin Biao died for being the "social basis for restoration". There was no end to it all, and he just couldn't take it. He jumped into a sluice and got pounded to death. He didn't drown. Under the sluice gate there's a channel for the backwater, and once you're in that the current swirls you round and round, smashing you against the base of the concrete dam. He went round and round for a whole day with a big crowd watching because they couldn't work out how to get him out. They had to use a crane in the end. He hardly looked human. Bones sticking out everywhere. His face, hands, feet were all gone. Doesn't bother me now. It's as if it was someone else's father. My heart's hardened.

I went into a construction brigade at the end of 1971 as a plasterer. I was fifteen. It was hard, and the money was lousy, only twenty-one yuan a month, and five of those went to my mum. Getting into the chemical factory was easy. It's a long way out of town, and it's bad for you working with benzene and methanol all day, so there weren't many takers. On top of that there's a big fire risk and you're surrounded by dangerous chemicals.

I knew all the risks but I didn't want to waste the rest of my life just plastering over cracks. I wanted to be in a factory, in heavy industry. But when I got in the factory I found it was the same old story. Heavy industry is just a whole lot of piddling little jobs all added together.

Have you read *The Human Factor*? Graham Greene shows that there isn't much of a human factor in what the security services do. And that goes for just about everything in life apart from small trading in the free markets.

I know I ought to be satisfied but I can't settle down. An operative just has to do what the gauges tell him to – it's dead boring. When automation's gone a bit further we'll all be replaced by machines. We're just machines. Doesn't matter if we've had a quarrel with the wife, or the kid's sick, or it's a holiday, or what, we always give the same orders – "Open Valve B2 in Number 4," "Close the spill valve," and so on. But it would be much more inhuman if we just pressed the buttons we felt like pressing – there'd be fire and explosions.

That's why we like travelling – apart from me, that is. Besides, we make a lot of money for the country. If everyone else had our productivity the country would be doing fine. That's why we can enjoy ourselves with a clear conscience.

I've got a little girl. She's one, and she looks like me. My wife works a long way away and the transport's bad, so she stays in her office hostel most nights. We get over 130 a month between us, and over 50 of that goes on the kid. Nearly all of us here have got families – we could never afford a trip to Beidaihe if we paid our own way.

I reckon every generation has its own problems. We all have our own joys and sorrows; we're all trying to make a decent, secure life for ourselves when there's no such thing to be had. If you're lucky enough to be born into a good era you can leave something behind you when you go. But if you're born into a bad time and you can't put up any sort of fight against it then you leave nothing behind you.

Life's like this train. If the station it gets to is Beidaihe you can have a great time. But if the station's just a halt in the desert with nothing to eat, nothing to drink and nobody around it's still your station. We didn't lay the track and we can't choose where to stop.

8

SERVICE

Mail

Qingdao. Liu Baolian, forty-one. Mother of three. We borrowed bikes to accompany her on her round.

You have a set delivery round and a schedule for it. Qingdao is hilly. You'll soon be complaining. One particular stretch on this round is very bumpy. I'm used to it of course.

There are lots of postal workers in Beijing, so why come all this way to interview me? You want a medium-sized city, an average route and a middle-aged woman? Well, I meet those conditions. But my route's better than average. Easier than the ones the young ones do anyway. They try to look after me.

The load varies. Depends how many letters people have written, and we can't control that. On this round I always have a few hundred letters and it can go over a thousand. There are more and more newspapers and magazines. The really big circulation ones are *Popular Film*, *New Sports*, *Martial Arts*, the *People's Daily* and the *Guangming Daily*. Then there are postal orders, and we have to get people to sign for registered items. As a rule, the peaks come in late December, and then again just before Spring Festival. It never seems to ease up. Whatever happens we still have to do the whole round. Still, it's nice if you don't have to get on and off the bike too often. I know this route very well. It's the best, there are no cul-de-sacs to waste time on. Of course there are advantages to a light load. I don't mind being slow, but I don't like stops. If I don't have to stop too much I can go back to the office early and get on with my own things.

I'm from the countryside and I used to be registered there. It's very difficult for peasants to move into the city. I was lucky. During the Cultural Revolution my husband was in the army. In 1968, his unit was sent to Shaanxi to "support the left". He was allowed to have his family with him so that got me and our two kids into a town. As an army representative in a factory out there he managed to get me a job. I was put on a cutting machine because I was unskilled. As an army dependant I didn't have to go through the trainee stage so I began as a grade-one worker. The following year I was promoted to grade two. Then I had our third child so I got maternity leave. I hadn't liked the city before that. Small county towns in Shaanxi aren't much, compared to the countryside of east Shandong. And things were such a mess in the Cultural Revolution. What with factionalism and fighting there were times when you couldn't even buy much to eat. But when I had the child I realized the town was best. There I was, not working, but still getting grain and maternity pay. Peasants never do so well.

My husband was transferred to civilian work back here in Qingdao. I followed him and got a job in the Post Office. As simple as that.

I could already ride a bike when I started on the post, but I was out of practice. I'd only ridden a man's bike before. The hardest thing to get used to was the strict work schedule at the Post Office. It had all been pretty relaxed in the factory. I've done six years here now, so I'm used to it all. But there's going to be a systems review and we'll be pushed even harder. It's all part of the economic reforms.

We work very hard but if we make a mistake and annoy someone they can be really rude to us. They'd never dare go on at a policeman or a doctor like that for fear of being arrested or getting the wrong medicine. They know we're hardly going to tear up their letters. We serve the people the same as they do but we're looked down on. Still, that's only a minority. Most of them are nice.

Yes, some of the old streets and courtyards were renamed in the Cultural Revolution. Revolution Street, Red Guard Road, that sort of thing. Nothing too outlandish. We still managed to deliver everything. We asked the residents to inform their correspondents of the present names to save us trouble. Here's a funny one for you. Just look at the address.

c/o The Wu Family Residence (Grey bricks and a large balcony)
The end of a winding sidestreet by
MALIN VILLA (Two storeys and a red roof)
Qingdao
CHINA.

Please open and forward.

I don't know how many hands this has already been through. It's somewhere on my round. Malin Villa is a convalescent home now. But we still have to find the sidestreet. The letter's posted from Holland: probably someone in Taiwan, writing to relatives through a connection there. Maybe they've been out of touch a long time. Actually if he didn't know the address the best thing would have been to put the person's name, Qingdao, China, and mark the envelope, "Overseas Chinese" or "Taiwan compatriots, seeking relatives". If we have the name we can get the address from the Public Security Office. If there are several people with the same name, we just work our way through them. If this "Wu Family Residence" no longer exists, then the sender's wasting his time. The envelope is marked "Please open and forward", but unfortunately we can't: it's forbidden by the Constitution. You get some peculiar ones posted in China too. One addressed to the policeman at such-and-such a crossroads for example. Usually, they're letters of thanks, but they could be complaints. Sometimes the street name and number on a letter look right, but there's no one of that name at the address. We try various standard things like reading 68 for 86, 7 for 1, 0 for 6, and so on. If after all this we still can't find the addressee, the letter is treated as dead. Even if there are two mistakes we may manage to deliver. I sympathize with people and I feel responsible. I always think how I would feel if I were the sender.

I don't get many letters. Just four or five from home each year at most. When my husband was in the army he didn't write much but I got a postal order for ten yuan every month, twenty at New Year.

I didn't have a lot of schooling. I sometimes have problems reading given names but then I just use the family name and shout, "A letter for you, Mr Zhang," or whatever. Trouble is, once I've got to know them well, it's embarrassing to ask their full name. I can nearly always manage the family names, I know all those characters. If a strange one does crop up I just call out the house number. I don't like to show my ignorance. Sometimes you get really illegible addresses. When I'd just started the job, I complained to someone. He was annoyed and said I was ignorant. Well, that's true, but at least my characters don't look as if I'd written them in my sleep. Now I always try to be polite. It only costs the public four fen for a stamp to send in a complaint about me, whereas I lose a six-yuan bonus. So long as they're happy, I am too. Some people are very kind: they offer me lemonade in the summer and invite me in to warm up in the winter. I don't accept though – I'd get behind schedule. It's against the regulations.

Sometimes I get upset, like when an old person waits for a letter every day and it doesn't come. If only their children would write, it would be such a comfort to them. Some people write often; sweethearts may write twice a day. And then suddenly it stops. Either they've broken things off or they've got married. Young people waiting for letters get desperate; old people seem embarrassed. Others make jokes. The old man at the next house is one of those – "Seeing to your plants, Grandpa Zhao? No letter from your son of a bitch today. No, no tea thanks. I must get on." Grandpa Zhao is such a nice person. His son's in the army. Usually writes about once a fortnight. There's not really one due but the old man's always hoping. When there isn't one he calls him a son of a bitch. He's a retired miner.

Policy has changed. It's no problem to have overseas contacts now. A few years back, no one dared. This one's a remittance from abroad. It doesn't say it's from a bank, but I recognize the sender's address. I can't say much for this family, the Lius. They're stuck-up. I'll ask them about the funny address though.

No good, she didn't know. She'd been to Malin Villa but she insisted that there was no such place as the "Wu Family Residence". And her cheeky grandson said if I was so sure it existed, I'd better find it for myself. He's out of work, just an overseas Chinese layabout. I knew this letter was going to cause problems. That's the eighth house I've asked at.

Now that my children are big and I've a bit more energy, I like thinking about what's in all the letters. This next couple are members of the Writers' Association. They get lots of mail. Registered items, printed matter, packages. I don't know how they have time to read it all. He's given me lots of magazines still in their wrappers which I pass on to my daughter. He told me not to give their address to any young would-be writers. As if I'd know any. Mind you, I've got a young would-be worker at home. My kid's waiting for a job.

This talking is slowing me up. I usually get here about eleven o'clock. I'm sure this one's a court summons. It's registered, so I'll need a signature. Letters don't frighten people but telegrams do. They're usually to announce a death or to get someone met at the station. I've never heard of one to announce a wedding. This woman's out and her letter's underpaid. There's four cents owing on it. Oh well, we'll be kind and leave it for her.

There are lots of things I can't tell you. It's in our rules that we have to preserve state secrets though they don't say what the secrets are. Suppose someone's making some sort of official complaint. It would be wrong to give them the mayor's address, wouldn't it? The Post Office is a very important organization. We have to know what can be said and what can't. Don't write all this down.

I'll have to go on trying with this one. At least we've got one thing clear. The "Wu Family Residence" was probably where that grocer's shop is now. Some of the older people in the office may know more.

Are you tired? You get tired if you do it every day. I've another delivery at half-past three. I'll pick up the letters and start out again.

At Your Service

Sun Jingkui, male, works in a crematorium.

Don't imagine that we come straight out with it to everyone and say, I burn stiffs. I tell them I'm in the Public Utilities Bureau. That's no lie, we do come under the Bureau. The Public Utilities Bureau and the Public Security Bureau have a lot in common: they're both in charge of people, one of the dead, the other of the living. And people are more afraid of us than of cops, as if we were stiffs ourselves. There's nothing scary about corpses, but people are scared of us. So much the better. "I'm from the crematorium!" We can scare you to death, then we burn you up!

Me and my mates, we always keep our spirits up. You may think it's funny for us to be cracking jokes but that's because you don't understand our job. You all imagine us working away grimly. Fact is, we don't wait for the end of the memorial meeting, we've perked up while you're still mourning in silence. We make wisecracks: "We're the King of Hell's doormen," "We've got a contract with the city hospital," "We'll be at your service next." Because we're looked down on, does that mean we can't have a joke? Of course some people despise us. They think we only do this because we're not fit for anything better, that we're failures. In fact, we're educated, civilized people.

Everyone has to die, but no one wants to see what happens to the dead. Death is going home, but who wants to switch on the TV and see what it's like? Besides, whether a crematorium counts as the last stop on the way home or the first stop is hard to say. Look upon death as going home, they say, but you're not yet home when you're dead. You still take up space on earth till we've turned you into ashes.

We take our work seriously. Do our best for the dead and treat them all well. No sloppy jobs. We do it mainly for the living, to set their minds at rest when they see them. We have a joke: Burn them well because one good deed deserves another. When we're dead they'll do us a good turn. Like finding us girlfriends, or changing us some foreign exchange certificates.* Foreigners who die in China end up in the crematorium too.

I was born in Beijing, in Dongsi. I finished senior middle but failed the college entrance exam. I waited for a job but nothing turned up. When I was fed up with waiting I had a fight with our district committee and the section in charge of people leaving school. They said, "There's a job in the crematorium, will you take that?" Yuck! It was the last thing I wanted.

My mistake was to tell my old man. He said, "Jobs are all the same. Somebody has to do them." He preached at me – all the usual clichés – but I was determined not to take the job, so I just kept my mouth shut. After that he kept on and on at me for loafing. His nagging drove me wild. After another row I stomped off in a frenzy and signed on for the crematorium. Before I went I swore, "Don't worry. I shan't quit till I've cremated you!" He never batted an eyelid, just said, "That's fine, just fine."

Honestly, it's my father you should write up, he's quite a character, honest, good-hearted, broad-minded – a real old Confucian. He joined the revolution in 1946, but he's still only deputy chairman of his factory's trade union. Sometimes I tease him: "How long have you worked for the revolution? Thirty-odd years? Nearly forty? Where's it got you? Men who didn't join the Party till 1964 are already ministers. You, you've wasted your whole life." He couldn't care less. "I'm no good, no education. This job suits me fine. I'm no match for those whizzkids." Then he goes on about piddling little household chores, or rushes off on his "business". There aren't many people with his sense of duty. A man quarrels with his missus, a kid falls ill, someone's short of money – they all turn to the trade union. It's a place where government organizations and the people meet. The most it can do is issue subsidies.

Stick it out for a few days in the crematorium, show you can take it, and you're okay. There's no test. If you're mentally prepared you won't find it too scary. Besides, we're materialists. Death is like a light going out. All that about spirits or ghosts is just rubbish. People killed in car

* Needed to buy high-quality and imported goods.

crashes, explosions or fires are a horrible sight, sickening, that's true, but they're not ghosts. They're not so bad when you get used to them. The hardest test, if there is one, is not despising yourself. In other words, you've got to build up your self-respect. Never mind now about loving your job. The main thing is to love your life, to be sure that it's worth living, and that even a job like ours is a worthwhile way of spending your life.

It's easier said than done.

I started as a porter, loading the hearse, calling from house to house to fetch the old folk. Why call them old folk? Because it's mostly the old who die at home in their beds. Talk of "dying" doesn't sound good either, better say they "passed away". We're a civilized country, China. We don't put things too bluntly. We prefer euphemisms. In three and a half years on this job, I've found out what people are really like. Some relatives laugh, others cry; plenty only put on a show of mourning. It's husbands and wives who weep with real feeling. With colleagues it's usually genuine, and the children too. But not the children-in-law!

When we start carrying the stretcher out, some relative who thinks he knows what's what will say, "Turn east and carry him out head first." When we're in the yard or the street, some of them bring a plank to put over the dead man's head, to pretend he's in a coffin! Goodness knows how many of them are Party members or Youth Leaguers, but I can assure you there are superstitious Party members. In the villages it's even worse. They want all the frills, right? We're an old country and a young one too, a mixture of old and new. I know, I've gone into the history of funerals. Most people know perfectly well that there's no heaven, no hell, and no future life, but they still go in for all that mumbo-jumbo. They feel if they didn't burn paper money they'd be committing a terrible wrong, letting the dead down and defying their own sense of what's right.* What they believe is one thing, and what they do is another. I've often wondered which counts more when it comes to a funeral, common sense or conscience. We don't like to interfere, except maybe to say, "Are you ready now? We must get moving."

There are painful scenes: the father has died and his wife asks their son whether he's going to burn the paper money for his father or not.

---

* By tradition, now officially condemned as superstitious, symbolic paper money is burned for the use of the dead in the afterlife.

You can tell they've been arguing about it for hours. The son is nearly fifty. He looks at us, then at the rest of the family, and makes up his mind: "I'll do it!" Takes off his army jacket and kneels down to burn the paper money. By the time we've loaded the body into the hearse, he's back in uniform, ready to go to the crematorium for the memorial meeting. I feel sorry for him and offer him a lift. We don't normally do that. We take the dead, not relatives, although we're allowed a couple of the family with us to go through the formalities. But he sends a young soldier with us to handle things: he has his own car to go in!*

It's right to uproot superstition, but you have to make allowances for human nature too. Anyway, I've seen a lot in three and a half years. It's too bad I can't write. If I did, I'd have great material, all the things I've been telling you. People don't always practise what they preach, and you can't blame them, especially these days.

Of course there's a back door for burning the dead. Everyone has relatives and friends, right? Some use the back door to speed up the cremation and jump the queue; others want it delayed, want the body refrigerated. They're generally waiting for relatives from far away. Even my father's asked me to open the back door. "Kui, my lad, I want you to do me a favour . . ." "Give me the name and address," I said. There was no messing about, and the hearse was on its way.

I'm not bad at the job. In summer decomposing corpses stink! When it rains or snows we get covered with mud and slush. But it's our job, isn't it? Every year I get a commendation for my good work. You get plenty of those in our outfit.

But there are no stories, films or TV programmes about us. You've got to have professional ethics. You can't upset a family in mourning. The dead don't know what's going on, but if you rough-handle the body the family will think you callous. Treat the dead well to comfort the living. But sometimes we're really put out by the things they do, dressing the body in good clothes with a wristwatch and a whole set of bedding. What use is all that to the dead? These last few years it's been a bit better: most corpses don't wear watches. I've heard some people are afraid we'd steal them! When I die I don't care if I'm cremated naked. The money's better saved for the living! Why burn it up?

In the Cultural Revolution a lot of people came to terrible ends, killed in struggle meetings, beaten to death, or driven to suicide, whole

* A mark of a senior officer.

families even. I was too young for that though: I'm only twenty-four. I wasn't even a "little red soldier"* then.

"Unnaturals" they call them: for unnatural death. Those girls are so pretty, it's terrible seeing their families crying their eyes out. They shouldn't do themselves in just because they've been crossed in love. When you're dead you can't enjoy a good meal, and no one will see you, however well made-up you are, right? The family's tears aren't much use – why didn't they do more for the girl when she was alive?

When you've seen a lot you get tougher, but when parents lose their children it still breaks my heart, especially now that we have family planning and one child to a family. Young people and children mostly die of illness or accidents. Medicine often wins the race with death, but if it comes to a fight, death usually wins. There's a limit to what the doctors can do. Cancer isn't always fatal, but once it's spread you can't do much about it. And what about other diseases? Life is short and each day brings you closer to the grave.

More die in spring and late autumn, and around festivals, especially the Spring Festival. My old colleagues say that in the old days most people died in winter, but not any more. That shows how good socialism is. No more frozen corpses in the street. No, I don't know much about politics; it's all what I've learned on the job.

In my spare time I read all sorts of books: literature, philosophy, history. And then I meet all kinds of people. Everyone comes to us when there's a death in the family; so that gives me insight into society.

Sometimes there's a fight. One person says, "Go ahead and cremate him." Someone else says, "No!" If it gets really hairy they'll threaten to hit anyone who burns the body. They might want to keep the corpse as material evidence, so as to get hold of some money or property, or to have the dead man's name cleared. None of that's anything to do with us: we've got our work docket. Without an order from the Public Security Bureau to keep the corpse, we have to cremate it. For instance after a car crash or a death during an operation the family can be most unreasonable, and even come here to make a row. They may feel they've been wronged, been paid too little compensation. Not all of them are so difficult, by no means all.

With the economic reforms the crematorium hasn't made any contracts with its employees – too many technical problems. If I

* Children too young to be Red Guards.

contracted to run it I'd put up a couplet on the gate: "All mortals must die. Don't leave ill-will behind you." And over the lintel I'd write "Look ahead." That would be for the living, naturally, to persuade them not to go on so about the dead, not to be blind to everything except money.

It's mostly the drivers and electricians who get fed up with their jobs. So why don't they sit exams to do something better? Fact is, they're not up to it. Most people in our trade are forced to it because there's nothing else they can do. And if no one did it, there'd be corpses everywhere.

The last two years I've been remodelling and making up corpses. I learned how from books on cosmetics and barbering for the living. It's usually very simple: you powder them, rouge them and comb their hair for their families to see when they pay their last respects.

It's harder with road accidents and industrial accidents when maybe the skull's smashed in or the nose and mouth are missing. The family and friends still insist on holding a memorial and viewing the remains. I use whatever I can: cottonwool, papier-mâché, plaster, grease paint, artificial hair. Whether the result's a good likeness or not I can't say. As long as half the face is left I can usually manage. Otherwise, I have to work from a photo, a single flat view, and it's not so good. But people expect the dead to look different, so that helps. Then there are old revolutionaries who've worked hard all their lives. When they die, other veterans always come to view their remains. I feel I owe it to them to make sure that they leave the world looking good. There are fewer and fewer of those old comrades now, so it's sad laying them out. They did a lot for our country, but they end up in the oven too, and that's that.

If the body is damaged, you can show the head and the feet and put a cardboard shape in between, with clothes on, under a sheet. That does the trick. You come out of the womb covered in blood, and if you're in an accident you die in the same state; but I can't send you into the furnace in that sort of mess. Some cases are hopeless though. They come in little bits in a plastic bag. Laying out's an art, but it only lasts a few hours before it goes into the furnace. Goes without saying though, the family's very grateful. The artistic effect lives on in people's hearts.

I wash my hands and I take baths. If we're run off our feet I may forget, but in any case we use spoons. We don't eat with our hands. However, if someone's died of disease, we make sure we use disinfectants. With traffic victims there's no need: the day before he was healthier than me! My wife's always worried about whether I've washed thoroughly. She doesn't realize we have much better facilities than at her Highway Bureau. Oh yes, my pay and perks are above average.

My wife's just an ordinary woman. I've read novels and stories about women doctors and university graduates marrying morticians; but real life's not like that.

I think about my work, life and a whole lot of other things. For instance, should I ask my father's factory to take me on as a worker when he retires? That's easily settled. Other things I can't decide about and probably won't have by the time I go up in smoke. I often think about our little girl. She's nearly one and a half. When she's bigger will she be ashamed to tell her friends and the kids she's at school with that her dad works in a crematorium? Will she tell them? I doubt it. I doubt it very much.

Don't identify me when you write this up. I've my own point of view and my own ideas but I don't want to be famous. Let's go. Come and see what my place is like. No trouble!

Vieux Paris

The temperature forecast is stuck at 39° centigrade. Chongqing.*
We wanted to find a downstreamer – someone from the lower
reaches of the Yangtse – who had settled here during the Anti-
Japanese War.

We went to see the master hairdresser Li Xuechu at the
New Image Hairdressing Salon. Although retired, he is still an
adviser to the salon. He took us to see another retired hairdresser,
Mr Xu.

A covered vegetable market that is also a street where peppers,
aubergines and white gourds are piled up. Behind the stalls are a
number of old, black doorways through which staircases can be
vaguely made out.

In the presence of master hairdresser Xu Dexiang, who talks
Chongqing with a north Jiangsu accent, Mr Li is happy to become
a listener.

I don't feel a stranger here, no. I've been here for half a lifetime. Back
in my old home in Yangzhou my parents have both passed away.
Besides, I suppose the weather's getting better here. The winter fog
isn't as thick as it used to be, and the summers aren't so hot. Or
perhaps I've just got used to it. Life's the same for us wherever we
are.

Did you have your hair permed before it was cut? Was it layered? Did
you get it done at Quartet? Quartet was made up of three second-class
salons and one first-class salon from Shanghai that moved to Beijing
and charged the top prices there. That style's not bad. But the women
here would never have it. They don't think they're having their money's

* Chungking, as it used to be known in English.

worth unless they get a head of tight curls. The people here don't understand. They're too ignorant. Can't be helped.

Chongqing wasn't as provincial in the old days as it is now. This was the wartime capital.* The wives of the Shanghai big shots all came here with their husbands. The work we did was the best in China. There were a lot more styles than there are now, ones you've never ever seen. We weren't going for a natural effect or trying to bring out the feel of the hair itself as we do now. We went in for classical styles in those days, and that meant a lot of work. Times have changed, and lifestyles too. Who wants to go to the salon and spend all that money to have their hair done just for the one occasion? Classical styles are only at their best for a single day, and you have to go to the salon just to get them combed. Women will only do that for their weddings. There isn't much difference between people's incomes these days: the highest is only four or five times the lowest, if that. In the old days – well!

I went to Shanghai when I was fourteen to start an apprenticeship in a salon. Do you know what it meant, being an apprentice in the old society? When you signed your articles you signed away your life. First of all you had to act as a servant to your mistress, looking after the kids, emptying the chamber-pots, cooking breakfast. Then you had to sweep up all the hair cuttings, hone the master's razors, and wash and steam the towels. Only after that could you start learning your trade. When I'd stuck out three years of that – it wasn't easy – and served my articles, the Japanese started bombing Shanghai. It was utter chaos. Like everyone else, we ran away, and we kept on running till we got here.

Troubles or no troubles, once you got here you had to carry on with whatever you could do. I hadn't been here long when another down-streamer hairdresser got me into Vieux Paris. In those days there were three groups of hairstylists in Chongqing: locals, Hubei people – they came here after the fall of Wuhan† – and downstreamers from Shanghai and Nanjing. Of course, we downstreamers had all the classiest salons. Vieux Paris and Nanjing were both run by down-streamers in those days. When the Japanese bombed Chongqing we all split up and went round the villages carrying basic barber's equipment on carrying poles. After the bombing was over we came back to the salon. In the salon we always talked downstream and absolutely

* Of the Kuomintang government between 1938 and 1945.
† To the Japanese in October 1938.

refused to learn Chongqing. We all ate at the salon too: the boss put up the money and docked it from our pay – we really did eat out of the same pot then. We each worked on our own account, and the work we did was all terrific. If a newcomer joined us you could tell from his first move where he'd learned his trade. It's still true now. If you make enquiries about who the top-class hairdressers round here are, they're nearly all downstreamers, and they've all retired. But there aren't many of us left here.

After the Japanese surrender in 1945 quite a few hairdressers went back to Shanghai and Nanjing. The ones who left first did well enough. There were two currencies in circulation then: *fa bi* here, and the Japanese puppet government's money there. Right after victory the money here was worth many times more than the money there, so whatever you took with you multiplied in value. But how much money could people like us take back? I went downstream too, and worked in Shanghai and Nanjing. Then I came back here. You weren't free when you worked there: too many dos and don'ts. The rules and regulations had got stricter than ever during the Japanese occupation. For example, hairdressers weren't allowed to wear watches or rings at work any longer, but I didn't know. One of the cleaners in the salon kept pointing at my wrist without letting anyone else see what he was doing. The penny didn't drop. Then the boss, who had been sitting up in the gallery, came over, snatched the watch off my wrist and thrust it into my pocket. Their idea was that if a hairdresser wore things that made him look rich, waiters, schoolteachers and the like would be scared off.

I couldn't take their stupid rules. I'm too quick-tempered. So I came back to work in Chongqing. (*"Yes, our Mr Xu is one of our really top hairdressers. His ladies' hairstyling is terrific. The only thing is that he's a little bit difficult." So said Mr Li.*)

Chongqing stopped being the capital after victory, but our business didn't slacken off. There were still a lot of funny customers around. You name them, we had them. Dance hostesses, girls hustling, they all did good business in Chongqing, and so did we. Trade didn't fall off after Liberation. Right afterwards everything looked good and everyone felt very happy, so we were busier than ever.

We had a new salon built after Liberation, and these are the old premises that were divided up for the staff to live in. This house isn't at all bad. You never saw what houses used to be like in Chongqing, half underground, damp and stuffy. The dust from the street came in through the windows – and so did the spit passers-by hawked up. We were still doing a roaring trade in 1958. *("People thought everything was possible in those days – we invented any number of new styles," put in Mr Li.)* But once any political movement started our business went through the floor. Of course we were affected by the "tiger hunt", the "three antis", the "five antis", the campaign against Hu Feng,* and all the rest of it. I tell you, nobody can beat a hairdresser when it comes to spotting political changes.

Take the campaign against Hu Feng. All the educated people stopped coming to get their hair done right away. They were like rats, terrified of being noticed, remembered and dragged into the case. If you ask me, that campaign was what started educated people on the downward slope. Every time there was a movement our business fell off – the anti-rightist movement,† class struggle in 1962, the "four clean-ups" in 1964, and so on till the beginning of the Cultural Revolution in 1966. By then the only women's style left was bobs. We were still doing some perms before that. But after we were made a joint state–private business in 1956, I wasn't much bothered about what sort of trade we were doing.

Back at the time of Liberation I was out in front of the workers in making revolution. I was pretty thorough. We dropped the old tradition of all messing together at the shop. I very nearly joined the Party, but my membership was never confirmed. *("Mr Xu was too difficult," Mr Li repeated.)* I just couldn't get on with our branch secretary. We never saw eye to eye about the salon. He didn't know the first thing about it. There were a lot of things I just couldn't take. I used to say what I thought, and I didn't have any control over what was happening, so I kept losing my temper and lost my candidate membership of the Party too.

They have an easier time there now that I'm not bawling them out any more. I've retired. If I'd stayed on as an adviser like our Mr Li they'd have made my money up to what I was earning before and I'd have got bonuses too. But that wasn't for me. My freedom's worth

---

* The first three were movements against corruption in the early 1950s. The last, against the writer Hu Feng (1902–85), began in 1955.

† Of 1957–8. The following political campaigns were all part of the move towards leftist policies that culminated in the Cultural Revolution.

more than a few coppers to me. It would have been more than my health was worth to watch the disgraceful way those youngsters work and keep my mouth shut about it. But if I spoke up I'd be asking for a row. It's best for everyone if I keep my distance. I took a trip to Shanghai and Nanjing at my own expense, and went into Violets and the Number One Hair Salon on the Nanjing Road to have a look at how they work. It was fascinating, but you lay people wouldn't understand. Hairdressing's an art, with its scissors-cuts and razor-cuts. Your movements have to be rhythmic and regular – it looks nice, and saves effort by cutting out a lot of unnecessary activity.

I really love this trade, but I absolutely refused to let any of my six children follow in my footsteps.

All of them are working now, apart from the youngest, who's still at high school. I'd sooner they were hotel staff than in this trade. Huh! Take a look around: you'll soon see how far behind Shanghai we are. It's not only the styles. We simply don't do the work as well as they do. Not that we're stupid. We're just too cut off here.

Right or wrong, this is where I've made my life. Some of the hairdressers from downstream who left after the Japanese surrender went to Hongkong and carried on hairdressing there. They opened beauty parlours and became their own bosses. Some of them have been back in China on visits in the last couple of years. They came to have a look round Chongqing and invited us all out for a meal. They spent a hundred yuan per table. Fantastic! In Hongkong the boss has to work harder than his employees – in fact, he's always the last to knock off. It isn't easy money.

We're no stupider than anyone else. But suppose you contract to run a hair salon here, do you get the right to get rid of people? In the old days the boss had the right to hire and fire. If someone didn't work properly he was out. That was the only way to keep your customers. These youngsters nowadays, they'll do a set quota of work, but all they care about is speed. If you won't take trouble, this trade isn't for you. People come to the hairdressers for a rest and a bit of luxury. If you don't get their hair clean when you wash it they'll be uncomfortable and they won't come back another time. If the staff get paid much the same however they do the job, you lose customers. I wouldn't contract to run a salon unless I could fire people.

I'd sooner stay at home and make a bit less money. Being happy is what it's all about.

As Mr Xu waved goodbye Mr Li said very quietly, "Do you think someone like him could sit around doing nothing? For this trade, the main thing you need is a hairdryer, which costs a hundred or so. You can make up your own cold perm lotion. So if he works at home and charges three yuan for a cold perm and styling it's cheaper than in a state-run salon and he's making a good profit. As an adviser to a salon I can't do any of my own work on the side. Last year he was asked to give classes and teach some students in Daxian county, and he did some styling too. Came back with over a thousand in his pocket." Mr Li gave another quiet chuckle.

Schoolfriends

About 3000 women and a scattering of men have gathered in the old-style courtyard to celebrate the 120th anniversary of the founding of the Bridgman Academy for Girls, now Beijing's Number 166 Middle School.
Cao Shizhi. A woman of thirty-five.

I graduated from junior middle school here in 1965. This friend of mine was my classmate, and she's also a colleague in the Number One Department Store where I work now. I suddenly recognized her when I got the job two years ago.

We had to look all over the place to find the one room for our year – all the classes of 1964 to 1968. There must be hundreds of us, but the classes of the 1930s and 1940s had a room to each year although there are only a few of them here.

This suit I'm wearing is company uniform. Managers wear woollen worsted, department heads a wool mixture, and we two wear this man-made stuff. We're at the same grade as sales assistants.

I didn't go on to senior middle school here. I thought it over and decided on technical school. I hadn't much chance of getting into university so it wasn't worth staying on here. My marks were nothing special, and for another thing there was the problem of my family's political status. My father was a clerk in the Shanghai Bank. He started work there before Liberation and stayed on until he retired in the 1970s. There was no problem with him. He wasn't the sort of person who gets involved in politics. It was my mother. She'd been a housewife until she began to teach in a night-school after Liberation. In the anti-rightist campaign of 1957 petty intellectuals like her who didn't keep their mouths shut got picked on. She was sent to a labour reform camp outside Beijing. They rehabilitated her a few years ago. My

[177]

brother couldn't get into university because of her, and became mentally ill with depression. There were four of us in my family. He was the
only boy. I'm the youngest. My two sisters went to university but I
wasn't as clever as they were. No one at home gave me any advice when
I was deciding what school to try for, so I made the choice myself. The
women of our family are all alike. We all take after our mother: we
don't care about domestic matters. We're much more interested in the
outside world.

The technical schools advertised for students in the papers. I applied
to quite a few that were linked with heavy industry – engineering,
metallurgy and power. I didn't think I'd make a good nurse. I ended up
at the Beijing Commercial School, my sixth choice. It trained purchasing agents. I thought it would give me the chance to travel and involve
me with heavy industry. I didn't realize that school had no links at all
with industry.

In the end I had only one year there, followed by ten years spent as a
shop assistant in a mountainous area outside Beijing. I wasn't allocated
the job. I got it because of the policy of sending people to the
countryside in 1968. For the first four years I was in a village supply and
marketing co-op. I worked in the commune shop for the other six. We
sold everything from silk to garlic in that little shop. The hardware
department stocked tyres for carts, door hinges, the lot. We bought
all sorts of things too: timber, medicinal herbs, mountain haws,
scorpions, eggs, nuts and pigs. When we bought a pig it had to be
butchered, then its meat was sold in the shop. Of the four of us working
there I was the only one from the city. The others were locals. We took
turns at doing the cooking. We had a horse-drawn cart to move out the
things we purchased in the mountains. I learned to do everything
except kill the pig.

It didn't get me down. We educated young people were supposedly
being "re-educated by the poor and lower-middle peasants" and I
accepted this completely. Indeed, I was doing rather nicely. I wasn't
too far from home. I didn't have to do farmwork and I got a wage:
twenty-six yuan a month for all those years. The commune shop
wanted to promote me to buyer. I really didn't want to do it because it
involved a lot of travelling. I was thirty and I wanted to settle down.

I started on the slow process of getting back home. As I wasn't so
very far away and was in a salaried job it was hard for me to get back to
the city. I had lower priority than young people who had been sent

down to work as peasants. My first move was to swap jobs with a driver who worked for the Capital Iron and Steel Company. I moved to Capital Steel as a worker and he returned to Huairou county where his family lived. Next, I started to hunt for another swap so that I could do the sort of work I had done before. Of course it was all difficult. I had to fix everything myself, with a bit of help from my friends and relations. My own family were useless. In the end I found someone who worked in a department store near the steelworks who wanted my job in Capital Steel. We swapped, I worked there for a year and then I was transferred to Beijing. I've been here four years.

I get fifty-four yuan a month. I don't know what grade I count as. It's all rather mixed up. Do you know what grade we are? *(She addressed this last question to her colleague who replied, "We're paid as graduates of technical middle schools. How come you get fifty-four when I only get fifty-two?")* Oh, I still get the extra two yuan I started getting in my year in heavy industry. I think technical school was the right choice for me. Senior middle would have been a waste of time then because the universities stopped recruiting in the Cultural Revolution. Two years ago technical-school graduates all got an extra wage increment. I get quite a good bonus, about thirty yuan a month. We accountants get the average bonus. Sales staff in the electrical department can get as much as fifty yuan. Since June there's been no limit on bonuses. Before that, we got only ten or twenty a month. With the economic reforms in Beijing, our bonuses will be taxed next year, so we'll get less.

The old lady on the platform was our Dean of Studies. She organized this celebration. They want to use the anniversary to raise money for the school. The school was founded with money from an American woman, Mrs Bridgman, as a private missionary institution. During the Japanese occupation it was taken under government control as the Beijing Number Four Middle School. When the war ended it became private again under its old name. After Liberation, it was first known as the Number Twelve Girls' Middle but after the Cultural Revolution it went co-educational as the Number 166 Middle School. It was one of the best schools in the whole country. This year it got 160,000 yuan. At its lowest, in the 1970s, the grant was 60,000 yuan.

My sister was at school here before she went on to read Chinese at Beijing University. She's a keen opera fan. When she graduated she wrote to Jiang Nanxiang – he was the Minister of Higher Education then – to ask for a job connected with opera. What a nerve! In those days people were really . . . Anyway, she was given an editing job in a publishing house which dealt with opera. The school asked her to help produce a commemorative booklet and see if she could get all the famous alumnae to write for it. She has done it all in her spare time. I didn't join anything in the Cultural Revolution. My family belonged to one of the "five black categories",* so I wouldn't have been eligible. We were driven out of our old house to live in a little place nearby. The policy now is to restore houses to their owners, but we still haven't got our old home back.

I'm not married yet. Friends have introduced me to more men than I could count but . . . I've got a boyfriend at the moment. He's forty-four. He's got a fifteen-year-old child. His wife died of some illness. At first I kept finding fault with him but then I realized that even my two sisters, for all their ability, felt frustrated with their home life, so I stopped. He'll do. We'll probably settle soon. I'm thirty-five, but I feel as if I'm forty.

---

* The "five black categories" were landlords, rich peasants, counter-revolutionaries, "bad elements" and rightists. Her mother was a rightist.

9

OFFICIALDOM

Jargon

From south of the Yangtse to north of the passes cable radio announcers right down to village level try to use as much official jargon as possible. They all have the same basic style, despite individual variations.

An aquatic farm with a Party secretary and a manager.

In the first place, on behalf of the 120 staff and workers of our farm I must express our sincere thanks to the journalist comrades from Beijing and to the leading comrades from the county for coming down to the grass roots to direct our work.

Allow me to report on the basic circumstances of our farm. This farm of ours was founded in 1983 with the fullest support from the provincial, prefectural and county leadership, as well as from the foreign trade departments. We were also given selfless aid by fraternal farms that had started before us, and helped by the peasant comrades of nine rural districts around here. So the main credit for what we've achieved must go to them, to the Party and the people. The reason why we were able to start the farm, get our first crop, start exporting and start earning foreign exchange for the country all in the same year was in consequence of the economic support and political concern from the leadership at all levels.

For a range of understandable reasons, including the sabotage of our country's inshore fishing industry by the Lin Biao and Gang of Four counter-revolutionary cliques, our country's king prawns have long fallen far short of meeting domestic and export market demands. Only after the Third Plenum of the Party's Eleventh Central Committee* did

* When the Deng Xiaoping reform policies were launched in December 1978.

aquatic production here receive its due attention, develop from nothing, and win some achievements.

This farm of ours enjoys the benefits of weather, place and people. The weather is the east wind that has been blowing since the Third Plenum, as I mentioned a moment ago. By place I mean that this poor country of ours has over 7000 hectares of coastal mudflats that haven't yet been developed and put to any other use. By people I mean the concern of the leadership at all levels.

In accordance with the directives of the Party's Central Committee our farm has reorganized its leading group. Two university graduates have joined the leading group, one as farm manager and the other as deputy Party secretary. We have thus fulfilled in a preliminary way the requirement that the leadership should be revolutionized, intellectualized, rejuvenated and specialized.

During the first period of Party rectification . . .

As regards our trade union, youth and women work, and culture and recreational activities . . .

Management is of the highest importance . . .

In brief, our farm has grasped the seven words, the seven aspects, the seven . . .

In order to enable more of our products to enter international markets faster and to satisfy domestic demand, we have . . .

Output? Last year we caught nineteen tonnes, which was seven tonnes of prawns after processing. It was all exported.

There's nothing to say about me. You can't have publicity for the individual! The credit for everything must go to the Party and the people, right?

I was born in 1932, joined the revolution in 1950, and joined the Communist Party of China that same year. Before I came to this farm I was the Party secretary of a people's commune. My wife? The old woman's a farmer.

We welcome you to come again.

Section Chief

Liu is a salesman in a branch of the state-owned Xinhua book-
store chain. He was cagey, and clearly suspicious of inquisitive
strangers. He volunteered no information and refused to answer
some of our questions.

I'm twenty-seven. I was assigned to this bookshop after finishing middle school. I'm in charge of the literary section now, with thirteen shop assistants under me. Of course I serve behind the counter too.

We can't let the customers help themselves from the shelves, or the books would disappear. Last year we tried direct access to the shelves for a month and our section alone lost over 700 books. The state had to make good the loss. We opened the shelves on instructions from above; and when they told us to close them because we were losing money we did. I don't know about what they do abroad and I can't remember what it was like before the Cultural Revolution. Maybe in the future there'll be open-access shelves, when there's a higher standard of public morality. But now even selling them over the counter we still lose books.

If we catch thieves we fine them. We haven't got any legal right to, but we can get round that: we charge for the book, then confiscate it and tell the thief he can have it when he brings a written self-criticism with his unit's official stamp on it. The last thing shoplifters want is for their employers to find out about them so they never come back. They're fined the price of the book. I can't see anything wrong with that. If anyone's to blame it's the shoplifter, or perhaps the manager, but not us sales staff.

If we suspect people we make them undo their bags or clothes to show us. We seldom make a mistake; when we do we apologize. Whether we have the right to do that or not I don't know, but I've yet to see honest customers refuse to open their bags or unbutton their jackets, and clear themselves.

My salary is thirty-eight yuan a month. It's enough to keep myself without any help from my parents, but I don't give them anything either. I'm saving up ten yuan a month for my wedding. I've got more than 700 yuan now.

I've been out with several girls, but it's never come to anything. They always call it off. It's no disgrace when they dump me. It's their fault, not mine. Besides, it's a load off my mind.

I meet these girls through introductions, and first we go out together. If we hit it off we can go steady; if not, that's it. I want a girl with a good character, a clean political record and a kind nature. Looks don't matter. No, they really don't, so long as you get on well.

We haven't got any university graduates here. Our leaders are basically of two sorts. There are the retired officers who know next to nothing about the trade and have to learn on the job. Then there are ones like our manager. In 1951 he was a sales assistant in a Xinhua bookstore in the north-east. Then he was gradually promoted to a section head, vice-manager and manager. Of course he knows the ropes and he's reliable, but he's nothing special. Our ablest people are mostly the department heads. They were booksellers back in the old days of joint state–private ownership. Our manager's worked hard for thirty years. He sets us all a good example. No, I don't want to become a manager – I'll do whatever job I'm needed for. Some of our manager's old colleagues are still shop assistants. The novelist Shen Rong once sold books too, and now she's writing them, but she's an exception. I don't envy her. I know my own limitations.

Yes, some of my colleagues say my only strong point is that I'm not hot-headed. No good comes of it. One rash movement and you'll pay for it for the rest of your life, and your kids will too. A comrade in our district office told me she did brilliantly in senior middle school, but because her father was a rightist no college would take her – she had to work in a shop. Now her father's been cleared and rehabilitated, but she's nearly forty, and she's got no hopes at all. So people should watch their step, keep their cool, and not make trouble for themselves and their children. This has happened all too often. It's better to keep your head down.

In middle school I joined the Youth League and was active with the Red Guards. I was really somebody! But a few years in the shop opened my eyes. In every political campaign we take a load of books off our shelves and send them to be pulped. Of course, since the fall of the Gang of Four there've been no more literary inquisitions. But writers who make mistakes still have to criticize themselves, and that can't be comfortable. So I've always swum with the tide.

Generally speaking, the biggest editions are about two million nationwide. That includes political books, works by national leaders and regulations. In special cases, Chairman Mao's works for instance, ten million copies are sold. The only books in our literary section that could sell like that are thrillers. The smallest editions are about 2000 copies, for second-rate poetry or boring history booklets.

If books published for policy reasons lose money, the publishers carry the loss, not us. We know some books are bound to lose heavily, quality art books for example. That doesn't affect us either. There are a lot of books that sell like hot cakes but don't get reprinted. The readers want them but they don't appear. Hasn't happened so much recently, but there are still some. It's nothing to do with us. For instance the Chinese translation of the *Decameron* isn't being reprinted. I can't give you any examples of Chinese books – I have to watch what I say. Well, then, *Ren A Ren** sold out very fast, but can it be reprinted? It's an unhealthy book. It must be a bad book. Why else would it be withdrawn? It's been criticized in the press, hasn't it? We have to do what we're told. Our superiors understand the principles involved and can take the broader view. We can't just sell the books that move fast. We've got to take politics into account, not just money. Money can be counted, but not political damage.

Sometimes we make the customers buy another book with the one they want, although in theory we're not supposed to. Too many kung-fu adventure stories are bad for young people, so with each they have to buy a copy of *The Unification of China by the First Qin Emperor* to counteract the poison. *Sex Information* and *What Newly-weds Need to Know* sell quickly too, so we make the customers take a copy of *How to Repair Electrical Appliances* with them. You'll find that other shops go further. They make you buy two works of literature with each copy of the comic book *The Champion Boxer*.

Generally speaking we make twenty cents in each yuan, but that has to cover taxes, stock damage, building depreciation and wages. We

* Dai Houying's novel, published in English as *Stones of the Wall*.

tried the responsibility system for a month, then gave it up for various reasons. For one thing, the bonuses for staff who over-fulfilled their sales quota were such a small fraction of the gross profit, it wasn't worth their while. Instead they took good books, the best-sellers, home to sell in their spare time – and pocketed all the profit. We couldn't have that. There were other reasons too which I'd better not go into.

Of course I'm in favour of reform. The Party Central Committee has called for it. The question is how. We can't scrap the iron rice-bowl.* You can't have everyone doing their own thing. As I see it, we should obey our leaders. Those old comrades know what to do.

They understand about going all out to mobilize the masses, and about democracy and centralization. A bookstore isn't a purely commercial set-up. There's a big difference between selling books and selling vegetables. Books are propaganda. I hardly ever read novels. I like films, preferably Chinese. Foreign ones are too confusing for me. My colleagues are different: they go for Japanese and American films, which I hate. In the evenings I watch TV or think over my work at home. After all, I'm a section chief. I'm quite content with any job I'm given – I'm serving the people!

No, I can't answer that. No comment. I can't tell you that either. I don't think we're overstaffed. Some of us sell books and make out bills, others take the money; that's our system. The sales assistants don't take money, and the cashiers don't handle books – what's wrong with that? We all think it saves trouble. You can't handle both books and money. Anyway, a few backward characters might help themselves. Just suppose you were suspected of embezzlement: how could you clear yourself? This is our system!

I've already said too much, more than I'd normally say in ten days. A section chief has to set a good example.

What do you mean, cagey? Oh well, think what you like. Everything I've told you is the truth.

Of course I'm like the rest of my generation, but I'm quite satisfied. I haven't got any special worries. I'm not looking for trouble.

* Lifetime job tenure.

Lawyer

In this city of over a million people the legal advice centre is a new and almost unknown establishment. It is in a small house next to the stadium and has only two outside telephone lines. Not even directory enquiries knew either of their five-digit numbers, which are not to be found in the thick 1982 phone book.

Zhou Yi, lawyer.

I'm from the outskirts of Beijing. Before Liberation we were upper-middle peasants – that's the class status we were given after Liberation. We had a little surplus grain, all scrimped and saved by my father. Because we were a bit better off my father started getting fancy ideas, and he sent me to school. Not the old-fashioned village school – I went straight to the "foreign academy". My family thought the old-style schools were useless, and that only the "foreign academy" would get you anywhere in life. It was during the Japanese occupation so the textbooks were stuffed full of their propaganda for "co-prosperity" and "amity". We started learning all that traitor stuff in class one.

At the end of my second year the Japanese surrendered and we switched to new textbooks – Kuomintang ones this time. In senior primary school we had civics lessons, which were quite like politics lessons nowadays – all about legitimate rule and citizens' duties. I didn't mind those lessons – I knew it all backwards. It was easier than Chinese or arithmetic.

Our place was liberated a term before I would have finished primary school. As I was supposed to be educated they made me a clerk in the village government. In those days an "intellectual" like me was a real somebody. There were some children of landlords and rich peasants better educated than I was, but they weren't trusted. I joined the Party when I was seventeen and became the village Party official, which is what they called the secretary of the township Party committee in those days.

Before the switch to co-ops in the mid-fifties we got off course. We had another division of land in the countryside, not landlords' and rich peasants' land, but the middle peasants'. To be honest with you, I didn't believe in it myself, especially when my own family was getting hit. But I soon put such ideas out of my head. Back in the early days of Liberation there'd been a directive from the Centre banning landlords' and rich peasants' children who'd joined the ranks of the revolution from interfering in the land reform in their home villages. I took it to heart. Later on there was another directive from the Centre ordering us to stop hurting middle-peasant interests, which showed I'd been right in the first place. Not that it was any use being right. I hadn't discovered the problem logically – it was just an instinctive reaction caused by my class nature.

I didn't have to pass an exam to get to university: the village authorities told me to go, and I went. The People's University in those days was really just a training school for cadres, and I wasn't exactly thrilled when I was put in the law school. I didn't want to learn how to fight lawsuits, but when you were sent you had to go. Besides, I was going to university to learn how to hold power on behalf of the people, as they used to say then.

Basically, it was the Soviet legal system. The only proper laws China had then were the constitution and a few other lesser laws such as the Marriage Law. As for a criminal code or a civil code, we didn't have them, and people were still arguing about whether we needed them. Gradually I got into the subject and started enjoying law.

Legal bodies in the old society were instruments for oppressing the common people, markets where silver was traded for lives. In the new society we had to have our own legal forces to serve the people.

Later on I was called a rightist, and unfairly too. It was all because of a dissertation I wrote. In those days there was a lot of pressure to write dissertations before you graduated. Mine argued that the Kuomintang's constitution and laws were just confidence tricks and that there had never been rule of law in China. They picked on this and said that I'd deliberately phrased it so as to include New China. I really hadn't meant that – I'd never have dared. Now everyone's maintaining that our old legal system was defective, but I can't claim to have been saying that in the fifties. Other people read that into what I'd written.

There was another reason too why I was in trouble. My teacher said my dissertation was interesting, so when he was labelled a rightist, I got burned too. The logic in those days was that anything the enemy approved of had to be bad. I didn't dare to defend myself. When my fellow students criticized me from what they said was an irrefutable revolutionary viewpoint I'd never have dreamed of contradicting them. It wasn't a courtroom debate, and anyhow I'm no hero. I just wanted to get through the crisis.

I really wanted to "wash my face and change my heart". I criticized myself for dear life and denounced others for the wrong things they'd said. I wanted to atone for my crimes. Everyone's said something wrong at some time or other, haven't they? At the time I thought I was proving my loyalty to the Party. I'd joined the revolution when I was still a kid, so it was my home, what held me together. I really was scared of being chucked out of the revolution's ranks. But now I have to admit that during the anti-rightist movement I was a coward. I like films and TV programmes about rightists, but I have to remind myself that they're just stories. I wasn't like them. Nowadays everyone says that the Party was wrong then. Huh! At the time we all felt in our hearts that we were the ones in the wrong.

Crying and snivelling about it wouldn't have done me any good at all. The fashion then was for struggling with people to their faces and denouncing each other behind their backs. During the "four clean-ups" political campaign* and the Cultural Revolution anyone could join in. But it was all very unscientific. That kind of accusation isn't anything like direct confrontation in court – the cases are often full of holes. I said a lot of terrible things about other people behind their backs.

When the Soviets had just started building their worker–peasant regime after the October Revolution, they were ruthless about suppressing counter-revolution. When we were doing everything the Soviet way we copied that too, and took it further as well. But was everything Soviet right? And didn't we overdo it all? Mind you, at the time I didn't dare think things like that. Perhaps we underestimated the stability of our people's regime: we weren't like the Soviet Union back in its early years. But I only realized all that later.

Of course I got kicked out of the Party. As a "rightist who'd attacked

* Around 1964.

the Party" there was no way I'd be allowed to stay in: that was simple logic.

I was sent to the countryside for a year. They were being kind to me: it wasn't as bad as Qinghai or Ningxia.* Later I was transferred to a job in the county's labour office, and there I stayed till I was rehabilitated. As a "dead tiger" I wasn't given too bad a time during the Cultural Revolution, but I had my troubles, of course. Although my crimes had been serious they took off my rightist label in 1961 for good behaviour – I'd returned to the ranks of the people. At first I thought I really was out of trouble, but it turned out to be no such thing. Although some of the pressure had been taken off me, there was new pressure – it seemed you never stopped being a rightist. The rest of my life looked hopeless. Only in 1979 was I properly rehabilitated, my name cleared and my Party membership restored. Economically, I'd suffered too. I never got any rises unless they were being given to everyone. So I was promoted a couple of grades, which gave me an extra fourteen yuan a month. Only our Party would have the guts to admit and correct its mistakes like that. Why else could anyone say there's hope for the Party?

In 1980 I was transferred to the district people's court, and in 1982 to the legal advice centre. I was back in my own profession again. A lot of my fellow students are still doing other things. Because legal work has been neglected for a very long time, a lot of law graduates are in administrative jobs. They won't come back to the law again, even though there's a call for them to do so. As for me, I don't like the profession, because I was made a rightist when I was studying for it and so I was never able to practise. Besides, I think it's going to be one hell of a problem getting a healthy and complete rule of law.

Our law is part of the people's democratic dictatorship and fundamentally different from capitalist law on the big issues of what it protects and what it suppresses. Of course a lot of provisions are the same. No laws anywhere give you a ten-dollar reward for murder or arson. Some people have the wrong idea. They think that under the people's democratic dictatorship you can't apply the same legal criteria to everybody, because that amounts to using the law as an umbrella for bad people like landlords, rich peasants, counter-revolutionaries or bad elements. And they want to include people who

* Areas where the living conditions for prisoners and exiles are generally poor.

once had a bad status but have had it revoked, and even their children. There are still some comrades who'll say in a civil dispute that it's class vengeance if the son or daughter of a landlord or rich peasant has hit them. But you can only have people's law when everyone is equal before it. Only a few years back nobody dared say that. But some comrades, even some leaders, have still got it in for us because we "don't serve the proletarian dictatorship". Anyone would think that only unequal laws like those in South Africa were right.

Although the courts aren't places where you trade silver for lives any more, quite a lot of cadres still think they're places where they can trade power for lives. We always resist their pressures. The key problem is that so many people are ignorant about the law. I'll give you an example. A Party secretary calls us and orders us not to defend someone because he's a "bad person". Well, if the factory Party secretary can decide that someone's no good, what are the police, the procurator's office and the courts for? We might just as well let the factory run its own court. Still, things are a lot better than they were a few years back. Slowly we're getting there.

You press people get it all wrong when you write about the Public Security arresting a murderer or a thief. Even if someone's been caught red-handed and there's cast-iron evidence, what right have the papers to reach an instant verdict before he or she has been tried by the court or even indicted? The foreign way of referring to someone as a suspect or the accused is far better.

People don't like bringing civil disputes to the courts or to us unless they've got themselves really badly entangled. I suppose that is characteristic of us Chinese. And what we really do if they come is to mediate. Even court hearings are aimed at solving the problem at issue without any loss to anyone's dignity. What we say is, "We welcome you to come here." Yes, write that down. We really do welcome everyone to come here to solve their problems instead of causing the grassroot units and the leadership trouble by going to the factory director or Party secretary to complain about a fight with the neighbours. Let everyone stick to their own trade.

We'd like more staff transferred here. We're short-handed, short of able and energetic people, but we've got no housing. To this day I'm still in the county labour office's accommodation.

My wife is an accountant in the fruit company, and they've got even less housing. The two of us and our two sons who are at middle school have to squeeze into one and a half rooms – just twenty-two square metres – with no lavatory, let alone a kitchen.

Things will gradually get better. Even if we can't move, our sons will leave after they graduate. I've told them not to have any crazy ideas about marrying and settling down in our place for the rest of their days. It's public housing, and they can't inherit it.

I'm a lot bolder than I was when I was a rightist. You do learn something from experience.

United Front

Liu, deputy head of the United Front Department of a county committee of the Communist Party.*

After shaking hands he sits across a conference table from us and opens up his notepad to read out some case histories and a string of statistics. As he talks he gradually loosens up and pushes his little notebook aside.

So you see, this work of ours isn't easy! Talk to the comrades working in other departments and it's "Oh, you have it pretty good all day long, shaking people's hands, enjoying the best food and drink – our own local delicacies and imported cigarettes like 555s and Marlboros" . . . but I'm telling you straight, I can't get used to those brands! I prefer our own Qianfoshans. Seeing how we're always coming into contact with all sorts of people from abroad, people imagine that we enjoy lots of special advantages! But can we ignore the regulations on dealings with foreigners or Party rules? Nobody notices all the piddling jobs we have to do, cleaning up after others.

This is a small county, not as open to the outside as Fuzhou or Amoy, but we're kept just as busy. Elderly overseas Chinese come home to their roots and find that their old house is still occupied. We have to contact the housing bureau, the neighbourhood police station, the current occupants' work units, as well as the occupants themselves – you can't force them out, and you can't beg – but it comes pretty close to begging! Before the old folks arrive from abroad, you have to wash every window, polish every tea table and whitewash all the walls. I'm not kidding! Out in the fishing grounds, when our fishermen get into

* Responsible for relations with non-communists, especially with people from Taiwan, Hongkong and Macao, and overseas Chinese.

[195]

disputes with fishermen from Taiwan, Hongkong or Macao over fishing rights, there's the coastguard, the police and the Fisheries Management Commission, but they're not satisfied till they've made a complaint to the United Front Department! Sometimes it comes to blows, and our fishermen forget themselves and wound people on the other side. Maybe our fishermen are in the right, but the compatriots* know the score and complain to us. You can't just tell them the rights and wrongs of the matter, or refer them to the law, because United Front policy is involved. You begin by treating their wounds, and keep on telling them how all compatriots from Taiwan and Hongkong are family here until they're mollified and realize what they've done wrong.

A few days ago one of our fishing boats collided with a Taiwan boat. A typhoon blew up right afterwards, and both boats came into harbour for shelter. Our boat was contracted out to private use and wanted compensation from the Taiwan fishermen. Yesterday the captain of the Taiwan vessel told us he had to leave port. We couldn't impound the boat and keep them here – when a boat is detained, the Taiwan side makes all sorts of wild charges, and it's embarrassing; but when they sailed away, our fishermen came demanding 800 yuan for ship repairs from us. I told them, "Take it to the maritime arbitrators." The fishermen said, "Hey, you let the boat go. Are you working for the Kuomintang?" I've just telephoned to ask what to do. This was all pushed off on us by the Maritime Affairs Department. They blamed us for letting the culprits leave and refused to get involved.

We get the same sort of trouble with the tax people. A lot of Taiwan compatriots come over on fishing boats to visit relatives and they buy mainland products to take back.† They say they're gifts for friends and relatives, but sometimes they're impounded as contraband. So the Taiwanese say that "the gentleman in the United Front Department" gave them permission, and then the Customs Bureau and Revenue Bureau both start taking us to task. Here's the problem: other units work according to rules, and regulations, but not us – we have to use explanation and persuasion, and not let the compatriots suspect that we're doing it for the United Front, because that puts them off. It all depends on experience and flexibility.

* Fellow Chinese not from the mainland.

† The prices of some Chinese medicines and other products are lower on the mainland than in Taiwan.

I'm a local. Joined the army in '54, was promoted to second lieutenant in 1960, and was assigned to the county in 1972. Originally I was in the county Armed Forces Department, but two years ago the United Front Department expanded and I was transferred here as deputy department head. I lost rank, but what does it matter? It's for the revolution!

I'll never get promoted. No chance. To be promoted as a cadre now you need two things: qualifications and youth. I went into the army from junior middle school, and I'm forty-six this year. I've no hope.

But – just between us – do all those kids with diplomas work out so well? The leading group in our county was reorganized last year. We were sent a new deputy county head of thirty with a degree from the teachers' college who'd been teaching mathematics in middle school till then. College graduation counts for two grades, so he's a grade-twenty-two cadre with the use of a car and driver. Needless to say, he was given housing right away. They call it a "younger, more intellectualized leading group, with cadres whose ability and political integrity are equally matched", but how can you measure ability and integrity? He owes it all to his degree. Not many people in our county have higher education, and hardly anyone with a university degree was assigned to the county level. Everyone who got promoted in the county and the communes this time is from the teachers' college, and so is the new deputy mayor.

The long and the short of it is, they don't have what it takes to be officials. Do you think a middle-school teacher knows what happens in a county office? Was he worried! He knows less than the Party committee's messenger. They say he can't eat and can't sleep for all the people seeking him out all day long, and even waylaying him on his way home to solve their problems. But what can he solve? He's hopeless. Not everybody has it in him to be an official. His kind may make good teachers, but they're not cut out for office, just as the county head wouldn't be a good teacher. Frankly, there's really no way anybody's going to take him seriously. I'll be damned if I'm going to take his crazy orders. I'm doing my job, and to hell with him. Anyhow, my United Front work isn't within his purview. My outfit is under the Party committee. I'm in charge of the Taiwan Division and the Overseas Chinese Division. The comrades are clear about who's in charge – us, not him.

Before the leading group was reorganized, we had plenty of people struggling for power. Those who'd been retired weren't willing to leave, and cadres in units that had been merged with each other were fighting to hold on to their positions, so there really was a rumpus. Nobody expected this flood of officials with diplomas who couldn't take charge or get people to obey them. By the time the Central's policy got down to our level, it all boiled down to two inflexible principles: diploma and youth. Some were not so young; and as there aren't any college graduates at the township level, graduates from secondary technical schools take their place. The old cadres have the experience, but people ignore that. The newcomers have to do everything themselves and make their own mistakes first. Old cadres retire, perhaps on the early plan. You have to go at sixty, or they'll make trouble for you. But they should give retired cadres a little decision-making power. Why is it they provide all the amenities for them, but won't give them any work to do? In my opinion, there are some old comrades who're more willing to stick their necks out and take on responsibility than the young cadres, not to mention being less selfish and more upright.

We old soldiers tend to be direct and go for quick solutions. We don't like a lot of talk about "information" and "efficiency" when nothing get's done. A lot of things took some getting used to as a civilian. Demobilized officers get a raw deal now. There's no time to get a degree as an army officer working your way up the promotion ladder. During the Cultural Revolution, a batch of army cadres took over local civil government, but it played havoc with the image of the army and corrupted the thought of some cadres.

But you can't get promoted just for long service in the army any more. You've got to be young and educated there too now, and it's even less flexible than in local government. Above certain ages you can't be battalion commander or a regimental commander. I think the army *has* to be younger. It has to be able to move and fight; commanders must go for days without sleep. Old men can't handle that.

Civil government ought to be a little more flexible, but they want to save themselves trouble and avoid stirring things up, so, in the name of "implementing the Central's policy without any deviation" they've ended up with some iron rules, and – if I can say a "reactionary" word or two – "Mama and Papa just stand to the side, it's all up to Junior, and Grandpa, his guide". They haven't begun to solve a whole series of fundamental problems, like what to do with people in the prime of life, the first echelon, and so forth. How long does a master train his apprentice? Three years. So, even in a period of transition, you have to get a bit of on-the-job experience to start with. Army officers come from the ranks, and from the military academies. They understand the organizational structure and the psychology of the soldiers and junior officers. They know how to command in battle. But a civil official, humph! Some teacher walks through the door of a Party committee for the first time in his life and becomes its secretary, or a department head, and all just because of his diploma. Did he earn his diploma at cadre school? At a Party school? No – from a teachers' college. What does he understand? There's no professional knowledge without experience.

Senior comrades already have experience, and they've paid the price for it, so why have a youngster beginning again from scratch? Sure, they say, "Help him on to his horse and go with him on the first leg of the journey." But once he's jumped up on to that horse, some senior comrades don't want to help, and he won't accept the help of some others. He insists on galloping off by himself, not letting others come with him. Me? I'm past it. I'll mind my own business and let it go at that. I'll retire in a couple of years. I can't quit till then: I'm not old enough, though I can't be promoted, either.

Why is everybody rushing for those diplomas? If the young people in the county committee all register with the television and night universities, and even study at the office, who'll do the work? Quite a lot of our young people used to do very good work, but now they've pushed it aside to study maths, physics and chemistry – they don't do justice to either. There are for sure a lot of people who think they can't get promotion without a diploma; otherwise, would they all be in school? But they've got no alternative, and they really might get ahead with their degrees one day.

10

LONERS

Irreproachable Conduct

A small town bounded to the south by the Sanggan River and to the north by the railway. A bell tower still stands at the crossroads in the centre. Where the bell once hung and over the doorways are inscribed stone tablets: ancient ones commemorating people of irreproachable conduct, modern ones for revolutionary martyrs.

Most of the houses around here are built of adobe, some roofed with traditional tiles, others with modern ones. The buildings in reinforced concrete are government offices and joint state-private shops. The signs on the adobe-built shops mostly indicate that gongs and cymbals are made or sold within. This is the traditional local industry. A popular song blasts out from a loudspeaker hung in a doorway. As we draw nearer we see that this shop-sign reads Audio Centre. To the left is a shop which repairs Hongkong electronic watches; to the right "Modern Trends" sells up-holstered furniture and aluminium basins.

The middle school, the alma mater of a number of well-known people, is in a narrow winding lane just off the main north–south road. There are several rows of grey-brick buildings beside a field in which stand two basketball posts.

She teaches science in this school. She is thirty-seven and unmarried.

It's no crime not to marry. In general I get on well with my colleagues but because I'm not married they always make me feel the odd one out, different from the rest. Lots of students come to see me here and that's okay, but male colleagues couldn't. Gossip is a terrible thing.

I live among the students. I like teaching them. What chance do country children have of broadening their experience except by getting an education? All that most of them have to look forward to is going home to work the land. So they're really keen to learn. If a student is prepared to make an effort, I'll do anything I can to help, whether it's a matter of coaching, finding some money or fixing something up. Country children are honest. It's the students who keep me going.

Although it's so near, I haven't been into town for two weeks. What's the point? They all know I'm an old maid, even the smallest children. I don't know them, but they all recognize me and point me out. Why should I make myself a spectacle? The students bring me back salt and soap and anything else I need.

This is my home town. I was thirty-one when they started holding college entrance exams again in 1978. Another year and I would have been over the age limit. I didn't dare apply for university, so I put down Hebei Teachers' College. I was the only woman in the whole county to get in anywhere that year. My family all thought I would go far but I ended up back here.

The Cultural Revolution broke out when I was in the third year of senior middle, and about to do university entrance. I was very, very ambitious in those days – I wanted to go to medical school. Partly perhaps because my mother was ill, and also because I'd got good marks. I realized early that with a bad class background like mine my only hope was to do well at school. My father left China in 1950 and we lost touch. In 1972 we had a letter to say he was in Hongkong but we didn't dare reply. My mother was a housewife until Liberation, then she did a crash course for cadres and came here to teach until ill-health forced her to take early retirement. In the Cultural Revolution, the others were all rebelling, but we belonged to one of the "five black categories"* so I kept my head down. I did all sorts of things. I was a street vendor, and then worked as a contract labourer carrying earth and sifting sand. I kept the two of us on my eighteen yuan a month.

I started a temporary job here in 1970. I taught two mathematics courses, was a class tutor and stepped in for any teacher who was away. Well, if you've finished senior middle school you can manage most things. I earned twenty-four yuan at first, then it went up to twenty-nine and finally thirty-two yuan. These days if bright students don't earn much I tell them to compare themselves with me.

When I became a member of the permanent staff in 1972, entrance exams were supposedly being reintroduced. I was nursing my mother

* Her father was probably classified as a counter-revolutionary.

and correcting assignments at the same time. Our house had no glass in the windows and there was even ice in the kettle. My mother's circulation was poor but when I held her she warmed up a bit. I'd have lit the stove but we had no coal. She begged me to ask the leadership to get her into hospital – but would they have bothered about a retired teacher like her? "Let me get those students through their exams for senior middle school first," I said. "For them it's the chance of a lifetime. Then I'll fix up the hospital for you." I felt it would look bad taking leave to look after her in hospital when I'd only just been made a regular teacher. The upshot was my mother died. What's more my students' exam marks were no use to them, although they were particularly high that year. After the Zhang Tiesheng business* it was decided to select them on the basis of "revolutionary spirit".

When you're unhappy it undermines your health. After my mother's death I simply went to pieces. In 1974 I came down with hepatitis and neurasthenia. I also had a stomach haemorrhage and myocarditis. As soon as I was taken off the drip, I went straight back to my classes. Immediately I felt my life was still worth something. I kept on at my books all the time I was ill: I told myself that if I wasn't going to be an educated woman, I could at least be an educated ghost.

Now I was alone I lived in the dormitory by the main gate. There was no janitor so you couldn't lie down for a moment without someone knocking at the door to ask the way somewhere. During the reading week at the end of term, some girls whose homes were a long way away moved in with me. One night someone outside shouted that there was a thief. The girls were too frightened to move so I grabbed a chopper and chased the thief off. It was very lonely being the only person there in the holidays. I asked the principal to let me have a little room in the back courtyard where the teachers' families lived. "Nobody's stopping you getting married," was his reply. "The rules say that single people have to live in collective accommodation." Collective indeed! I was living all by myself. What harm was I doing to anyone? Why should single people be refused their own rooms? So I did as my students suggested and moved into an empty room in the back courtyard.

The school authorities were furious. They swore at me and I lost my temper and told them I'd die before I moved. They took the case to the

* Zhang handed in blank college entrance exam papers, together with a political tirade against exams. He was subsequently hailed as a hero in leftist propaganda.

county education department and someone came to sort it out. He was quite sympathetic and said that as I'd already settled in, I shouldn't be asked to move. The principal felt let down and threatened to resign if I wouldn't give up the room. Then he cancelled my classes. I told him he had no right to do this and deprive my students of their lessons. It wasn't even a good room, just a storeroom, dirty and full of rubbish.

All I want is justice for us single women. Only children are doing fine these days, so why should women who are on their own be given such a hard time? We're not distracted by housework, we don't take maternity leave and we don't have to miss work because of sick children. Some mothers take it very easy at work, as if they deserved some reward. That's not fair at all. In other countries people are eager to employ single women. Now that we're adopting so many other things from abroad, why don't we take up that one?

I had to struggle to get this room I'm in now, too. A lot of new accommodation was being put up, but they weren't going to give me any. The leadership said if I wanted a room I'd have to partition an area off. They'd give a grant of 400 yuan, and I'd have to provide the materials and hire the labour. Nobody else was treated like that. When I told some of my former students, they promised to get hold of the materials for 400 yuan and to do the work for nothing. After all, they were parents themselves by now and had built their own places. The oldest are thirty-one now. Some are cadres, others run their own businesses. They finished the job in a couple of weeks. The men did the building while the women cooked. They built a little lean-to kitchen for me as well as two rooms. They said that though they'd failed college entrance and would never get very far, at least they could feel happy they'd built their teacher a home. After it was finished I was ill again.

My students often ask why I never married. I tell them it's simple. I was eighteen when the Cultural Revolution began, and it went on until my mother died when I was twenty-six. Then my health collapsed. By the time I'd finished college I was nearly thirty-seven. People don't understand. They think I set my sights too high, or that I'm cranky, or have had some infection I'm ashamed to reveal. At least it's better than during the Cultural Revolution when unmarried people were accused of being secret agents sending off messages in the middle of the night.

I get on okay with my neighbours although there are problems sometimes. They couldn't understand why I wanted to buy a desk and a cupboard when I live alone. So was I meant to mark homework hunched over on my chair all my life? And they asked me why I bothered making dumplings just for myself at Spring Festival.

My health's still bad. I get ill every year when the graduating class leaves. If I don't feel well I go to bed with my clothes on in case I have to call someone to help in the night. One summer I had a reaction to the drip and started to shake all over. The students were scared and called the principal, but nobody came. I don't want them. I'd rather be left alone. But they are unfair.

I saw an article about a nun who's deputy head of the Chengdu Buddhist Association. I wrote to her but never heard back. Sometimes I think it would be nice to find somewhere quiet to study Buddhist scriptures. But I've got no room to turn to religion. All I can do is believe in my students.

I talk to men and boys a lot in my work. Frankly I think a lot of men are pettier than women. Marriage can be just a series of trivial quarrels. Marriage for its own sake is stupid. It's tiring enough being out at work all day, without having to be on your guard against someone at home and sharing your bed with a virtual stranger. What's more I don't understand at all why loose women get on so well, unlike us serious women. I can't fathom this "sexual liberation". Marriage is a serious matter. I could never switch from one man to another. Why do women always let men deceive them? It's not as if we were any less intelligent than them.

I've never had a boyfriend or had a secret crush on anyone. When I'm travelling I might feel drawn to someone I see, but then they go on their way and that's the end of it.

I'm sure I'm not the only single woman to feel the way I do. I want to appeal for equal rights for us. I wrote a letter to *New Outlook* and they published about a third of it. Perhaps they thought it got too complicated. Extracts were reprinted in various papers. Then I really did have problems. I got dozens of letters every day, sometimes as many as a hundred. Some supported me or poured out their woes – these were from women. Others told me what to do. I tried to reply to all of this group. The other 90 per cent were proposals of marriage. They thought I'd been advertising for a husband! The writers said they were from 10,000-yuan households, that they had fridges and colour TVs or that they were cadres with thousands of yuan in compensation money for their suffering in the Cultural Revolution. Some letters were really obscene. But I don't want to marry. I've got cirrhosis of the liver, I've had haemorrhages and viral myocarditis. All I want is rights for single people.

My students are my only comfort and I get on well with them. After they graduate some end up as cadres, some as thieves. Once I told a student I'd had ten yuan stolen and he made the thief give it back. When our alumni get married, I send a present, but I don't go. If I did, people might stare at me instead of the bride.

I never thought that the leadership would take any notice of my letter in *New Outlook*. But they did. They said I'd implied they neglected me. In the staff appraisal at the end of the year I'm always put in the bottom 5 per cent. I complained about being in the lowest group when my class had the best marks. "As you're so good at writing, put it in the papers," was the principal's reply. And I know I'll have more trouble now we're going to have our professional gradings fixed. Letters to the county education department and visits from higher officials are no use in the end. As soon as the high-ups leave he says: "Don't you forget I'm the principal."

My only fault is that I'm different from other people because I haven't married.

Misfit

Xiao Huiying, twenty-two. As she talks she makes little gestures with her fingers. From sunset until midnight we sit on the flagstones in Tian'anmen Square. She speaks; I speak; sometimes neither of us makes a sound, and we sit there quietly.

What am I? No one, as far as respectable people see it. I haven't got a permanent job, and I don't belong to a unit – all I've got is a residence permit. I'm a citizen. But then I'm not an ordinary citizen either. Am I like one of your average citizens?

Basically, I don't care whether people understand me as long as they'll acknowledge my existence. But even that's hard, because in many people's eyes I'm beyond the pale, some kind of monster or loony. Lunatics are as human as the rest of us, but because they're crazy they get treated as if they didn't belong to the human race any more.

Just look at all these people in the square – whole families out to cool off. So many Beijing people are still living in rotten conditions. Forget air-conditioning; they haven't even got electric fans. We're a poor country, and we want to change – but how? The only way is to get rich. The trouble is there are too many people wanting to get rich and too few prepared to find their own way. There's so little spirit of adventure: people are too used to plodding. Too many people will only go into action when their backs are against the wall. And a lot of others simply muddle along. So I'm a loner in my thoughts as well as my actions.

My father's a worker. My mother's a housewife. When the two of them start on at me and call me "mad" and "weird" and say I'm asking for trouble I think to myself: just look who's talking! All their brothers went to university, and those two didn't even make it through primary school! I just don't get it. How could a businessman and a factory owner have produced such a pair of weirdos as my parents? They were misfits and rebels themselves. My father's father had a furrier's shop. He's dead now. My grandfather on my mother's side had an ink factory, and he's dead too. He died when they searched his house during the Cultural Revolution. Nobody struggled against him; he just frightened himself to death.

With a background like that I didn't exactly shine at school. In 1979 I joined the army – not the People's Liberation Army, the army of unemployed youth. I was really fed up and started having rows with my parents. And when things came to a head I jeered at them, "It beats me where you found the energy to produce me at a time when you were half starved to death!" I was born in 1961, in the middle of the three years of natural disasters. But I don't look at it like that any more. I'm beginning to see how it was: the harder the times, the stronger the urge for survival. And people often get driven to doing things they wouldn't normally have dreamed of doing – not your so-called "civilized human beings". People are all monsters. What we respect is precisely the opposite of what our animal survival instincts drive us to. Humanity and human dignity are often no more than a joke.

In the spring of 1981 the street committee got me a job with a transport company doing odd jobs. I earned less than twenty yuan a month. Before I'd been there long I met a man who worked in an oilfield, and for some reason we fell madly in love. It all happened so quickly. We were in love with figments of our own imagination. Twice I went secretly to the oilfield to visit him. At night I slept in the women's dormitory and during the day I watched him work. Later I fell out with my parents over some trivial thing and ran off and stayed there for over a fortnight. When I got to see more of him I found I wasn't as keen but I was still prepared to marry him even if it meant losing my Beijing residence rights and transferring to work in the oilfield with him. The problem was he wanted me to stay in Beijing and act as his "home base". He hoped I could find him a job there. But there was no chance I'd get him transferred to the city. Even the children of top officials have to be prepared to go a long way from home and settle for a few dozen yuan a month in the sticks. When that failed he hoped – no, he actually suggested – I swap jobs with a woman at the oilfield whose husband was in Beijing. She was willing to slip me 2000 yuan in exchange for my job and my residence permit. But it went against all my principles: I've always wanted to be in control of my own life.

I came quietly back to Beijing without a tear. And when I got to the door of the post and telegram office at Beijing station I went in and sent him a telegram: "Two dreams shattered." Whose dreams? Mine and that of the woman who wanted to transfer to Beijing. He'd know what I meant. I was just going to pay for it when the big station clock struck six and I burst into tears. After I'd cried myself out I went and paid. The assistant looked at my message and took my money without a word. But as I turned to go I heard them saying: "And I thought someone in her family had died!" "Head case!" Normally I would have sworn at the so-and-sos, but I hadn't even got it in me to do that. So I know I'd had all I could take.

I still love him. Or at least I still love the image of him I have in my own mind. I was in love with the "moment in paradise" I'd turned it into. When I got home my parents wept for joy – they'd thought I was dead. They were as happy as if they'd found a new daughter. They didn't realize it wasn't the same me any more. I went back to the transport company and had to write a self-criticism for disappearing for twenty days without leave. But that wasn't good enough for them. They wanted me to write exactly where I had been on what day and with whom. I got the message all right: they thought I'd been having it off with someone! That made me sick, really sick. And I said: "Right, I'll pull my trousers down and show you I'm still a virgin. Will that stop your suspicions?" I wouldn't admit I was wrong. My attitude was thoroughly bad. I refused to reform, and I wouldn't accept their authority. So they threw me out. I said: "Thank you all so much. Your concern about chastity should be an example to all the kings, emperors, ministers and generals in history." If the truth were known they could have won me round with just a little coaxing. Some petty officials are so stupid. When they get heavy with people like me it only puts our backs up. Some get driven to thieving and prostitution and end up as menaces to society.

So I became a loner, but I was more energetic and also a lot more confident. For months I didn't read anything, didn't go to the theatre, didn't go to a single concert. I just practised typing as if my life depended on it. The aim was to make my living. After that I joined an unemployed young people's typing centre, and I landed myself a job typing English commercial documents for the offices of big companies in Beijing hotels. Now I'm earning three or four hundred yuan a month. That sounds like an astronomical sum to anyone in public employment. In fact, my old classmates look up to me. Some people look down their noses at me and say behind my back: "She may be doing all right for herself now, but she'll be in the shit before long.'

We've got people doing research on China's reforms, analysing what's led to the economic take-off in Hongkong and Taiwan, or studying the Soviet Union, Yugoslavia and Romania. But others are still trying to go back to the way we used to do things in the sixties.

I give my younger brother fifty yuan a month. He's just started at university and he thinks of it as a student grant. All the rest I spend. It goes on clothes, good food – I have several different dishes a meal, beer, soft drinks – on books and concerts. I don't give my father or my mother a penny; nor my sister. We all earn and we're financially independent.

Money's no object. There was this Xi Xiulan concert I had to buy a ticket on the black market for. Paid a fortune so I'd get a proper seat not just a perch right up at the back. Actually the amplification was so good it wouldn't have made any difference. And I don't even like pop music! I began to think about this and I realized I was only there to be able to say I'd gone. The whole thing bored me so I walked out halfway through. The hopefuls still waiting outside couldn't believe it. Well, I'm not like them. Nothing means that much to me. I'm too realistic.

I think I could write. At any rate, some fiction or something. But I've never written a word. There's no money in fiction, and I'd only be making trouble for myself if I wrote everything I think. Besides, where's the fun in painting a nude with yourself for model?

There's a Japanese man who wants to marry me. But I won't have him. I'm earning 400 yuan a month here; what would a typist get there? And when he starts to talk about supporting me that's even worse. I'm not having that. I've only just managed to establish my independence. I'm not marrying a foreigner and that's final; you won't catch me bowing and scraping to them. I've got my principles, even if it's not easy to say exactly what they are. I don't have a problem of sexual needs because I've never actually gone the whole way with anyone. I'm a virgin. After being in love once I feel too weary to fall for someone again. Anyway, if it didn't work out that would finish me altogether. I'd probably just start sleeping around. It's lucky, just as it was lucky I didn't lose my Beijing residence permit. Yet it's also a greater loss than that, isn't it?

When we finally parted he said it was because I was too modern: he couldn't control me. But why should he? I don't want anyone having control over me. But I would like to be able to depend on a man. How do you explain that? Life's full of mysteries. But what your average Chinese man is looking for as a suitable wife is a girl who'll cling around his neck. A girl to cling around his neck who can also earn her keep. That's my analysis. And it's the tragedy of a lot of people today.

Can you walk me home? There's a stretch ahead where there aren't any street lights — it's just an alley. And I'll have to climb over the courtyard wall: the main gates will be locked by now.

On the Road

Yang Shouqian, nineteen, has a beard at least six inches long, shoulder-length hair, and a small straw hat with a red tassel. People wait outside his hotel just to catch a glimpse of him.

In the last year and a half I've covered over 17,000 kilometres – 3900 on foot, and the rest by bike. I'm just nineteen.

I wanted to go, so I went.

I'm from Jiamusi in the north-east. In primary school and up to the beginning of my third year in junior middle school I was a good student, always got top marks. But by then I'd had enough of boring old textbooks, so I quit school in the second half of my third year. I studied at home instead. If I'd finished junior middle I'd have gone on to senior middle and taken college entrance. But it's very competitive. I might have had to study something that turned me off, then been put into a job that meant nothing to me and been a complete failure. So instead of letting other people mould me I decided to find my own niche. My classmates and teachers thought I was a screwball, out of my mind. They came to our place to get me back on track. They wanted me to be a good boy and read the same boring old texts as everyone else. But I knew what I was doing. There was no turning back. Social pressure was mostly family pressure.

Come the ideal society, the family will have to go. My dad – it was mostly him – is a good father, a good feudal father who likes beating his kids. He's beaten me since I was that high. I grew up under the whip of feudal despotism. There was no arguing with him: he always kept a whip ready to give us a flogging. He's a doctor of Chinese medicine, polite to his patients, and foul to everyone else. My father said he hadn't kept me in school all those years for nothing, and he made a big thing about getting my graduation diploma so I went back and passed the exam for him.

Next I needed work. Had to wait for a job, right? But what I really needed was to understand society, so I could make my own judgements. I worked for three days in a construction brigade, then "retired". I spent a whole winter getting to know local people: workers, peasants, bums, drop-outs, all sorts. I wanted to find out how they lived and what they felt about life. I'd decided to leave Jiamusi in spring and travel all round the country.

On 21 March 1983 my father bawled me out again. "You've been going on for days about this big trip. How come you're still here?" In fact I was all set. "Don't worry, I'm off tomorrow," I told him. "Go on then," he said, "and don't come back. Good riddance!" So with this blessing I split.

At 4.30 a.m. the next day I set out on my fact-finding journey on foot. I felt pretty bad as my friends came to say goodbye. "You can't come all the way with me," I told them. "We'll see each other again." Though it was early spring, the north-east was still covered in snow and ice. All I could see behind me was this expanse of white with the smoke stacks of Jiamusi sticking up like grey pillars. I headed along side-roads towards Harbin.

I had twenty yuan my grandad had given me for the Spring Festival. He called it money to "weigh down the year", to try to stop us youngsters from growing up. It's a folk belief: if you grow up, you'll grow old and die – better not to grow up at all. If you think about it you can understand something of what's wrong with us Chinese. My parents? Not a penny! Just curses. They hadn't wanted me to go. They even gave the municipal Youth League secretary an earful. I'd asked the Youth League for a letter of introduction, because without one I'd have had trouble every step of the way. I lied to them, said I was waiting for a job, was twenty-five and wanted to see the country at my own expense. Sounded plausible, so they wrote me the letter. But when they found out I was only seventeen, and my parents were dead set against me going, the fat was in the fire. They wanted the letter back. That's why the secretary came to our place. My dad was fool enough to swear at him, so I managed to win him over in the end. We young people can usually understand each other. I told him, "When I said I was twenty-five you believed me and agreed to write me a letter. That shows I can pass for a twenty-five-year-old. Now you want it back just because of my age. That's crazy. If you think I can pass for twenty-five you should have faith in me. You screwed up, but don't be in such a hurry to backtrack. My family were bound to be against it. Let's work on the old people together."

"Comrade Yang Shouqian is on a fact-finding walking tour; please look after him." That short introduction smoothed the way for me, though it wasn't all easy. After leaving Heilongjiang I hoofed it through Jilin, Liaoning, Hebei and Tianjin to Beijing, 3900 kilometres in all. I wore out three pairs of shoes. The letter of introduction saved me a lot of money, since local governments, Youth League offices and other units gave me food and a place to sleep. Most of them seemed eager to help me – I don't know whether from admiration, scepticism, surprise or even pity. Some of them cold-shouldered me, as if I wasn't serious and would give up and go home if they didn't give me a bed. Sometimes I stayed with old peasants and their equally hospitable dogs and fleas. Sometimes I slept out in a sleeping-bag and if it got too cold I would run around to warm up. Didn't bother me – I'd asked for it.

I wasn't out to break any long-distance record, only to understand society and investigate folklore. After reaching Beijing I bought a bike and a simple camera. I earned the money by practising medicine while I was finding out about local folklore and listening to the villagers' tales and gossip. With the prescriptions passed down in our family I cured quite a few patients who had common diseases. The countryside's still short of doctors and medicine. The "barefoot doctors", who had a bit of education, have gone off to make it as traders. So I took their place as an itinerant quack.

By the time I left Beijing I'd picked up a couple more ways of earning cash: teaching martial arts and coaching youngsters in philosophy and history for their high-school entrance exams. But I never have any money to spare. Right now I haven't got a cent to my name. The other day I figured out that these eighteen months have cost me only 1800 yuan. People don't believe this, because it costs that much just to live in town, and I've bought a bike, a camera and several hundred yuans' worth of books. But honestly, I've only spent 1800. And I earned it all myself apart from twenty-five really ill-gotten bucks, the twenty given me at the Spring Festival and five more you'll hear about presently. I don't mind being broke, I can always earn more.

In Guangdong I couldn't be a quack, since there were no patients, and nobody wanted to learn martial arts; so I went to a restaurant, told the boss that I was starving, and asked for work. By washing dishes and chopping firewood I got good meals and three yuan on top of it, enough to keep me going for two more days. Someone said my journey had great publicity value, and I should get factories to provide me with free gear to promote their stuff. Or I could raise subscriptions; but I didn't know who to approach or how to do it. Lots of local papers wrote me up, but no factories were interested in me, only an unemployed youngster who tracked me down. He was dead set on coming with me. He was the pits! Once when I'd gone hungry for three days I asked him for a mouthful of malt extract: he refused. He was scared he'd starve to death! I'd done everything for him, taken him to Shanghai with me. So I sent him packing. I can't stand guys like that. The ordinary people I met along the way were better.

I cycled through Hebei, Shandong, Jiangsu, Anhui, Shanghai, Zhe-jiang, Guangdong and Guangxi, and spent three months on Hainan Island. That part of my journey was about 15,000 kilometres. The south wasn't like the north – they were very big on class struggle! I kept being run in by the police or the militia. My letter of introduction cut no ice with them. They simply didn't believe I could have come all the way from the north-east on my own, so they'd throw me in the slammer as a vagrant while they checked up on me. After it had happened often enough it didn't bother me any more. I'd tell them what I was doing and ask them to contact Jiamusi, then take a breather in the cell. Sometimes I was there a couple of hours, sometimes seven or eight, depending on how long it took them to place a long-distance call. Once the Jiamusi Public Security Bureau assured them that I wasn't an escaped convict they'd cheerfully let me go. They'd even say nice things. At the check-point on the border of the Shenzhen Special Economic Zone I got detained as usual. When they let me go, I said, "That's not enough. I've got to see your special economic zone." They said it was impossible without a permit from the Provincial Security Department. "Well then, ask for one," I said. "You've called up the north-east, so what's the problem about calling Guangzhou?" And I got the permission of the Provincial Security Department to see round the Shenzhen and Zhuhai special economic zones.

Sometimes I got taken for a healer with magic powers, sometimes for a schizophrenic. In one temple the nuns kowtowed to me as a re-incarnation of one of Sakyamuni Buddha's disciples. But very few people believed that I was investigating local customs. I call myself a "high-class beggar" or a "semi-itinerant quack". Aren't begging and cheating social phenomena too?

In the north-east and the north I was hardly bothered by the police and militia. But I ran into bandits more than once. That was when the nationwide hunt for the two Wang brothers* was on and quite a few city crooks were holed up in the hills. I ran into some of them. Once a couple of bastards held me up. I told them, "I haven't got any money. I'm on a fact-finding tour." They told me to strip, and we started arguing. After a while one of them slipped behind me. Was I lucky! This guy behind me took a swipe at me with his stick, but it was just when I was shifting my weight on to the other foot because I'd been standing in the same position too long. He missed me, but smashed the other bastard's face right in. So I kicked the guy behind and said, "Some muggers! You need a few lessons from an old hand." Then I cleared off fast. That was scary! If he hadn't missed I wouldn't be here today.

Another time I came across a good bandit. When he grabbed me I told him, "I'm broke and I haven't eaten for a whole day. I'm on a social study tour." He didn't believe me, of course. Demanded to see my papers. Would you believe it, a bandit wanting to see your ID? When I showed it to him he said, "Good for you, pal! I've not been doing well the last few days: I've only taken five yuan. But you have it." I didn't want his stolen money. "I'm helping you out, pal," he fumed. "If my money's not good enough for you I'll kill you!" I looked at his stick and was afraid he'd really kill me with it, so I took the money and ran. Behind me I heard him saying to himself, "Wouldn't take money? Who on earth refuses money?" That five yuan was a headache to me. If I left it by the road somebody else would pick it up and it would still get spent. But where was I to hand it in? I had to keep it and try to put it to good use. Those were the other five ill-gotten bucks I mentioned just now. I often think about that guy. I hope he's gone straight.

I've written over three million words so far. I write up my diary every day. I've also taken nearly 4000 photographs that Youth League committees and local government cultural bureaus have been very helpful about developing for me.

My three days in Shanghai were the most frustrating. I'd collected a whole lot of stuff and written a long account of my observations, as

---

* Two gunmen who killed a number of policemen and were on the run for months till they themselves were gunned down.

well as an article on marriage. I showed it to an old folklore specialist. "This article of yours," he said, "well, it . . . it smacks of spiritual pollution." Because I mentioned communal marriage and promiscuity. "These things, well, the masses have forgotten them. So why bring them up?"

That wasn't the first time I met with this kind of reaction. I feel we've got to analyse the inner logic of the development of our Chinese folk customs and folk literature. Stands to reason, doesn't it? But when I speak of a cultural transition zone between relatively backward and relatively advanced cultures, the usual reaction is, "What's a 'cultural transition zone'? Did you make up that expression yourself?" Language is a tool to express ideas and communicate, so why shouldn't I coin a phrase? But no! Because I'm too young, I haven't got the right. They claim that old terminology can express new ideas quite clearly. Seems to me that from the thirties to the eighties the study of folklore has been at a low ebb in China. Practically nothing new has come up. Folklorists in the US and Japan have made big advances, and by taking over some of their new concepts we've jumped, as it were, from grade three to grade five. But we can't just copy foreign methods blindly. It isn't like building computers. Their theories aren't always correct. You've got to draw on different social sciences, and even on maths and statistics, to study our Chinese customs. So I say that the study of folklore in China today is in an embryonic stage.

I've been asked about the political significance of what I'm doing. The person who asked that question sure didn't know anything about folklore. I'm trying to understand the emergence and development of different cultural communities with the aim of correcting some of our national defects. How else can we put them right? For instance, why are peasants everywhere so afraid of family planning? Why do women go into hiding to have their second baby? You have to start by getting some ideas about the influence of material life on people's thinking, on their views about life, on clan relationships, on their sense of family responsibility and so forth.

My next investigations will be of aboriginal wild men. In the history of civilization, in the history of mankind, could there have been a group that turned away from modern civilization? Could there be a community that stopped evolving, a community still in a prehistoric stage? I want to discover some wild men – the missing link in human evolution – and find out how they developed. Of the world's four great mysteries, the Loch Ness Monster and the Bermuda Triangle are abroad, out of my reach, and I haven't the equipment or theoretical know-how to study UFOs. I can only study the wild men. That's why I've let my hair get long and grown a beard, and got my mother to make me a fur coat.

In December I'm going to Guangxi, then in the spring to the Shennongjia Mountains in Hubei. I know that a lot of people have searched already without success. Even if I do find them, I'd rather live with them than catch one. That's the only way to get to know them and study them. Genuine zoologists don't study tigers in zoos. So when people ask me, "Young Yang, when are you going to catch a wild man?" I just smile. I only might bring one back with me.

I shan't leave the Shennongjia Mountains until I've succeeded. When I was in Beijing a few days ago I climbed the Great Wall as a sort of farewell gesture. The Great Wall is the symbol of our nation, but it's no longer able to protect us. It's a fantastic part of our cultural heritage, but now it's falling to bits, ruined by people and by the elements like a dragon hacked apart.

What do I need? Photographic equipment and a small tape-recorder would do fine. I'll borrow them and give them back later. No, I don't collect contributions, don't know how to. But if any of your readers want to help me, they're welcome to.

Good Looks

She is so strikingly beautiful that nearly all men stare at her whenever she goes out.

Dad had a watch and clock business before Liberation. Afterwards it was made into a joint state—private company with him as manager. Later he was dismissed for corruption so he went into something new — he did odd jobs in a fried-food shop. I was born in 1955 and soon afterwards the family got really poor. I didn't go to kindergarten. I just played with other children in the alley. I spent the whole day on the street. They weren't too bothered about me at home. I had two elder sisters and a kid brother. With three daughters what would it have mattered if one died? That's how it is in poor families.

I was poor-to-middling at primary school. I hardly ever got a good mark. When I was in class four, the Cultural Revolution broke out, so I had another few years running wild on the street. Then, in 1969, I drifted into middle school. It was in my second year there that I realized I was beautiful. Of course people had always said I was a pretty little girl, but I thought they were just being nice. Obviously by the time we were at middle school we weren't completely ignorant about sex, but we didn't know all that much either. I couldn't help knowing that several of the boys fancied me. They were always trying to please me and showing off.

When I had a period, I was sure to find a big bar of chocolate in my desk. At those times we didn't do morning exercises, so the boys could work it out. I still don't know who it came from. But every time I quarrel with my husband, I think, "If only I'd married that one." Of course it's just a dream. Anyway, kindness isn't enough. I want a real man.

You think I was lucky? Only thirteen and boys falling for me already!

Of course they were just interested in me for my looks. I wasn't very kind. When we finished school we were all split up. There were just three of us girls sent to the same production team. Before I went, I dumped all the boys' notes and letters on the table and said, "You can each take the ones you wrote." You can imagine how this really upset things in the class. When I was older, I could see how horrible I had been. None of us knew what love was really like. We were just fooling around.

That year I was fifteen. All of us went to work in the countryside. Well, a few stayed in town. The ones who could pull strings.

My commune was in hilly country. Some boys from the class which had been sent down the year before began to chase after me. I fell for one of them. I suppose it was because I was rather lonely. I only saw him a few times. The older boys were good to me. When I was going home to see my family, they queued for my ticket, got me a seat, carried my luggage – everything. Just to see me a bit longer. They liked to get a seat beside me so that when the bus went over a bump they'd be able to lean against me.

We tried to level some of our commune's land. One of the older lads hurt his foot on a stone. It was in plaster so he just had to sit in the village waiting to get better. I used to go to chat to him. Sometimes I'd take him some chicken. The older boys often brought me chicken or dog meat which they'd stolen from the peasants. I can't say how it happened. I don't know how he had the face. But anyway, he asked, and I let him. I was sixteen years old. I used to think it would be really something – but when it happened, I found it was nothing at all. I was a girl beforehand, and when I got up I was still the same girl. I hadn't turned into a grown woman. But the feeling I'd had for the other boy disappeared after that. There was nothing left. I waited anxiously for my period because I was afraid I might be pregnant. I didn't feel very pleased with myself but I didn't feel guilty either. I didn't really like the boy, it was just curiosity and confusion. I couldn't help it. I never wanted to marry him. That simply wasn't on the cards. Afterwards I didn't see much of him.

Once I was back in the city, I was sent to work in the factory canteen but I didn't last long. You see, every day the queue in front of me was the longest and they were all men. Some of them were so shameless they wrote me little notes on their food tickets. I took no notice at all, but afterwards the person who checked the food tickets would tease me about it. I had to ask for a transfer and started driving a crane, which was very easy. As usual, everyone looked after me. Once, the crane cable snapped and a big shaft fell down, just missing a fellow called Ye. If it had hit him it would certainly have killed him: it weighed over ten kilos. Ye was only a young worker but he gave me a real earful. There were very few men who would blow their top with me – they were too much in awe of my looks. I admired him for having the guts to swear at me. I didn't want to drive the crane after that, so I got myself transferred to work on a precision grinder. That was very light work too, because it was electronically controlled.

Later I found out that Ye's dad was a very distinguished engineer. He'd been a farm boy who'd managed to win a government scholarship to the United States. Brilliant he might have been, but when his wife died, he married his children's nurse. What's more, he was really horrible to the children of his first marriage. He only cared about his pretty new wife. "I hate all pretty women," Ye told me. I think that was what attracted me to him. Isn't life strange?

Lots of people introduced me to likely boys. Some young workers would come to my home to chat me up. Even on the street, perfectly respectable men would come up and ask me if I had a boyfriend. "No, I haven't," I would say, "but I don't want to find one on the street." I went out with a trade union official for a few months. We were introduced by a colleague. We got on all right. He was a good man, reliable, a Party member and he had prospects. But later, when I told him I wasn't a virgin, he didn't want any more to do with me. I can't blame him. I admired him, he was a principled man. Up to then, I hadn't cared for him that much. But after we broke things off, I felt I loved him.

I've always felt that all women hated me – they're afraid I'll steal their men, even the ones who haven't got boyfriends.

Next I was introduced to a boy whose father had hundreds of thousands of yuan. They'd been bankers before Liberation. If I'd married him I'd have had no more worries. I wasn't afraid of him – he was rather effeminate – but I was afraid of that money. He loved me. When I was getting married to someone else he gave me a lot of presents, terribly expensive things. "In future, even if things are very hard for you, I won't be able to give you anything," he explained. So I accepted them. "I'll be a married woman soon," I said. Then he said, "If you want anything from me now, there's still time. Afterwards it'll be too late." He patted me on the shoulder. "I've never yet even kissed a girl," he said, "and I'm not going to break that rule now." He went away.

Last year he got a wife with better class origins and higher social standing than mine. They set up a modern, well-equipped home. He wasn't very happy afterwards so he went away to work in the Shenzhen Special Economic Zone as an accountant. Since then, we've just had business dealings. I give him Chinese currency and he buys me things from Hongkong. He always shows me the currency exchange receipts with the rate for the day. He plays straight with me.

He knows I'm not very happily married either. "If ever you can't bear it any longer, just call on me," he once said to me. "I'd still marry you willingly and set up a new home with you."

He meant that he would break up his first marriage. So I wouldn't do it. I couldn't, and I wouldn't have wanted to.

I got married to a technician when I was twenty-seven. It was all based on fantasy. I had wanted to marry someone who knew how to struggle. It was too romantic. I don't want to talk about him. I think we've both got an idea of what'll probably happen . . . never mind that I'm about to become a mother. Even if we wanted to make it last it wouldn't work. It's hopeless.

When my husband heard what had happened in the countryside, he wasn't upset and he didn't blame me. In fact he was pleased. Why? Because I was spoilt goods. He used to worry that I was too pretty, that my value was higher than his, so we weren't equal. When he found out, it lowered my value in his eyes. I knew how he felt. It wasn't tolerance. It was selfishness, real selfishness.

All the same, he isn't the worst. The really bad person was that boy in the countryside. I remember he said that once you turned off the light, it didn't matter whether someone was pretty or ugly. It was all the same. It was all fucking anyway. That was an awful thing to say.

Since I've been married, men have kept chasing me just the same. I did fall for someone, a man who wasn't after me. I invited him to come to see an exhibition with me and afterwards we ate out together. "Well," he said suddenly. "We're both grown-ups. We're both adults. Right?" And that was the end of it. Wherever I go, it always seems to lead me back to the same place. There are a lot of things I would like to know – and yet, if I do get to know them, what use are they?

I've had some problems in my life, but on the other hand, some things have been made easy for me. If I want to buy anything, I always find the male shop assistants are most attentive. If I queue for returned tickets at a theatre, someone is bound to give me some. And yet I feel I get further and further away from people. Can this be all my fault?

Beauty is my only advantage, my "capital". But I always seem to like the people who don't take any notice of it. The pity is that I don't have anything else to give.

11

CRIME AND
PUNISHMENT

Inside

The road that leads here used to be called Coffin Shop Lane. It has been renamed Self-Renewal Road.

Beijing Municipality's Number One Prison. The Fifth Brigade. This has been a jail since the Qing Dynasty. The buildings are shaped like a hand with its five fingers outstretched.

The little finger is a corridor of long, narrow cells. The prisoners sleep in two-tiered bunk beds, sixteen to a cell. Every man has a shelf in a small, unlocked cupboard for personal belongings. The striped sheets and white quilts are folded with military precision. A guitar hangs on the wall of one cell, and in the corridor are red lanterns to celebrate the Spring Festival. There is a display of paintings and a wall newspaper run by the inmates, as well as little red, yellow and green flags and charts referring to hygiene and work.

The palm of the hand is the main entrance and a hall, around which are a number of small rooms. The first room to the left of the entrance is the warders' duty room. In the next room lives the political instructor of the Fifth Brigade. It is about nine square metres, and contains a single bed, a wash-stand, a small cupboard and a two-drawered desk under the glass top of which are photos of his son and of himself and his wife.

Guo Zheng. Thirty. Political instructor of the Fifth Brigade.

We take only long-term prisoners. The work we do in this brigade is pretty specialized: making moulds for the manufacture of plastic sandals. All those shoes from the Qinghe Plastics Factory you see in the shops come from here. Double Golden Horse nylon socks are from this prison too, but from other brigades.

It takes two or three years, training a skilled worker in our trade.

That's why we choose long-term men. We haven't got a single historical counter-revolutionary here, and only one active counter-revolutionary.* He came in during the Cultural Revolution. He wasn't against the Gang of Four – he was against everyone. He was a technician in a design institute who wrote in his spare time and spread his stuff around. He's still resisting reform. When the other prisoners are watching television he keeps his head down and won't look. They're nearly all common criminals now, youngsters most of them. Our technical manpower's fallen 50 per cent in the few years I've been here. That's because the more youngsters we get, the worse-educated our intake is. So we have to start off with two or three years of remedial teaching, and that means keeping an eye on them while they learn, because if we don't, they don't. They can't even string a couple of proper sentences together – they can only talk dirty.

So you want a youngster who's a legal illiterate serving a long sentence and can show you something of the reform process. I reckon Gai Lujun would fit the bill. He's a murderer who came here in 1978. Originally he was on a suspended death sentence, but later that was commuted to life imprisonment. A couple of years ago it was reduced to fifteen years. He's reformed well.

Me? I graduated from junior middle school in 1971. I was sent here after being demobilized. In those days the demands here were very tough, and you had to be a Party member. I joined the Party when I was in the forces. I was in signals. When I first heard I was being sent here I was . . . well . . . My family are workers.

Most people work on a three-shift system, but here we say we work three and a bit. Let's start with the three main shifts. By regulations, the prisoners get up at six, so we have to be up even earlier to supervise them getting up, followed by ten minutes for roll call. They get twenty minutes for breakfast, and while they're eating we use the time to deal with various things like quarrels between the prisoners, censoring incoming and outgoing mail, reading prisoners' reports on their thinking, and so on. Those twenty minutes go by in a flash, which is why we've all lost the habit of eating breakfast. At ten past seven the prisoners go to the workshop to start work, and we have to go with them. They break at 11.30, start again at 12.20, and knock off at five.

---

* "Historical counter-revolutionaries" are past opponents of the regime, by contrast with "active counter-revolutionaries", who are still opposing it.

After supper they do their washing. The prisoners have study from 6.30 till eight, with half an hour for the latrine in the middle of it. At eight we check the cells and have a head count. Lights out at 8.30. Those are our three shifts. The extra bit is that while the prisoners are asleep three of us have to sit in the duty room to stop fights or cope with emergencies. Two of us do half duty and stay till 2.30, and one does a whole duty and has to stay till 6 a.m.

We're badly understaffed. There used to be eight warders in our brigade, but one got into university and the old political instructor's ill, which leaves only six of us. One's a woman, and as women comrades can't very well be put in charge of male prisoners she can only do paper work, so she doesn't count. We should have at least fifteen men, to make the ratio of supervisory cadres to prisoners 15 per cent. We've got 120 prisoners at present. It's just about impossible to get a free shift on holidays. I haven't had a day off since the Spring Festival. When you've been too long on the job, you really can't take much more of this strain. Our old political instructor had a cerebral haemorrhage last year, and he was only forty-nine. We've got to be on our guard all the time. The three big kinds of trouble here are escapes, fights and suicides. Of course, escapes are the most serious. Most fights are just scuffles, but they can get dangerous. The year before last a fight broke out when the prisoners were working. One of them was chasing another with a cutter from the workshop in his hand. I was completely unarmed. By the regulations we don't normally carry our truncheons, and there was no time for me to go to fetch mine. They were fighting like tigers. Luckily I'm young, so I just grabbed a metal bar and charged in. I tripped the one in front over. Once they saw I was a warder they bottled out, and the fight stopped. After that I had to wear my tongue out on them. It took a whole day to get them both to admit they were wrong, criticize themselves and promise not to do it again.

We do have suicides. It wasn't in our brigade, but not long ago there was a prisoner who was devastated when he didn't get officially praised at the end of the year. The reason was he'd reformed well and was pretty stable emotionally: he was left off the list so that one of the new prisoners would get some encouragement. But he thought we'd lost confidence in him, and ate a whole heap of nails. We rushed him to hospital for emergency treatment. He was saved. It took a lot of talking to make him feel better about it all.

The prisoners aren't allowed to lie down during the day, not even on their rest days. Amusing themselves is okay, but they can't lie down. There's no way of knowing what's going on in their heads while they're lying down. They've got to spend their time reforming themselves. They can't be left to their own devices for a moment.

We know about the home background of every single man – how many people there are in the family, how they're placed, and what attitude they take to him. We think about it all day while we're on duty. You're trying to size the prisoners up, and they're trying to size you up. If you're fairly easy-going and they try anything out on you, you come down a bit harder on them and they'll behave themselves after that. You mustn't let them find out what makes you tick. Some new comrades give too much of themselves away to the prisoners, and we have to warn them as soon as we can.

When you're with the prisoners every day, morning, noon and night, you get to know each other pretty well. So you can't afford to get slack. For instance, if you get up five minutes late in the morning now it's winter, one of the prisoners will fetch you your washing water. But you can't let yourself get lazy like that. You'll get hooked on it, and when he commits some minor breach you'll find yourself wondering whether to tell him off or not.

Basically, I'm in here round the clock. I don't usually get home. We're an advanced collective, which puts us under more pressure, and means we organize more activities. Two days before Spring Festival prisoners and staff held a tea party. The next day we had to collect the prisoners' reactions to it.

On the day itself the prisoners' relations were invited into the prison. For the next three days we let some of the prisoners have their wives stay with them. We chose ones who were reforming quite well but whose wives were getting on badly with their mothers-in-law, hadn't been married all that long and wanted a divorce. That's what young people are like. In 1980 nineteen of our prisoners or their wives wanted a divorce, but after we'd worked on them seventeen gave up the idea. We do everything we can to stop divorces. It helps with reforming the prisoners in jail. We supervisory cadres vacated our rooms, but there were still only three rooms for four couples. There was one couple whose relationship was quite good, so we just gave them one day together before they vacated the room for another couple.

This last Spring Festival one of the prisoners lost his father. He was the only son, so we got permission from higher authority to take him home so he could see to his father's funeral and talk to his family.

We encourage the prisoners to study, so that they can be useful people when they go out. Quite a few are taking the exams for a junior middle-school diploma. The state recognizes the diplomas issued by the Adult Education Office. Last time we had fourteen men pass in both mathematics and Chinese, and others who passed in just one subject. These are some of the certificates. We couldn't possibly put their photographs on them in the usual way. They've all got shaven heads, and by our rules they have to show both their ears, hold a board with their name on it, and stand in front of a height measure – they're the mug-shots for wanted notices if anyone escapes.

Gai Lujun will be here in a moment. You'd better not press him too far on the details of his case. When he was living in a temporary shelter after the earthquake in 1976 he was abusing his little sister. She was fourteen and he was seventeen. She got pregnant, and he was so scared about it coming out that he strangled her. It was quite near his home. He broke off some pine branches and found some leaves, put her body on them and lit them. He thought he'd get rid of the body that way, but he didn't even burn her skin up properly – she was still recognizable. He never went back to the scene of the crime. Because his case is so – you know – don't ask too many questions. The other prisoners sometimes give him a bad time because of it. By their logic robbery and murder are the greatest. You can ask him about anything else you like.

Originally they wanted us to get junior middle-school diplomas. None of us got that far at school. But we wouldn't pass even if we had three whole months to do it in, which we don't. We're all young in this brigade, apart from Director Mi who's in charge of the production side.

None of us young ones who are married get on well with our wives. We've got no time for the family. It's quite a problem to give the young bachelors who haven't got steady girlfriends enough free time to do their courting.

"Sir!"

When given permission to enter, a skinny young prisoner in black cotton padded jacket and trousers with blue sleeve-protectors comes in. He sits on the small stool by the door.

[233]

The political instructor explains to him briefly why we have come. "Tell them."

I'm Gai Lujun. I was born in 1959, started primary school in 1967, and carried right on through to senior middle school but didn't finish. I was seventeen when I committed my crimes.

Things were pretty chaotic when I was at primary school. It didn't matter whether you took textbooks to school with you, but you had to have your *Quotations from Chairman Mao*. All we did was dig air-raid shelters, learn manufacturing, do military training, practise farming and have meetings on the "living study and application" of Chairman Mao's works. I started junior middle school in 1972, and senior middle school in 1974. In those days junior and senior middle-school courses lasted only a couple of years each.

I don't think I can remember anything else very special.

In primary school I was an "activist in the living study and application of Chairman Mao's works", and in middle school I was a "three-good" student.*

Things were still rotten right after the Gang of Four fell. In 1977, before I was arrested, the school was a real mess. The teachers didn't have the guts to keep the kids under control. We did seven subjects in senior middle school, but you could go on to the next class even if you failed all of them. All our exams were open ones – you could look at the textbooks while you did them. I was one of the best students in the class, but I failed in two subjects, foreign languages and maths, even with the books open in front of me.

I used to like singing, recitation and all that sort of thing. You see, it was because I did all that quite well and nobody knew anything about the other thing that I was so scared of it all coming out. I'd have had no future and my parents would never have forgiven me either. That's why, well, you know, I killed her. The main reason for my crime was my bourgeois vanity.

The Cultural Revolution? I went to the Iron and Steel Institute and Qinghua University to watch the armed struggles and pick up propaganda leaflets. Everyone was grabbing them, adults and children too. Real fun it was.

Of course a lot of the kids at school had girlfriends or boyfriends

* Good in study, thought (i.e. politics) and health.

then. Some of them were quite open about it, and some weren't, but everyone knew. I was friendly with several of the girls, but I never – you know – with them. I wouldn't have dared.

Did anyone incite me? Yes, one man, an engineer in a factory near our school. He was a bad element, but I didn't know that when I met him. I used to go for a run on the school sports ground every morning and so did he. After a while we started talking to each other. He showed me some pornographic magazines, and when I was in trouble later on he was the only person I could turn to for advice. He wanted to get revenge because his class status was landlord and capitalist and he'd been labelled a bad element during the Cultural Revolution. But I only knew about that after my trial. He was sentenced to over ten years because he'd been carrying on with some other women.

When I got my suspended death sentence I didn't appeal. I reckoned I deserved capital punishment, and I'd got off lightly. The detention centre didn't feel the same as jail – it was sinister and scary, and I really wanted to get to jail. I'd heard of the Fifth Brigade here when I was in the detention centre – there were old lags there who'd been inside before. When the political instructor came to fetch me he told me that I could change myself by reforming and get my sentence reduced. That's why I tried hard to learn the trade skills once I got here. I'd only been training in the workshop about three weeks when there was a proficiency test. I did quite well, and I got a bonus for the quarter, although by the government regulations I hadn't been there long enough to get one. After nine months I asked to be allowed to work independently. I haven't committed any big mistakes in prison, and I don't reckon the discipline here is too strict. I've come here to reform myself.

The cadres are kind and you can't fool them. I'm not trying to flatter them to their faces, but they think of everything for you, even more than your own parents. They know which of the prisoners' wives want divorces and whose parents are ill. If there's a fight we have to get the cadres to sort everything out for us. Sometimes they ask us how grown men like us can kick up such a fuss about nothing. That makes us feel really awkward.

We were all keen to see the National Day military parade on television this year.* I'm a vegetarian, but in the rush I got given the

---

* A very big military review was part of the celebrations on 1 October 1984, the thirty-fifth anniversary of the founding of the People's Republic. Such parades are very rare in China.

wrong food for breakfast that day. Production Director Mi got an egg and cooked it for me himself. He said we had to move quickly as we youngsters had never seen a military parade. It's true. All I saw as a kid were the reviews of Red Guards in the Lin Biao period.

My parents must take some of the credit for my reform. I brought terrible disaster on my family, but they didn't abandon me. My father used to be a cadre in the Agricultural Machinery Institute, but when the Institute was moved first to Sichuan province, then to Xingtai in Henan, he got himself a transfer to Tongxian, just outside Beijing, so as not to be so far from us. He still only came home once a week, so he had very little contact with us children. My mother works in an ice-lolly factory, and with the time going to and from work we didn't see much of her either. My elder sister's been working as a cook at a university since she came back to town, and I've got a younger brother who's a contract labourer in the factory where my mother works. He's had kidney trouble since he was a kid, and he never got any proper education. I really do want to get out of here so I can do something to repay my parents. But I'm worried about the way people outside will treat me.

Of course some of the prisoners say horrible things to me too. When I was commended for my work, someone said, "It won't do you any good, they still won't reduce your sentence." Quite true. When the thirty-fifth anniversary of the People's Republic was coming up we were all wondering whether there'd be a special amnesty or sentence-reductions, perhaps even for the Gang of Four. No way, it turned out, not for them, let alone for us. But after I was sent here in 1977 my suspended death sentence was commuted to indefinite imprisonment, and since then that's been reduced to fifteen years at most. It's already two years since that reduction. Surely they won't keep me here from 1977 right till 1997.

We're all pretty interested in criminal law here. We'd better be. We spend any free time we get reading it up. A lot of us subscribe to the journal *Democracy and Law*. *("Every execution notice is posted here before it's posted outside," explains the political instructor with a smile.)* When all those notices about "severe blows" at criminals went up in batch after batch* we all realized straight away by comparing our

---

* In the campaign of harsh sanctions for criminals, including many executions for a wider range of offences than previously, that began in the autumn of 1983.

cases with those ones that over half of us would have been shot by now.

At the time I didn't think about anything except how to cover things up. My crime was discovered after only a week. My sister had disappeared. My parents were very worried about it, and so I had to be too. They went looking for her, and I went with them. I thought I was going to get away with it. Later they took me to the police station. They asked me in my first interrogation where my kid sister had gone, and I said she'd disappeared. Where, they asked. I said I didn't know. But when they asked me why I'd been breaking branches of pine trees I panicked. I thought they must know all about it, so I confessed everything.

I was in the police detention centre for a year altogether until my case was decided. When the others were talking about their cases I couldn't say anything about mine. I just read the papers and thought. They were always taking prisoners off to be shot, and every time I heard them taking someone away my heart started pounding. What about the legal process? In those days I didn't even know you had to be tried. The Criminal Code was only published in 1978,* and all I knew then was that you had ten days in which to lodge an appeal. I didn't get myself a lawyer. There weren't any lawyers in those days.

I knew I was going to get a suspended death sentence. My final statement to the court was, "I can blame nobody else for doing something so dreadful and falling to such depths because of my bourgeois vanity. All I can ask is that the government will give me a chance to repay it for rescuing me."

The judge said that in prison I had to reflect deeply on my crimes, work hard at reform and try to win a reduction of my sentence. My parents were hoping that I'd reform.

My parents weren't there because the trial wasn't public – they generally weren't in those days. I only ever heard of a public trial after coming to the Fifth Brigade. Do criminals ask for their parents to keep away from trials? I don't know.

Even in those days the cops from the local police station gave talks on law and order, but I didn't pay any attention.

I used to go to a lot of sentencing rallies. There were some on our school sports ground, and I went to others at the Workers' Stadium.

* It was openly published in 1979.

They even issued us kids printed outlines of the cases to discuss. When we'd heard about a case we thought was really terrible we'd shout, "Shoot them!" Then we'd hear about another, and it'd be "Shoot them!" again. The old ladies in the street committees talked the cases over too, and they joined in the shouting. It was only when I got here that I found most of the guys I'd been yelling about were doing time here. We're all in here together.

In my cell I'm the duty man, which is much the same as being a team leader. If people aren't getting along we have to calm them down, and if we can't we get the cadres in. The cadres are sizing us up all the time, and we're getting their number. If they're easy-going we play them up; but if they're tough nuts we watch our step. *(He paused and turned to look at Political Instructor Guo sitting beside us.)* Anyhow, fights have just about stopped. Well, if you think about it, you've both got all those years to do. It's hard enough as it is.

We're different from historical and active counter-revolutionaries. We're not against society, we just threaten it, which is why we have to be remoulded, recognize our crimes and become new people.

I'm learning how to paint. The teacher graduated from the Central Academy of Art. Of course he's a prisoner too. We've got a foreign-languages class as well. The teacher talks English better than Chinese – before he came in here he spent all his time with foreigners. I haven't been to those classes. I've heard that too many people are studying foreign languages outside.

We have Sundays off. That's when I wash my clothes, paint, and practise calligraphy. Before I got here, I didn't know how to unpick or wash a quilt, or make a new one. At home my mother and my big sister always did it for me. We all help each other with sewing – it doesn't matter how crude your stitching is. We usually get to see a couple of films a month, there's TV on Sunday mornings and twice a week, after supper. When you've finished your remoulding for the week all you want to do is watch television. Recently we've been allowed a bit more.

I know about the outside world through television and magazines. The brigade gets some magazines and we subscribe to some with our earnings. Apart from law magazines, I get *Younger Generation*, *China Youth*, *World Cinema* and *Popular Cinema*. And a literary magazine too, *Harvest*. I got 200 yuan last year. I sent 150 yuan home. These last few years I've hardly had to ask my family for any money at all.

I've got an apprentice to keep an eye on now: he's got to learn the trade properly. He's a thief. We prisoners aren't supposed to ask each other about our crimes, but sooner or later it all comes out. There were a lot of terrible things I'd never even heard of before, but you can't avoid talking about them. I've just got to try hard to reform. This apprentice I've got now, is he dumb! He's supposed to have finished primary school, but he can't even add two-figure numbers together.

The difference between life in here and outside? Well, we've got less space. The standard of living's lower, and we eat pretty badly. For breakfast and lunch we get cornbread, turnips and cabbage, and for supper bread made from wheat flour. There's meat on Tuesday and Thursday evenings. We don't want dumplings any more – we get them every week. When the others have meat I get an egg because I'm a vegetarian. The Muslims have their food cooked separately and get holidays for their religious festivals. Normally all the food is made by the prisoners who work in the kitchen, but we have to make dumplings ourselves in our own time.

My apprentice-master – he was released when he'd served his time – came back and told me that mould-makers are doing very well outside now, though I don't know what things'll be like by the time I get out. Plastics have got a good future, but I'm only a mould-maker, and without knowing the theory of it I might not be able to make a go of it outside. When I've done my time I'll be over forty.

Do I want to stay on here as a free worker after I've done my time, or do I want to go? Of course I want to get out. *(When he realizes that we have the special circumstances of his case in mind and are wondering how he'd be received outside he blushes.)* Yes, I still want to get out.

When I came in they were building the first flyover in Beijing at Xizhi Gate. From what I've seen on television there are quite a few of them now. I'd like to walk across one of them.

Political Instructor Guo comes all the way out of the prison with us.

Gai Lujun really has done quite well. When his father came to visit him here he said, "I'm a political worker, and I couldn't educate my own son properly, but you've done it."

I live quite close by – ten minutes or so by bike. I'm going home for a meal. When I can get a free moment I go home to play with the kid, but then I have to rush back here. I've no time at all to help with the housework. My wife understands. She works in a paper mill. We were at middle school together. I've been here for nine years now.

Foreigners will never believe that bad people can be reformed.

Son

Evening. A tall, slim and friendly boy gives me a ride on his bicycle as we happen to be going the same way. We take back alleys to avoid being fined by the traffic cops. His eyes, hands and feet all react very quickly in the winding twilit alleys. He does not stop talking for a single moment.

I'm nineteen, I've never had a job, and I haven't been to college, but I haven't been kicking my heels at home while I'm waiting for work. In spring last year I took the exams for industrial art college. I was one of the best at painting, colour and modelling. But the damn college turned me down. They were scared to take me. Because I've got "Served three years labour re-education"* in my file.

Did you ever hear about the gang that trashed the Foreign Trade Centre in 1980 and broke a few windows? I was one of them.

We didn't do it out of any principles or ideas, and we weren't out to get anyone in particular. It wasn't anything political. We were just fed up, bored out of our minds. Can you understand that? Some of the gang were sons of high officials – they'd got no chips on their shoulders. We were just b-o-r-e-d.

I've always lived a reasonable life, much better than a lot of other people. My grandad worked on historic buildings, but he retired a long time ago. My dad's a painter – quite well known. I'm his only son, so I didn't have to go without. I got on okay with the other kids at school. Their parents were all officials, and mostly quite big, so I felt sort of put

---

* "Labour re-education" (*laojiao*) can be imposed for up to three years by administrative decision without the courts being in any way involved. It is in theory a lesser sanction than "labour reform" (*laogai*) to which more serious offenders sentenced by the courts to imprisonment are subjected. Both forms of forced labour are generally performed in labour camps or penal farms.

down even though I was always the best at everything. They lived better than our family, than my dad, than me. There was something wild in them that kept coming out. I could never keep up with them. Perhaps it was jealousy on my part. I wasn't going to take it lying down. Perhaps I was being oversensitive. Some of the other kids' fathers pulled handcarts for a living, and as far as I could see they were happy enough. If you've got anything going for you, rely on yourself. If you haven't there's no point in being jealous. I figured that out for myself at labour camp.

I was a show-off then. When they were trying to nab us after the trade centre I could have got away. I'd left home. But I couldn't ditch my paintings. I went back to put them away so that they wouldn't get messed up when the cops came looking for me. As I went in through the door there were the Public Security waiting for me. Well, since they'd nailed me, I thought I might as well take the whole rap. Better than the whole lot of us getting arrested. So as soon as I got to the cop shop I said I'd been the ringleader and it wasn't anyone else's fault.

As I was under sixteen then I was given three years' labour re-education. I worked at the foot of the Zhongtiao Mountains in Shanxi.

That's where I began to understand what it's all about. There were all sorts there – labour re-eds and convicts. When you're new in a place like that the other guys in the cell try to intimidate you. During my first day's work there they gave me a hard time, but I ignored them. That night I'd just lain down to sleep when my quilt was pulled over my head and a whole lot of them started beating me up. I took another terrible pounding the next night. A few more nights of that and I'd have been done for. So during work on the third day I found a chance to grab one of the bastards. I pushed him to the ground, held my shovel in his face and told him: "Tell me who's behind it or you're going to get this. I'm inside already, so I've got nothing to lose." That softened the bastard: he knew he was beaten.

That night I was on my guard. The moment I felt someone grab my quilt I was on my feet before they could cover my head. That caught them on the hop. Then they surrounded me. "Don't know when you're licked, eh, you little bastard?" So I grabbed the thermos and flung it straight at the swine who'd pulled my bedroll over my face the first two nights, I smashed it open on him, boiling water, broken glass and all. Cut him up from head to toe. You can imagine the mess he was in. The whole lot of motherfuckers caved in then.

We labour re-eds had thermoses in our cells. It's convicts who don't. We had our lights out at night, but they had to have them on. We'd just made mistakes, it was just "contradictions among the people".* Convicts are criminals, and that's completely different.

Anyhow, that's how I came out on top. There was nothing to it.

The days drag in there, and I started seeing things very clearly. I realized I'd completely wasted my good years. I wrote to my old schoolfriends – the other boys in the gang that smashed the place up – and told them what I thought. But the little bastards just laughed.

I didn't let that get to me. If I was going to get somewhere in life it'd all be down to whatever I could teach myself. So I went back to junior middle-school textbooks and started studying again from there. I planned on taking the college entrance exams when I got out.

Thank goodness they didn't transfer residence rights then: three years later I came back to Beijing.† I found that my old pals were all eating and drinking like there was no tomorrow, getting themselves girls, and wheeling and dealing. Hell! That was when I realized what a stupid idiot I'd been. I'd spent three years inside for them, and they weren't worth it.

I'm sitting in on the third year of senior middle school now. I pay fees, but I'm not registered. Don't need to. Chinese, mathematics, English, history and all that: I'll need it all in future when I take art college exams again. I'm no good at writing essays. I've got my thoughts about life, but I can't take middle-school essay titles like "The most unforgettable thing in my life" or "One of my teachers". They choke me. I figure those middle-school kids who just study mindlessly are real idiots. The fuckers think they know it all, even though it's all out of their books. Even if they get top marks I don't reckon it means anything. Mind you, I feel I'm a wash-out myself, really pathetic. As soon as the classes are over I pick up my bag and clear off. I don't talk to them or have anything else to do with them. No point.

I still have to live off my father. I want to get into college. No other plans. Any school will do. Someone like me'd be just as good at college

---

* Which, according to Mao, were much less serious and could be resolved by less forceful methods than "contradictions between the enemy and ourselves", in dealing with which harsh methods could be applied.

† As part of the draconian anti-crime measures of 1983 large numbers of city people had their urban residence rights cancelled by administrative order and were sent into exile, often to the underdeveloped north-west.

as those stupid bookworms, though I've got no way of proving it. I don't believe the colleges will always turn me down.

I get on okay with my grandmother. Old folk are blind to your faults – they still love you. The worst is my old man. When I went off for labour re-ed he went on at me about how he'd always brought me up properly. Sure, I went wrong, but that doesn't make him right. Sometimes quarrels get so bad that I have to clear out, and run away from home.

I hang around the streets. Sometimes I fix myself a night at a friend's house. It's tough in winter, but I won't go to my gran's. Would that be running away? You're broke, you can't change your clothes, and eating's a problem. Once the cops almost threw me into the detention centre as an illegal vagrant from the provinces. Luckily they decided I wasn't one before we got there. "Clear off," they said, "and stay home. Don't you get cold, hanging around the streets in midwinter?"

I've got one place, and it's really good. The Yuanming Park.* I love the ruins and the vegetation run wild and the sense of space. There's nobody around. I know how its colours and scenery change through the year as well as I know my own home. It's my den. I could take you there and make a little shelter deep in the bushes with thick walls of grass all round and a little patch of sky above. You can lie there and hear nothing except the wind in the grass. I read and paint there. If I come across couples I clear off. When it's snowing from a grey sky, and the ground is white, and I'm under the dead, black branches of the trees I really feel I'm the only person in the whole world.

* The site of an enormous palace complex in the north-western outskirts of Beijing burned by British and French troops in 1860.

Hero

Ma Youhang, thirty-five, medium height, wearing olive-green uniform, softly spoken, non-smoker.

He is a member of the Communist Party and a national hero and model in the public security front. He is now deputy head of the Tianjin Railway Public Security Office. He won his first-class award for valour in the Tianjin Railway Station shoot-out of 16 August 1980 with three young men who drew guns in the police station. The two surviving gunmen were later executed.

The publicity about me has got to stop. I don't want to disappoint you, but there's nothing to write. First, we all do the work here, and I don't count for much. Second, whatever I did before, by the standards of my responsibilities it's not enough. Third, there are over a hundred other public security heroes. Fourth, it all happened over four years ago, and you shouldn't go on being held up as a model for ever.

I've got one kid, a daughter. Even heroes aren't allowed a second child! Several of us at work have got daughters – we're going to form a fathers-in-law association. One good thing about having a daughter is that it makes it easier for me to tell other people at work to limit their families. My wife's a bookkeeper at Tianjin Station.

I was in the third year of junior middle school when the Cultural Revolution came along in 1966. After being forced into the "struggle, repudiation and reform" of the Cultural Revolution I was sent to the countryside to temper my red heart. I was in Siziwang Banner in Inner Mongolia, near the frontier with the Mongolian People's Republic. It was cold, and pretty rough too.

I was the second child. None of us was allowed to stay behind to look after our parents because my father was struggled against as a "capitalist roader" – he'd been in the Hebei Procuratorial Commission. My mother was a "capitalist roader" in the middle school I went to. I saw her being the target of struggle meetings over a hundred times. There I was, watching my own mother on the platform having her arms held up and twisted behind her.

I was found a job in 1971. My father had died the year before, but they didn't hold a memorial meeting for him or rehabilitate him till 1979. The job they gave me was on the railways, at Erenhot. They wouldn't let me back to the city – I had to stay in Inner Mongolia, but at least I had a wage. I'd been living without any hand-outs from my parents ever since leaving school. I guess our generation of cadres' kids are more capable and get things done because we had such a tough time. We're not like cadres' spoiled brats these days. My mother was all by herself in Tianjin and she really needed someone to look after her, but it wasn't till 1973 that I was transferred back to Tianjin to be a policeman at the railway station.

I didn't mind the job being tough, but I really hated the idea of being a cop. I had a terrible impression of the police in those days. A classmate of mine had been beaten up and framed as a thief when he sold his own bike. The cop who handled that case was a real bastard.

But when it comes to jobs beggars can't be choosers. I was determined not to be like that guy. I still feel the same way – but I can't be sure I haven't been a bit affected by our occupational disease.

The joy of security work is winning other people's safety and happiness. Take arresting pickpockets, for example. On the face of it, all they steal is money. But that money might have been a once-in-a-lifetime opportunity for the victim. Yes, the victim may have lost all the hopes and happiness of a lifetime.

With my comrades, I've arrested thieves, robbers, murderers, confidence tricksters – all sorts. And I've run in people pretending to be overseas Chinese or from Hongkong or Macao. There was one girl spoke good Cantonese and was very well dressed. I soon caught her out by asking a few simple questions about Guangzhou and Hongkong. She was a Tianjiner, and she was looking for a pick-up. She said someone had taken some of her foreign exchange certificates to buy her ticket and had run away with them. But what she really wanted to do was to hang around in the first-class waiting room. She was definitely up to no good. We told her off and fined her. What would have been the point of locking her up?

There was a girl when I was in Inner Mongolia from the same sort of background as me – national bourgeois. But she went off and married a cousin in Hongkong. She's in Houston in the USA now. At the time I despised her for running away because she couldn't take it. Now I realize that the way things were then she didn't have a chance. I hear she's doing all right in America. She's a real overseas Chinese now.

I live with my mother. It's a state-owned apartment in an old house. It was originally assigned to my father, and they haven't tried to kick us out.

When that incident happened I was a sergeant. I'd been patrolling with a woman comrade, and when we'd got the three criminals into the nick I didn't like leaving her by herself outside: it was dangerous at night. I'd just reported it all to the comrades in the police station and was leaving when firing started inside. If I'd organized things better we'd have dealt with it much faster. As it was we lost a comrade. So I have mixed feelings about being honoured as a hero: another hero was a dead hero. Still, our whole police station was honoured collectively.

Later I was promoted to deputy head of the police station, then head in 1982, and people's representative. It's wrong, the way I'm made a labour model year after year. *(In 1982 Ma Youhang caught a swindler on the run who had defrauded people of large sums of money; in 1983 he arrested a robber and murderer who had caused an explosion, and with his colleagues he solved a major case of theft.)* My salary is eighty-seven yuan a month – not bad for someone of my generation.

If you've only got room for one policeman in your book it really shouldn't be me.

Self-help

It was autumn, the hottest time of the year in that city, and we were melting. Had you met the manager of the Self-help Youth Service Centre in the street you would probably have taken him for a civil servant or a young university instructor.

Nor would you have expected him to be so intelligent and articulate.

Thinking and ambitious young people should devote some cool, calm reflection to the time-lag that our People's Republic has created.

Before the Cultural Revolution my life ran quite smoothly. My kindergarten, primary and middle schools were all good. But once the Cultural Revolution broke out I became a pariah.

I had to beg. Would a fifteen- or sixteen-year-old do that unless from dire necessity? Perhaps I was too honest. I couldn't steal, I couldn't rob, and I had no family or friends.

I got a job as a petty trade-union official after the fall of the Gang of Four. This was thanks to my parents' efforts: it was only when they'd been "liberated" that they could look after me.

I reckon that if young people living in this age of reform don't dare reform themselves it's a sign that they have no ideas. We've already wasted a lot of time, and the only way we can make up for that is through our own efforts. This age needs our generation to produce scientists, entrepreneurs and politicians who will press further ahead. At the very least we ought to do something for the unemployed kids who didn't actually go through the trials of the Cultural Revolution but got caught in the fallout all the same.

That's why I contracted to run a youth service centre financed by investments from my old employers and also by funds collected in society. My old work unit wanted something set up that would provide work for their own out-of-work youngsters.

Contracting is risky, but I've got confidence in myself. My wife's behind me too. Starting up is hard without a guaranteed income and the back up of a proper work unit. Even selling domestic electrical goods and hardware there are a lot of headaches.

The biggest one is money. The tens of thousands of yuan my old unit put up wasn't anywhere near enough for building and stocking our centre, and it had to be paid back too. We couldn't develop our business because we didn't know the right people. And unemployed kids are a real handful: you can't just let them do what they want.

But we've stuck it out for six months and made a start. Our seventeen youngsters are pulling in 110 yuan a month on average. That's better than in a state enterprise, but the work's harder. The fact that we've survived and built up some reputation shows that people want a new development like this. Also as the economy livens up we're much more competitive than companies that are only after money: service to society is our raison d'être, and so people prefer us.

Our assets are now worth over 100,000 yuan. We deal mainly in electrical goods, but we also supply specialist households in the countryside wholesale. We'll wholesale anything we can get as long as it's legal.

As I've contracted to run the centre I draw my salary and bonus from it, not from my old employer. Last month it was somewhere over 130 yuan. I can't have any privileges.

Looking back over my thirty years, my past was obviously unfair, but I can't go on complaining about that for ever. When I was young I had to beg, then I was packed off to the countryside and I didn't find a regular job till I was in my twenties. The fact that I've chucked that in shows how serious I am about getting involved in the economy and finding work for unemployed kids. I've suffered and been tricked, but I've worked and sweated for my country. My only regret is that at thirty I still haven't done anything much for it.

In my speech to the prefectural Youth League congress a few days ago I said, "The minds of our generation have been buffeted and washed clean in the torrents of life. Our generation is determined to create our own lives through our own efforts. By helping ourselves we are working for our country and our people."

The following January a friend told us that this interviewee had been arrested.

The findings of the investigation and interrogation were that he had "taken advantage of the economic reform policy to collude with others in China and abroad in speculation. . . . The Self-help Youth Service Centre suffered more losses and is now being reorganized. . . . The resale of a motor vehicle alone involved the embezzling of public and private assets equivalent to over 16,000 yuan. . . . Incontrovertible evidence fully accepted by the accused . . . prosecution for fraud and speculation . . . sentenced to twelve years' imprisonment . . . dismissed from his posts. . . ."

12

GETTING ON

Avionics

The first day on which Beijing's Yanjing Hotel is open to Chinese customers. The western restaurant. A white-haired old man and his wife.

Places like this should always have been open to everyone. Back in the 1950s the Friendship Hotel was a residence for Soviet experts. The big restaurant there was always empty but Chinese weren't allowed to eat in it. When I went in once and sat down a waiter came over and said, "Hey, comrade, this is for foreign experts." I said I was an expert and asked for the menu. The food wasn't anything special.

I've seen quite a lot of the world, but the only places I've come across this sort of thing are in China and the United States, where blacks aren't allowed into some places. That's the racial arrogance of some American whites. But with some of us it's self-contempt. That's why I say big hotels should be open to the general public.

A few years ago I was in Germany on a tour of inspection. Suddenly going out after all those years of not being allowed abroad meant that the prices there came as a terrible shock. It felt like going shopping in Wangfujing with only thirty cents in your pocket. All I brought back was some coffee, beans that is. Instant's no good, not even Nescafé, compared with the coffee you've ground yourself. *("He's a coffee addict," his wife puts in. "He can't live without the stuff. When they were having struggle meetings against him during the Cultural Revolution one of his crimes was 'drinking coffee like hot water'.")*

("What do you want?" the waiter asks. "You've got to order whatever you want all at once." He takes the order and goes. "They certainly aren't very polite," the old man's wife comments. "All that 'What do you want?' They ought to say 'What would you like?' or 'What will you have?' And I wonder if the food will be any good.")

[253]

I've heard they've got a good western-style chef here. Hors d'oeuvre, hot entrée and a dessert, all for only seven yuan. You've got to know how to order – the point is to eat well, not to throw your money around. I've been a man for a good meal all my life, especially since the Cultural Revolution. Our armchairs, carpets and other furniture got burned or smashed up, and we haven't replaced them. We've got no savings: can't save.

I've tried all the main styles of cuisine. The people who eat worst are the Germans. The longer I lived in Germany the more strongly I felt that the Germans, who do everything else properly, don't know how to eat. Mind you, that was a really tough time for them. When I went back in 1981 the service was a lot fancier, but the food still wasn't up to much.

I've been to all the western restaurants in Beijing apart from Maxims and Minims, the two new French ones. Maxims is only for foreigners and Minims for Chinese. You won't catch me in either of them. *(These two restaurants were opened by Pierre Cardin near where Beijing's Chongwen Gate used to be.)*

Funny place, Beijing: the fast-food places are more expensive than proper restaurants. They're joint ventures. Put a few foreign words on the sign and the price shoots up. But fast food isn't competitive here. We Chinese have got plenty of time on our hands. If we go to Donald Duck's for hot dogs it's not for a quick snack but to treat someone to western cuisine.

Every four or five days we squeeze on to a bus to go shopping downtown, then find somewhere to eat. We saw in last night's paper that this restaurant was going to be open to "outsiders" today – foreigners are the insiders now, and we citizens are the outsiders . . .

My name's Hang Xiaozu. My family was very poor. My father and my elder brother were both out of work for a long time, and they had to sell our property to keep us alive. I learned very early that you had to have a skill. My aim in life then was to be a radio engineer.

In the 1920s radio meant transmitters and receivers with big valves and everything else. When I was studying at senior middle school I built radios for my rich schoolfriends for free. I was learning skills at their expense, and grateful to be given the chance.

At university I was in the department of electrical engineering. These days there are lots of different departments, but there was only the one then, and it was divided into what we called "strong electrics" and "weak electrics". "Strong" was electrical engineering and "weak" was electronics. After a couple of years my family couldn't afford the fees, so I had to start earning enough to pay them and keep myself. I set up a couple of radio stations in Hangzhou. Before that there was only a government station that went off the air by day. A rich student got me to build one at his home for fun. That earned me enough to get through university, and won me a little fame, too. After graduation I was taken on by the Hangzhou telephone company to put up a radio station for them.

We didn't have electricity at home, so to make the radio equipment I had to use our charcoal stove to heat up the kind of soldering iron used for soldering tinplate kettles. I made some batteries myself so that we could have a tiny electric light at home. A small businessman saw it and he got me to make some car batteries for him to sell. He got stuck with them though because the owner of another battery shop that opened up later had better connections with drivers. When I saw him sitting waiting for customers I made my mind up never to go into business. After the Japanese War you could make a sure-fire fortune with anything you could fly in, but I didn't go in for any of that. If you've got a skill you can always get by.

When I was a student I was chairman of the student union. There were a terrible lot of massacres those days: 30 May, 18 March, 3 May and so on.* We got the students on the streets burning Japanese goods and demonstrating. That's when I realized how weak China was. We were being pushed around, and demonstrating and burning wouldn't be enough. We had to learn technology for the sake of the country.

When I'd been working at the radio station for a time I got into the Eurasia Aviation Corporation. It was a joint venture with the Germans. There were joint ventures in those days too. I don't think there was much Chinese investment in it at first, but later on it reached fifty-one per cent of total investment, so it was a "Sino-foreign joint venture under Chinese control". When I joined it was a tiny outfit and they kept the technology secret from the Chinese. We weren't allowed to watch them repairing the planes. Chinese were supposed to be only assistants and deputies.

I was in the radio department, and my boss was a German who'd

* On 30 May 1925 unarmed demonstrators were killed by British-officered police in the International Settlement in Shanghai; on 18 March 1926 unarmed demonstrators were killed by the warlord government in Beijing; and on 3 and 4 May 1928 Japanese troops massacred several thousand people in Jinan.

never studied radio. He was just an ignorant aircraft radio operator. He'd lost a leg after peasants shot him while he was buzzing their sheep for a bit of fun. The company kept him on as ground staff. The Chinese manager had studied radio abroad, but it was all theory and he couldn't actually do anything. The two of them despised each other and were always at each other's throats. So I was promoted very fast – it was natural selection.

In the old days there weren't any radio navigation aids; the pilot had to navigate by maps and find his way by the lie of the land. That almost cost me my life. We had a foreign pilot who thought it would be fun to fly up the Yangtse, and he flew on till he got himself lost. Looking at the ground didn't help him at all – he couldn't even tell the names of the cities apart, let alone recognize them. He was never going to find his way to Nanjing. I knew we were circling over Suzhou, but the soundproof window between us meant we couldn't talk to each other. He couldn't read my gestures, I couldn't read his, and the plane was coming down. Well, it crash-landed in a town called Mocheng – that's a name I'll never forget. He couldn't do a thing and just sat there in the plane like a helpless ninny while I rushed off to phone in an accident report. Later on they imported big planes with navigation equipment. The Germans didn't dare touch it, but I found out all about it on the quiet. When the equipment broke down they wanted to send it back to Germany to get it repaired, but I insisted on fixing it myself. The manager agreed because the pilot couldn't fly without the equipment and the company was losing money. When I'd done it my prestige shot up again.

I made a copy of the equipment without telling anybody what I was doing. I was quite well paid at the time, so I could afford to make it at home. When the boss was away we tried it out openly, and by the time he came back from his holidays we'd finished. The flight tests had been successful, and I'd even improved on the original by incorporating American design features. The outcome was that the general manager sent me to study in Germany. We were the last group of students to go there – it was 1940, during the Second World War.

The other three who went with me all joined Lufthansa, but I wasn't allowed to. They said they weren't going to let me rip off any more of their know-how after I'd copied the navigation equipment. I demanded to be sent back to China, but our embassy was too busy pulling out to look after me, and they told me to stay on. After we declared war on

Germany I found myself a job with Siemens making airborne radar. I did that till 1945.

By then life was extremely tough. Although I was earning a hell of a lot there was nothing to eat and the British were bombing us every night. You stood a very good chance of getting killed. We weren't allowed to take cover when we heard the air-raid sirens; we had to stay at our posts. I'd worked out where the British bombs would have to fall to get us in their effective radius, but they only came close enough once, on my day off. The Germans didn't bother much about political checks. They just made me work, and do plenty of overtime. After VE Day I went to Vienna.

There were five victorious allied powers – America, the Soviet Union, China, Great Britain and France – but there was no Chinese flag at the victory celebrations. When I asked why, the authorities said they hadn't got one. I had though – I'd bought it in Hongkong and always hung it at the head of my bed. And I'd got an overseas Chinese woman to make me a party flag, the Kuomintang party of course. I didn't know the first thing about the Communist Party then: all I'd been told was that it was the "alien party" that never allowed the Kuomintang a moment's peace. The overseas Chinese there got me to organize an overseas Chinese committee. That gave us official stationery and an official stamp, so we could deal with the authorities and even issue legally valid marriage certificates. That was when the *Central Daily*** reporters Lu Keng and Yue Shuren turned up in Europe as war correspondents with the American forces and all of us Chinese had a meal of noodles together. (*"During the Cultural Revolution knowing Lu Keng made things really bad for us," his wife interrupts.*) Lu Keng used to be very patriotic in those days. I miss him. Wish he'd come back so I could see him again. I read his stuff in the Taiwan papers – he's still very hard-hitting.

The only Chinese consulate was in Switzerland, and they told me there I could get back to China on a displaced persons' boat. But why? We weren't displaced persons: we were experts that the country needed to get back on its feet. Later on I was sent some money from China to attend an international civil aviation conference in France with our general manager. After about six months there I was broke and the embassy had stopped looking after us. I had the chance to tell a meeting

---

* The Kuomintang's newspaper.

of overseas Chinese about what the embassy was up to. The next day the embassy sent my airline ticket round and told me to clear off, and lose no time about it. They were scared that I was going to stir up trouble for them. I flew Air France to Calcutta, changed to a China Airlines plane to Kunming, then took one of our planes to Shanghai.

By then Eurasia had been reorganized as the Central Air Transport Corporation, one of China's big two airlines. I became the chief engineer in Central. The chief engineer's word was law then – you didn't have to bother with endless discussions.

The Kuomintang was really good at winning people over. As I was a non-party figure they were very nice to me. I was sent on an inspection tour of the US to make up for the tough time they said I'd had in Germany. When the Kuomintang was getting ready to clear off to Taiwan they told Central to go too, but we played for time. When we couldn't put off moving any longer we went to Guangzhou and stalled a bit more, then moved on to Hongkong. Then we rose up and came back to China. The "Two Airlines Rising" it was called: us and China Airlines.

Communists were involved in the rising. My right-hand man in Central Air Transport had links with the Communist Party: he'd shared a room with Zhou Enlai when they were both at the Whampoa Military Academy.* I was on the committee we formed when we rose. Of the seven of us who had been in charge, some didn't come back to China, and some came back, then went again. I'm the only one left. We proclaimed our rising on 9 November 1949 then came back to Guangzhou to talk things over. The main problem was pay. There were several suggestions, but I agreed with the one that we should get enough to maintain our standards of living.

There was a row but I got them all to see it my way, and that's how we did it. The Communist cadres kept away from the meeting: they wanted us to sort it out ourselves.

When I was being hunted as a "tiger" during the "three anti" and "five anti" drives,† Zhou Enlai put in a good word for me: "Hang

---

* The Kuomintang military academy in Guangzhou from 1924 to 1927 where Zhou was a Communist Party representative.

† Against corruption, waste and bureaucracy by government personnel; and against bribery, tax evasion, theft of state property, cheating on government contracts and theft of economic information by business people. These campaigns were run in 1951–2. "Tigers" were main targets of attack.

Xiaozu couldn't possibly have done things like that. If he were like that he'd never have come back." The outcome was that from one day to the next the "tiger" became deputy chief of the tiger-hunting team. Whenever I met the Premier he'd always shake me by the hand and address me by name before I could say a word. He fixed for me to work in Tianjin, because there weren't any western-style houses in Beijing then, and he was worried that I wouldn't be able to adjust to life here. I was in charge of a secret factory in Tianjin, apart from being the chief telecommunications engineer for the Civil Aviation Administration and having three other jobs. At first I got a double salary – nearly 600 yuan a month – but in 1952 I volunteered to have it cut, so I get nearly 300 now. Prices were very low then, and the country had to be put back on its feet. It made me feel bad, taking all that money when I'd come back to share the hard times.

Later on my factory was put under the General Staff and I was made a colonel, the second highest possible rank for an engineer, but paid more than a major-general.

I did my bit in the fifties, but less in the sixties. Our people were dispersed. Then came the Cultural Revolution . . . I'm retired now, but I'm still an adviser. I'll do any job the Ministry of Space Industry gives me. I get up early and the chauffeur drives me to the office. I have to go in. I spend every morning there reading the big *Reference News** and other things. I can borrow the meters and stuff I need for repairing colour TVs. I used to do black and white sets, but not now. There's a whole crowd of old boys who've recommended me to each other. If your televisions go wrong do bring them round and I'll fix them for you but I can't take care of your friends' sets too.

My trip to West Germany in 1981 was the first time I'd been abroad in over thirty years. I managed all right – my German and my electronics were still okay. When I visited Siemens I found that my contemporaries had all retired: the younger people treated me as a grand old man. My old one-legged instructor had come back to Germany from Africa: he drove a long way to see me – he'd never imagined I could still be alive, and working too.

When I was abroad I did everything I could to save hard currency. Canned food was cheap, so I had it for every meal. Never went into a

---

* An informative secret newspaper that comes out twice daily and has a lot more news than the *Reference News* to which the public can subscribe.

restaurant except for official banquets. The comrade who went with me was meant to look after me, but I was looking after him all the time because he couldn't talk German. He wanted to buy a colour television. I took him to a lot of shops till we bought an old one for the equivalent of only forty yuan. I told him I could fix it. When we got back I hit it and it worked.

Yes, I'm very resilient. During the Cultural Revolution I was at the receiving end for eleven months. Because I'm such a gourmet they made me head cook at cadre school. Recently a cadre who's a Party member came to shake me by the hand and apologize for having given me a hard time. He was actually crying. "I mean it when I say I was grateful to you," I told him. "When you locked me up in a dark room you bought tobacco for me." He really wasn't a bad man. ("Look at that," his wife protested indignantly, "they persecuted him appallingly, and he's thanking them for it. They persecuted me too. It was terrifying. They said I was married to a spy, and after they'd interrogated me they said I was a spy too. We lost everything – carpets, leather-upholstered furniture, all sorts of things.")

They turned on her when they didn't get anywhere persecuting me. When I went to Germany last time some people asked me if I was going to meet my former wife, a German. Of course that wasn't on. She's in East Germany, and it would have been harder for her to get to West Germany than it was for me from China.

Our children have all left home. We don't give them money: they have to be independent. We have seven rooms, plus two lavatories, a kitchen and a pantry. The government assigned them to me, and we need them all. I won't have them living here. I use different rooms for different purposes. I've got five children, and only one of them had a proper college education. She trained as a teacher – she's in a middle-school now.

Oh dear, your prawns look terrible. We had real lobsters at the banquet to celebrate the thirtieth anniversary of our airlines rising. As thick as your arm they were, and this long. They were served with a cream sauce – what a sight for sore eyes.

Selling Flowers

*A summer's day in Nanjing. Girls are wearing orchids fastened to
their dresses. The delicate scent spreads through the city.*

*She is squatting on the ground in the small traders' market near
Xinjiekou, a faded red cloth spread in front of her.*

It's raining today, so business is slow. I haven't taken much all
morning. I don't have to invest much, but there's no profit in it.

When I was a child I saw the printed cotton tunics and silk scarves the
girls who worked in the city wore when they visited their mothers. I
longed to go too. Agents used to come to the villages looking for child
workers for the mills of Shanghai, Nanjing, Suzhou and Hangzhou.
One of them paid my family two silver dollars for me. My job was
reeling silk off the cocoons, lifting the ends out of boiling water with my
bare hands. Scalding hot it was. When I started I was still so small I had
to stand on a stool. I didn't get any wages for the first four years – only
my food. By the time I got my first pay the Japanese had taken the
factory over, but the only new person was the Japanese manager. When
the Japanese attacked Nanjing in the winter they burned the city and
killed all those people but they left the Japanese factories alone. Our
factory raised the Japanese flag, and our Japanese manager kept
us there so that we wouldn't get killed on the streets. Their army
slaughtered 300,000 people. Workers like us, poor folk, we had to
work for whoever came along. We went on strike for higher wages
sometimes, but not under the Japanese. We'd never have dared!

Nine of us girls rented a room. In winter it was better being all
huddled together. Every two months I'd save enough from my wages to
change for a silver dollar, then I'd get someone to take it home to my
mother. I didn't spend much: there was just my food and absorbent
paper each month – we women have extra expenses. Sometimes I used

to see an opera, and at New Year I'd have something special to eat. Mostly we ate brown rice, but later you couldn't even get that. When things went badly for the Japanese there was only "Patriotic Flour" – an inferior flour milled from acorns, millet and stuff like that.

When I went back home on visits, I wore a printed cotton tunic and a silk scarf too, but by then I knew that the girls I'd seen before coming home looking so fine had been scrimping just like me, to put on a good show. My village was in an "insecure zone" – what they call an Anti-Japanese Base Area these days. The Japanese raided it so the people at home suffered much more than I did. But though we were in enemy territory and they weren't, you could still send letters and money, and people could come and go.

I married in 1943. My husband was a mechanic in our factory. He sent a go-between to my family. I still bump into her sometimes – she was a factory girl too – we hold hands and find plenty to talk about. I was already engaged to someone else in the village, so I had to refuse him but he wouldn't take no for an answer. One night as we were coming off shift he had his way with me so I had to marry him. It's rough fellows who get what they want.

I gave him three sons and a daughter but I don't get a thing from any of them now. After Liberation life got better. Between us we got 150 yuan and a good forty kilos of grain coupons a month. We were doing very nicely. They were just starting family planning then. I didn't want any more. I wasn't going to be like one of those Soviet "heroine mothers". But he was set on it, and another little boy came along in 1958, the year of the Great Leap Forward. Originally the baby was for my husband's brother. He'd been married seven years with nothing to show for it. But his wife got pregnant when I did, so they didn't want our little boy. Mind, that kid wasn't even his. He was useless – someone else was the father. Anyway, things turned out very hard for us. My eldest was just starting as an apprentice in a factory; the next was twelve; the third one two, and the last a babe at my breast. And between the second and the third I'd had two more we let the midwife take away with her.

We could still get by: my husband was earning over eighty a month, and the eldest could take care of himself. Our second was at school; the fees were only ten yuan a month, so that was no worry. But times got hard again all over the country. Everything was expensive, and there weren't enough grain coupons to go round. My husband's rations were cut, and mine were already too low. The poorer you get the hungrier you are, and then you get ill. My husband and my mother-in-law both died in 1961. Who knows why? Hunger I'd say! But we had to keep going, the children and I. The residents' committee office helped us a bit; so did the factory. In those days a lot of factories started up farms, reclaiming wasteland, breeding sheep and growing a sort of green soup stuff. Chlorella it was called. You could eat it. The factory people told me to go and work on the farm temporarily, so I'd have enough to eat. Which was all very nice I'm sure. But I couldn't because of the children.

Somehow we got through. I used one of our two rooms to open a hostel for country folk coming to market. They paid in rice and other produce as well as cash. After a year or so the residents' committee denounced me and I was taken to the Public Security Bureau for questioning. I was on very good terms with some of them there. One of them had even wanted to marry me. But it didn't help now. They hauled me over the coals. "Illegal trading" and a "black hostel" they called it, and they closed me down.

At the beginning of 1963, the residents' committee sent me to work at a bookbinder's. I stayed there on a temporary basis, right up till three years back. Then I couldn't manage the work any more.

During the Cultural Revolution the children found out I'd been labelled a bad lot and they wouldn't have anything to do with me. I'd only done it for their sakes. Now the eldest is a cadre. When he'd served his apprenticeship the state sent him to university. His own kid's taking college entrance exams this year. My second boy went to university too; now he's a cadre in Shanghai. He used to visit me every year before he got married, but I haven't seen him for eight years now.* My daughter is the unlucky one — she's in Jiangxi! She went to the countryside with some older students before she'd even finished junior middle school. The others did all right for themselves: worked on the land for a few years until Jiang Qing fell and then back they all came. But she stayed in Jiujiang as a waitress. If you ask me, she wants to keep her distance from me as well. When she was having a baby last year I told her to come home so that I could look after her. But she never came. The youngest is at university here in Nanjing, living on campus. But when he's finished there he won't be wanting me either . . . Well, I don't need them to look after me.

---

* Unmarried employees living away from home normally get paid leave annually. After marriage, leave is infrequent.

I buy the flowers from the country folk who sell them at the Qingliang Gate from four in the morning. I bring them home, string them up and sell them in pairs. Every day I buy 200 – that costs six yuan. If I sell them all I can make four yuan profit. Out of that I pay sixty cents tax for my pitch. Sometimes, of course, I can't get rid of them, like today. I've got dozens left, and by tomorrow they won't be smelling as good. I'll restring them: one fresh one with one old one.

When the orchids are over I sell jasmine, and when that's finished there's cassia. In winter when there are no flowers I make tomato chutney. That's how I got by last year.

No sign of the rain stopping! There's no one about any more. Here, buy some. They smell lovely! Take some home to the children.

13

SECOND THOUGHTS

Going Back

He is twenty-seven this year, not tall, neatly dressed, back in Beijing from western Hunan to take an exam for acceptance as an MA student.

Two years ago he volunteered to work in very poor hill country, and was for a while a man in the news.

Let's start with my name, Yang Shangshu. In Chinese it sounds like "sheep up a tree". When I was in middle school, another kid said, "That's a funny name when there isn't a single tree in your village." I got so fed up with his teasing I smashed his face in for him, the little pig. I was punished for it, and got a black mark on my record which is still there. Everything from junior middle school onwards goes into your personal dossier. There used to be trees in our county – the year I was born there was a tree-planting campaign. That's why my grandfather called me Shangshu, "honour trees".

But the next year it was "Everything for steel", and all the trees were fed into home made blast furnaces. But I still think of "sheep up a tree" whenever I hear my full name, and it makes me uncomfortable. I prefer being called Little Yang or Shur – that was my nickname when I was a kid.

We were the first group of students to get into university by passing an entrance exam. I was the only one from my commune. We thought we were the greatest.

I got into the department of pharmacology at medical college, specializing in Chinese traditional herbal pharmacology. In my village I'd been quite a star, and in middle school I was the life and soul of the propaganda team. I played the Chinese flute and fiddle and sang too. When we had the first party at college I put myself down for a Chinese flute solo. Imagine what I felt like with my bamboo flute when all the students from the big cities played fancy foreign instruments I could barely put a name to, like accordions, violins, clarinets and European flutes. I messed up my solo and got hooted off the stage before I was even halfway through. I hid miserably away in a corner.

I lost both my parents when I was a kid, and my grandad had to bring me up single-handed. There was no money for musical instruments. My mother and father both died in 1960. Say it was illness that killed them if you like, but it wasn't very different from dying of starvation. The idea that nobody starved to death in the three hard years is crap. But you lousy writers kept quiet about it until 1981. What the hell were you all up to before that? I suppose writers had their problems too. Not many people have the guts to speak up when it means putting their life on the line. That's why I admire Liu Binyan – he's not like that.*

The MC at the concert, a girl in my class, came looking for me afterwards. "What are you so upset about? We're all medical students – this isn't a music college." She looked so sincere I fell for her then and there. I found out the next day that I wouldn't have a chance. Her old man was the deputy head of the faculty. He's a full professor now, and on the committee of the Chinese Pharmacology Association. I warned myself it was a waste of time and I'd look stupid, but it was no use. I chased her for a whole year. I was very discreet. I never even told her I loved her. Of course she knew: she could see right through me, while I didn't know the first thing about her. She didn't look down on me, and she didn't discourage me either. She just drew a little closer.

For that whole year I got more and more drawn into my dream, but my work went to pieces. My only moments of peace were when I was with her, never alone, but in class for forty-five minutes at a time. I thought then that I'd never be able to live without her. But I had to in the end, and it didn't kill me.

Our first date was in the second year. We arranged to go to the botanical gardens together to collect specimens. I bought the tickets and pinched some fruit. We had a picnic. There was one bun left over but I didn't pick it up because I didn't want to look stingy. There were lots of young couples arm in arm, or even hugging in the gardens. I was just plucking up my courage to tell her I loved her when we ran into the

---

* Liu Binyan, born in 1925, is an outspoken critic of injustice, which has often landed him in trouble. A collection of his writings has been published as *People or Monsters?* He was expelled again from the Communist Party in 1987.

student who'd played the clarinet. She was so excited and happy to meet him, I felt suddenly I didn't matter to her. So I didn't tell her how I felt – we just picked up our specimens and went back to town.

To me she was a priceless treasure, but to her I was just a lump of dirt. I was completely depressed. I hated her and hated her family. I wished I could become a real somebody overnight, so that she'd have to go down on her knees before I finally forgave her. I drank for the first time in my life, but I didn't get plastered.

After I'd calmed down I took my roommate's advice: "If you're going to be somebody, the first thing is to look reality in the face." There was no way I could forget the past, but I avoided her. By the third year we had a very heavy workload. Music and poetry were irrelevant now – all that counted was your marks. I'd worked with my grandad since I was a kid, seen a lot of cases and knew quite a lot about herbal medicine too. The first year I'd been preoccupied with my grand passion, but in the second and third years I studied hard while the others were into love and having a good time. So I came out on top. I'd adapted to my environment and recovered my self-confidence.

I went back home to the village every summer, but stayed in the town reading during my winter vacation. I couldn't wait to go back to the village, but the college was my way forward. You may feel at home in your village but your people want you to leave and be a success. It took me some time to realize that.

Practically all the others went home in the winter vacations. After the winter vacation in the fourth year the Communist Youth League Committee got people to write essays on their home areas. That put me on a spot. Mine's one of the most poverty-stricken places in the whole country and there's not much to write about there. In the end I wrote about a fight between a tiger and a water-buffalo. The buffalo won, but people killed it. I said it was a traditional story where I came from. It got into the college magazine, and into a literary periodical too.

I ended up doing well in my studies and having a bit of "literary" fame. Before I left to do an internship in my fifth year she gave me a book – Zhang Jie's *Love Must Not Be Forgotten* – with a note tucked into it: "Let's carry on with the outing we didn't finish last time." It came as a complete shock. Only then did I realize I hadn't yet won my independence from her. I quietly sounded out my roommate.

"Don't imagine that she only fancies you because of your high marks and your story," he told me. "She's a lot craftier than you are. You're the student who's got the best chance in the whole department of being assigned a job in a big hospital. Besides, traditional pharmacology tends to be a family thing. A top professor would be quite likely to want you for a son-in-law." I didn't agree and to show he was wrong I produced a whole list of students from well-placed families whose work was good. "They've all got powerful backers at home," he said, "and urban residence rights. None of them would move in with the professor as a living-in son-in-law. You're different. Students from the back of nowhere like you usually have to go home when they graduate. So if he kept you here in town you'd be in his debt for ever. Besides, he's just a hard-up professor who can't even run to a colour TV. Would a top cadre's son be interested in her? She isn't even pretty."

My roommate was from the country too – the same county in fact. He saw everything in the worst possible light and came right out with things. The sad thing was he was usually right.

She told me a different story. Said she'd gradually fallen in love with me after that disastrous performance. "It doesn't matter that you're a bit naive and from the countryside too," she told me. "Love is mysterious, not just mechanical reflection of superiority." That really moved me.

During the internship in the hospital those of us who were studying Chinese pharmacology practised in the clinic for Chinese medicine. We had to eat in the hospital canteen, and my food allowance simply wouldn't stretch that far. I had a scholarship of thirteen yuan a month, plus another ten a month from my family. That was enough for me in the college, but not in the hospital. She was always helping me out on the quiet. She said poverty made people pure and high-minded. That's the last thing it does. Poor people are only poor because they've got no option.

After my internship I was always going round to her place. Her father was nice enough to me – he came from a family of doctors of Chinese medicine too. Her mother was very particular though, and as I didn't have any good clothes I always felt uncomfortable and scared they were going to send me packing.

We two were a lot closer then – after we'd kissed I started to feel much less constrained. Sometimes I even teased the professor, trying to get him to admit that if smoking was so bad for you it was wrong for Deng Xiaoping to smoke. But he wouldn't admit that, not even to me, his future son-in-law, in private.

She wanted us to get engaged, and I was keen too. Her father persuaded us to wait till the college decided to keep me on after graduation. All the other finalists were trying to fix up good jobs. Nobody wanted to get sent to a village – especially not the ones who came from the countryside. My roommate wasn't. "I'll pass the research students' exam, then I'll have the right to stay in town. Once I've got a master's degree, I don't reckon anyone'll be chasing me back to the sticks." He always did things straightforwardly. He didn't use the back door – there weren't any back doors for him. He stands on his own two feet.

Just then my grandfather died. He had a fall on his way to see a patient and it killed him. He was seventy-eight. I decided to go and practise medicine. It didn't matter that my subject was pharmacology – I knew how to treat most illnesses. She took it very calmly – on the surface at least. She certainly didn't try using love to blackmail me into staying. We knew each other well enough by then. Even if we'd slept together it wouldn't have held me back.

She didn't ask me if I'd change my mind. It was on the morning when we had to put in our requests for job assignments. I felt that this was the moment of destiny. I could make my old dream of becoming somebody come true. But I wasn't the same person I'd been in the first year. Even if going home was fanaticism this was the only time in my life I'd even be able to indulge in such fanaticism. There'd be no second chance.

I would have had a splendid reason for staying on: pharmacological theory is almost a complete blank in Chinese medicine. We Chinese are researching it now. So are the Japanese, and going at it hard. With my own speciality, my family traditions and the professor's guidance I could have done something special for China. Things would improve in the village as the national economy changed for the better.

I stood there saying nothing. If she'd said a few words more I might well have given her the answer that would have made her happy. But my mind was on other things. My village is about eighteen kilometres by dirt track from the commune's clinic, and over thirty-five from the county hospital, half by dirt track and half by tarmac road. If I went home others would do the pharmacological research, but if I didn't the village would be without a doctor now my grandfather was dead. Any doctor would have done, but no one else would go. The others wouldn't even go to the county town.

I told her I'd got to go back. I even wondered about trying to persuade her to come with me, but then I thought that she had the right to choose her own life. Besides, the government guaranteed her the right to stay in the city. In the end we agreed to write often and give each other moral support. She sent me scientific journals every month, sometimes with letters enclosed and sometimes not.

By volunteering I'd "liberated" my roommate. The quota of assignments to our county was only one for the whole faculty, so if I went, he didn't have to. He had volunteered to go to the county hospital, but he'd been very clever: he put staying on at college at the top of his list, and going back to the county town only fifth. I was the only student in the department who volunteered to go back to his village, and a lot of the other students laughed at me for it. Some of them said I'd had a wife back in the village all along and was fed up with sleeping with that student, or that I was trying to use this as a roundabout way of getting myself a Party card. You name it, they said it. My roommate said I was a real friend. He got a research studentship in Changsha. I got commendations and a big send-off. Inside I was boiling with fury. If just one of them had gone I could have stayed in the city and got on with my pharmacology.

There was plenty of trouble in store when I got back. The Public Health Bureau wanted to keep me in the county town. They said life would be easier there. I turned them down and went home. Then they wanted to keep me in the commune clinic. They said I'd be sure to get promotion as the only regular graduate in the whole hospital. Promotion? Would someone who'd thrown away a career as a specialist in pharmacology want to be the boss of a little clinic like that? I refused that too, and insisted on going home. So I ended up as the only person in the village eating state-supplied grain.

My people didn't give me a warm welcome at all. Indeed, they were very cold. They'd let off firecrackers when I first went to college. This time they didn't even give me eggs and hot soup noodles the way they had when I'd gone home in the holidays. They thought I must have got myself into terrible trouble and been sent back in disgrace. Why else would I have come home? Who'd ever heard of a great scholar going back to his village? To them anyone who passed the college entrance exams is a great scholar. The story had somehow got about that I'd slept with a professor's daughter – it was the professor's wife in another version – and been purged by the provincial Party committee. The people in my village still call all foreigners Yankee devils, Japanese devils or "blackies". It's nothing to laugh about. That's what they're like. They're ignorant although they don't want to be. To them the provincial Party committee is a great power centre. They'd cheerfully stone someone to death for sleeping with another man's wife, so I got off very lightly indeed. In a moment I'll tell you about another great injustice caused by this ignorance.

A few days later there was a drastic change in the situation, not because of anything I did, but because my "achievements" were broadcast on the radio. "Even the wireless says our Shur's all right. He's something," said the villagers. To them, being something meant having some ability, being someone people could look up to. They were illiterate, but they really believed the wireless, as they called it.

I did get something done in the village. I saw many patients and did quite a bit of preventive work against local endemic diseases. But it was nothing special – I was just an ordinary country doctor. Sure, I went out in storms to see patients, and I gave transfusions of my own blood, but not often, only a few times. That's a doctor's duty – it's nothing to make a fuss about. In autumn last year a clinic was set up in our village, and a graduate of a health-care college was sent to work there. It's quite like a real hospital, with her and me as doctors, and four nurses paid by the commune. She was a "fixed-assignment student" who was enrolled from our county and sent back to the countryside after she graduated.

Once our village had the medical provision it had lacked before, the county hospital transferred me back to them. So I've decided to get back to my pharmacology. I'm not staying in the county town. After lots of delays they agreed to let me take the exams for graduate school to do an MA. If I get into the centre, I'll go on with my studies and if I don't I'm going back home.

I don't care what people say about me. The worst will be that I cleared off from the village, that I'd been taking a roundabout way to get ahead. Let them. I do want to get ahead. If the village doesn't need me there's nothing wrong in going on with my studies.

People hoped I'd hit it off with the girl who came to work in the clinic, but I wasn't interested. If I become a research student I'll find someone in Beijing. I don't want a wife who can't live in the same place as me: that would be a lot of unnecessary trouble for myself and for the state too.

I'm in the Party, a probationary member. What I see more clearly than ever is that I must make a go of this research and beat the Japanese. That's my ambition now and it's still very ordinary.

I've got another reason for coming to Beijing: that case of injustice I mentioned. There's a man in my village – let's call him Fourth Uncle – who built himself a house in 1969. He made up a couplet to paste on either side of the door:

> Blessed land chosen by Chairman Mao;
> May the Deputy Supreme Commander* come to this door.

Over the door was written:

> Stars of good omen shine on high.

It was the era of "loyalty" and "adoration". He was just an ignorant peasant who'd adapted an old couplet about the Jade Emperor or the Eight Immortals or whatever. That landed him in prison for seven years. To start with he was charged with slandering Chairman Mao and Lin Biao. Then after Lin died in 1971 he was in trouble for having honoured him. He was only let out after the fall of the Gang of Four. But by then he'd lost his family: his wife had remarried, and his son had died of some illness. He was told to look to the future. Nobody uttered a word of apology, and the villagers did nothing to help him. So he asked me to phone the offices that deal with such cases. They reckon that letters are no use for reaching top officials: you've got to phone. They don't know who you have to phone, or how. I want to write the case up for the authorities here and get them to sort it out with the county authorities.

Stupidity and ignorance. That goes for both the offender and the people who handled his case. If we don't spread education and civilization a lot more widely, "small-scale producers" will give the country a lot of trouble.

If I pass the exam I'll go to university and if I fail I'll try again next year. If I fail twice, that'll prove I'm not up to it and I'll go home for good. Whether I go back to the village will depend on how things are. If that girl can cope with the clinic by herself, I might well decide to go to the county town. They can force me to go there

---

* Lin Biao, then Mao Zedong's designated successor.

anyway. Besides, I'll have better conditions for research in the county town.

The professor's daughter is married now. To my old roommate. They're both in Changsha. It's a good place to be.

Philosophy of Life

An instructor in Marxism—Leninism who would not allow her name to be published.

If what I say gets published I can say goodbye to my Party card.

I'm very depressed, and so are a lot of my colleagues. Some of them admit in private, "The future of us who teach and study Marxism—Leninism is no more predictable than the future of communism itself." We're depressed because we care about what's happening to the country. We're not reactionary at all. We all feel a sense of responsibility, but there's nothing we can do.

For instance, the Chinese Communist Party has been around for over sixty years, and we've been building socialism for a good thirty, but what's the result? In a lot of schools there are fewer young Party members than in the old days when it was an underground organization. And how many members are giving everything they've got for the Party's cause? In the old days we used to say "Never mind what they say: look at what they do." Now you have to listen to what they say in private to tell whether they're really struggling for the Party. When I was teaching in a Party school nearly all the students were pretty high-ranking. They'd all got a bit of power. Some of them had young colleagues bringing them nice things to eat, theatre tickets and the like. The old fogeys knew perfectly well what was happening. They said to themselves, "They're trying to use me to get into the Party through the back door." What sort of party is it you can get into through the back door? For them, joining the Party is just a step up the promotion ladder.

I didn't use to think like this, but the more I think the more depressed I get. The campaign to rectify the Party might solve some things, but fundamental changes in the Party's ways of doing things and in its ideas won't come about overnight. The problems are obvious and some of them are very serious indeed. For example, if we had a referendum with a secret ballot in which people could say what they really thought, would even 10 per cent of our citizens say they really believed in Marxism–Leninism and thought that communist society would ever really come about? There's one very famous "living Lei Feng"* who said a few days ago that these feelings are "just a few pale clouds drifting across the sky". There he was, spouting away on the platform, and there we were, sitting below him and not believing a word of what he was saying. If people like us don't believe it, how can ordinary people be expected to?

To put it bluntly, if we're Marxist–Leninists who know that dark clouds will blow away sooner or later, why do we refuse to admit that at the moment they really are banked up over our heads? What I've been saying is very rightist, but I've still got to say it. If it's published and by some fluke one of our leaders sees it, it might make them think.

When I was at university we all used to lie in bed at night in the dormitory talking about whatever came into our heads. One of us said, "There are three types of Party members these days: people on the make, people on the slippery slope, and people who just care about their families." But I believe there's a fourth kind too: real Party members. They're what holds society together. The trouble is that ordinary people aren't going to pay the least bit of attention to all that old stuff.

The other day I saw a policeman stop a Red Flag limousine in the street for breaking traffic regulations. That cop had guts. And what happened? A top official jumped out of the car and gave him a tongue-lashing. Wasn't the official being reactionary against our socialist legal system? But the bystanders were all delighted to see the policeman getting his come-uppance – it was disgusting. Of course, it's true that the people's police sometimes throw their weight about, but as the representatives of the state they do have to uphold the law. That incident sums up most of what I want to say.

At university I studied philosophy. Then I did teaching practice in the university's own middle school. I taught principles of philosophy in the standard politics course. The kids accused me of peddling rubbish. "Just teach us how you get a high enough mark in politics to get into university and we'll be satisfied," they told me.

I want to teach real students, not the sort of plodders we had in the

* "Living Lei Feng" is used in a rather mocking way to refer to goody-goodies.

Party school, which was why I've got myself transferred to this institute. Students today, especially economics and management students, are different. They're not longing desperately to get into the Party. They say that in subjects like theirs you're freer if you're not a Party member. And when they talk about their ideals some of them don't beat about the bush: "Going abroad, or getting rich."

I still believe in Marxism–Leninism, but I don't believe that Marx had got all his ideas on communist society sorted out, or that he foresaw everything. If Mao Zedong Thought has to be verified by practice why shouldn't Marxism–Leninism be?

You want a thumbnail autobiography? Born in 1959, when quite a lot of places had "already reached communism", with free food in canteens, and every day being worth twenty years.* The result was that a lot of the years were equivalent to one long nightmare-filled night. My father was a Party worker who used to fight in the heart of the enemy, but now the enemy's fighting in his heart – he's got cardiac disease. My mother's a physics teacher, and she doesn't need to prepare her classes any longer: they've been the same for donkey's years, completely untouched by political changes.

I started school when the primaries reopened during the Cultural Revolution. When the Gang of Four was smashed I graduated from middle school, and passed the exams for university the year after that. After university I was first at the Party school then transferred here. Pay: fifty-six yuan a month. Like a lot of other girls of twenty-six, I'm still unmarried.

Let's stop here. I've got to prepare a class. I teach others about the philosophy of life, but I still get confused when I talk about my own.

* Reference to the heady illusions of the Great Leap Forward.

Red Guard

She was one of the original Red Guards from Qinghua University Middle School.

Repudiating the Cultural Revolution means more than calling it names: what we really need, especially people like me who were involved, is cool analysis and critique.

I was fifteen and in the third year of junior middle school when the Cultural Revolution started. It began with an academic dispute when Yao Wenyuan's article on the drama *Hai Rui Dismissed* came out in a Shanghai paper and was then reprinted in the Beijing press.*

We didn't have much idea at the time of what it was all about. I was against Yao Wenyuan for criticizing an upright official, whatever the social system. Yao's supporters said upright officials were even more deceitful. Then we forgot about our arguments as we were too busy preparing for the exams for entrance to senior middle school in May. But the whole thing hit the fan before classes finished.

I think the Cultural Revolution was triggered off through two channels – one was academic debate, the other was the grapevine: you mustn't underestimate the inside information we got from cadres' children.

My overall assessment of the Cultural Revolution is that it was an absolute and total mistake, not a question of some rights and some wrongs, this or that percentage. The Cultural Revolution was initiated by conflict at the Central Committee level; it was the product of parties

* The publication of Yao Wenyuan's ferocious attack on an obscure Peking opera *Hai Rui Dismissed* by Wu Han in Shanghai in November 1965 and in the national press the following month was the overture to the Cultural Revolution. The upright Ming dynasty official Hai Rui was used in the libretto as a symbol for Mao's fallen rival Peng Dehuai.

outside the Party and factionalism within the Party. In the later stages they lost control, but what about the beginning? Actually it was meant to be the way it was, to overthrow a bunch of people. And lower down it wasn't like now, with everyone wanting to keep order – some people at least wanted to stir things up so they could do what they couldn't do in normal times. For example, denouncing lower-level cadres wasn't just revolutionary enthusiasm, it was also letting out years of pent-up bitterness. Chairman Mao's speech about how it had taken him years to find the Cultural Revolution approach couldn't be more accurate. Chairman Mao was afraid of a "capitalist restoration", afraid of "the masses going through misery a second time", afraid of "bad people usurping the leadership at every level". He meant well, and it led to disaster.

Later, when he wanted to put the brakes on, it was too late, the careerists were running it. Our generation were educated for years into "infinite love, infinite faith, infinite worship", and – what's that other infinite? – "infinite loyalty". So, ablaze with righteous indignation, we were off. From our leftist standpoint, everything appeared to be to the right, and once the Red Guards had been formed, I joined in beating up landlords, beating up rightists and raiding people's homes. I thought that was the only way to be revolutionary – "revolution isn't a dinner party" – but what was it in fact? It was beating up bad people with leather belts. Then we went out on the streets, smashing road signs and neon lights; we thought they represented non-socialist ideology, so we replaced them with a red ocean of slogans and quotations. It was physically and mentally much more exhausting than school.

We debated the question of class. We believed that with the exception of the "new bourgeoisie", socialist class status was determined by your "class brand" and we divided this up into the "five red categories" and the "five black categories" – later expanded to seven – and the "red periphery" – urban poor and the like who were born into petty-bourgeois backgrounds. Later my family got attacked too, and once I'd lost my revolutionary cadre background, I reassessed my own values and came round to Confucius' ideas of "not imposing on others things you yourself dislike". I really understood how much the "seven black categories" must have hated us. The second issue we debated was the question of "Maoism". We believed that as Mao Zedong Thought was already a complete system, the only reason it wasn't called an "ism" was because the "bourgeois headquarters" had taken advantage of

Chairman Mao's great modesty. We were all for the term Maoism and used it. Then Jiang Qing said Chairman Mao was opposed to this and that settled that. We had great faith in Jiang Qing then.

You could probably take the period from June '66 to January '67 as the formative stage for the Red Guards. When Chairman Mao put on the Red Guard armband that Song Binbin gave him and changed her name to Song Yaowu on 18 August '66 it was a recognition of the Red Guards, including the name "Red Guard" itself. Before that you had Red Guards, Red Descendants, a Scarlet Army and Rebel Guards, but as soon as Chairman Mao put on that armband they all changed their names to Red Guards. The way I see it, the spontaneous "Works of Chairman Mao Study Groups" which burst on to the scene from classrooms and dormitories were the embryonic Red Guards. Before 18 August, Chairman Mao had replied to a letter we Qinghua Middle School Red Guards had sent him saying, "I support you. To rebel against reactionaries is right."

Just as in earlier Chinese revolutions, it was the young intellectuals who were the vanguard and the bridges in the Cultural Revolution, and the Red Guards were originally supposed to be an organization for middle-school and university students. The sad thing is that this "revolution" wasn't like earlier ones; the Red Guards had only just started up and were still in their formative stage when their mission was completed.

We were given the task of establishing revolutionary ties, going out from Beijing to light the fires of revolution elsewhere. But when Red Guards from outside came here, we started fooling around. Outsiders came into Beijing to enjoy themselves too – it was a free train ride, free food and lodging. The first time I went out "establishing ties", I was in deadly earnest about revolution. I went to Shanghai and Hangzhou to encourage others to rebel against "the reactionary line of the bourgeoisie", telling people that the Cultural Revolution was meant not only to overthrow Liu Shaoqi and Deng Xiaoping, but also to eliminate capitalist roaders in the political establishment at every level. When we came back to Beijing we got into fights with Red Guards from the north-east.

After that we formed pickets. They were like Red Guard military police. But they weren't much use since the Red Guards never had any unified organization. These pickets were pretty heavy, they beat a lot of people to death. If they hadn't, they would have had no authority.

Later they got arrested by the Public Security on Jiang Qing's orders. A few months later they were released at mass rallies as "little warriors who'd made a mistake" – that was at Jiang Qing's command too! The conflicts within the Red Guards were very heated at that point and from being completely fragmented, they became two big opposing factions. After the dispute with the north-eastern Red Guards I went off "establishing revolutionary ties" again, this time for fun. I went to Guangxi, Guangdong, Zhejiang, Fujian and Hunan. For the first time I felt confused and disappointed. In Hunan I saw a mother and her seven- or eight-year-old daughter begging. The little girl was singing for money. She had the *Little Red Book* held tightly to her chest and she was singing revolutionary songs. The mother was next to her saying, "Please take pity on us, comrades-in-arms of the proletarian revolutionary faction." I didn't make that up. If you write about the strange and tragic events of the Cultural Revolution, the last thing you need to do is make things up.

I didn't dare, I couldn't, question the Cultural Revolution itself, but I did start questioning the factional fighting. While I was out "establishing revolutionary ties" I saw how the Red Guards had smashed things up everywhere. In the summer of '67 as soon as Jiang Qing started advocating "non-violent attack and armed defence", the fighting got going in a big way.

The rifts that occurred between rival organizations weren't only to protect some people or overthrow others, they were because everyone had a different notion of what an ideal model was. They all claimed they were supporting the Central Committee and the Central Committee Cultural Revolution Group, but underneath they were all jockeying for power. Armed fighting was on the cards.

The fighting came to Beijing last. It wasn't until late 1967 that the big clashes broke out here and it'd already got wild in other places by then. In a year and more of butchering one another, the "young warriors" whose historical mission was already finished vied with each other on the historical stage. The only possible outcome was total collapse. On 27 July 1968 the "Worker and People's Liberation Army Mao Zedong Thought Propaganda Team" entered Qinghua University to put down the fighting. It wasn't until the 28th that they managed to hold their ground. It was 3 September before Qinghua Middle School got taken over.

The year before last, Qinghua Middle School held a school

anniversary so I went back to have a look. There were hardly any traces of it, having been the birthplace of the Red Guards. Only we veterans could still distinguish the odd scar of the fighting from normal wear and tear.

The armed fighting was almost like a religious war: it was fighting for beliefs. The blow to me came when I got home. My father, with whom I'd long before drawn a clear boundary line, told me to keep away from school. We had an argument, but I wouldn't back down. The next day I found a note in the room which said, "Dear Ting, the fight between Master Huineng and Shenxiu was for the mantle and the alms-bowl.* Father." I was stunned. That was a story from my childhood. Suddenly I saw what I hadn't seen before. All of this fighting was to establish who were the true disciples.

I broke away during the fighting. It went against my beliefs, I couldn't go on feeling so confused any more. Carrying the Cultural Revolution through to the end wasn't just the supreme command, it was also my own personal ideal. But I just couldn't keep up with things. I couldn't even understand what was going on before my very eyes. It had all gone way beyond ideals; if you'd been me you would have been confused and uncertain too. Later on, I got quite used to feeling that way but kept aloof from it all. I got involved in love. According to Li Xiaosheng in *Diploma*, people like us didn't have premarital sex. Not necessarily. I did, and not with just one person either. To say that now doesn't matter much, it doesn't take that much courage. If you've had the courage to face yourself for having been a loyal Red Guard, talking about your private life is no big deal.

The Cultural Revolution even found its way into relationships between people, between father and daughter, made them abnormal. Looking around at our ransacked home, I felt it was all completely meaningless. I idled away a few months until the call came to go back to class and carry out the revolution. But there was still fighting going on at the school so I went home again. During that period I spent most of my time fooling around and dating.

In '68 we were called on to go down to the countryside, although actually it was compulsory. Some of my classmates sincerely intended

---

* Huineng (638–713) and Shenxiu (606–706) were both disciples of Hongren, the Fifth Patriarch of the Chan (Zen) school of Buddhism. Although Shenxiu was the senior disciple, it was to Huineng that Hongren left his mantle and alms-bowl in token of recognition of him as his successor.

to be "integrated" and to "carry out revolution for a lifetime", but I was already turned off. Marx had enough ideas all right. It all depends on which ones you're using at the time. That's how I saw it then. I spent a total of eight years in the countryside and didn't return to Beijing to work in a factory until the end of 1976.

Some of them really got into it but I didn't. I often used to sneak back to Beijing and stay for six months or a year. That had something to do with the shakiness of my private life as well as the chaos of the Cultural Revolution. My first boyfriend didn't go down to the countryside. He left to join the army in 1968 and that ended things between us. I had a few others after that but none of them worked out. I didn't get married until 1977 and I have a daughter now. It's hard to say, but when she grows up maybe she'll get caught up in something confusing too – I mean, if there's something really big going on.

I'm a grade-four worker now. I lead a quiet life: nothing special, but it's okay. I read in my spare time, and I don't give a damn about night school or the television university. If they don't promote you because you haven't a graduation certificate, then so be it. You can only be yourself.

14

HANDICAPS

A World of Colours

He Bo, masseuse in a clinic.

I wasn't born blind. I lost my sight completely when I was eight, in 1955. In 1945, when the war ended, my father came back from France eager to help rebuild our country. But the nationalist government was more interested in preparing for a civil war, so it was hard for him to find a job. By the time I was born, in September 1946, he was working in the Jiangsu provincial government, completely disillusioned. He chose the character Bo for my name which means doctor as well as abundant, because the proudest day in his life was when he got his doctorate.

I started primary school in 1953. I was a very ordinary child. In the first term of the second year I began getting headaches from time to time. At first it didn't happen when I was playing, only when I was reading or looking at the blackboard. The harder I looked at anything, the more it hurt, and there was always a dark blur in front of my eyes. My work began to suffer, and I stopped getting good marks. It was worst in maths, because the teacher's writing was so faint. I couldn't see it properly. She came to my home to tell my father and he scolded me for not working harder. I told him my head ached but he didn't believe me: he thought it was just an excuse. He did take me to hospital but, strange to say, I had no trouble at all in reading the test chart. Later on my headaches got worse, and after I vomited twice my father realized I wasn't just making it all up.

"A tumour on the retina". That sort of tumour is always malignant. The only thing to do was remove the whole eyeball – that's still the practice today. The doctor said 95 per cent of such cases occur in children under three. I was one of the other 5 per cent. First they diagnosed a tumour in the one eye, and I had to be hospitalized to have it removed. All I could think of was how ugly I would look with only one eye! When they said I could have an artificial eye, so that no one could tell the difference, I stopped worrying. I'd still be able to see and the headaches would stop. Father was very upset. He'd heard that this trouble was hereditary. He said it must come from my mother's side because no one in his family had ever had it. Nobody could tell if that was true. She had left us in 1949 to go to Hongkong with some high official in the provincial government – I learned later that he was a section head and she'd been his secretary. A few years ago I heard that he'd died soon after, and she was teaching in a Chinese primary school in Indonesia. We've never written to each other. Sending letters in braille is expensive and difficult. Anyway I don't want her to know that she has a blind daughter on the mainland.

After the operation, father bought me lots of good things to eat and ordered the best food in the hospital for me. My teachers and classmates came to see me too. I was enjoying myself so much that I even thought it might be nice just to stay there!

A few months later my headaches started again. I didn't breathe a word, for I knew it would be all over for me – I'd be blind. When I got the artificial eye the headaches got even worse, but if I took it out they eased a bit. So I hoped for the best, thinking the artificial eye must be to blame. Then the pain got so bad I had to tell my father. A check-up in hospital showed there was a tumour in my right eye too. Seventy-five per cent of tumours on the retina occur on one side only; once more I was one of the exceptions to the rule. I felt I was finished. The doctors wanted to operate at once, but my father wouldn't hear of it. He insisted on waiting two months. The doctors said that would be risky. He said, "I'll take the risk. I won't hold you responsible if anything goes wrong. I want to take her on a tour, as this is her last chance to see the country before she loses her sight. It will make all the difference to her later on." He wept, and so did the doctor. I was eight then, but I'll never forget what he said.

We weren't well off. My parents' divorce hadn't cost much, it had simply been announced in the paper, but she was abroad, and father was only a middle-school teacher. He already owed money to his school for my hospital expenses, and now he borrowed 800 yuan from friends. Eight hundred yuan! At the time that was astronomical! Setting out from Zhengzhou the two of us went to Beijing, Xi'an,

Chongqing, then down the Yangtse to Nanjing and Shanghai. We both knew this would be my last chance to see all this.

Last of all we went to Kaifeng, where our family had come from. Step by step I climbed up the 78 stone steps of Dragon Pavilion, then looked down on Lake Pan and Lake Yang. Lake Yang, the lake of the Yang family generals, had clear emerald water; Lake Pan, the lake of the treacherous minister Pan Renmei, was muddy. We visited Fan Pagoda too. Its dark wooden stairway had golden veins in the wood. On each grey brick was a Buddha. Our old home was under Iron Pagoda, which isn't actually iron but dark-brown brick. As we left Kaifeng, on the train, father said "Bo, look back, there's Iron Pagoda and below it is our home. Have a good look."

I did look hard, but my memory of it is hazy now. I can describe it in detail because afterwards I conjured up mental pictures of it over and over again.

On the eve of the operation we went to see an opera. Before the operation all that I could see was light grey. I counted one, two, three . . . I knew that when I came to again there wouldn't even be that light grey, there would be nothing at all.

Since then, day or night, waking or sleeping, everything has been black. At first I didn't even have the faintest sense of direction. I mixed up everything, even the things just beside me. Each time I bumped into the corner of the bed or the table, I was sorry I hadn't taken more notice of them before my operation. I should have memorized their exact positions. By degrees I learned to "see" again, relying on my hearing or sense of smell and touch. Sometimes without any of these I sensed changes in the world around me.

Father slowly paid off his debts, ten or fifteen yuan a month. When he had paid off all but fifteen yuan he suddenly came down with hepatitis. That was when I was about to graduate from the school for the blind. When my teacher told me he was ill, I sensed somehow it was serious. Very soon he was in a coma. He was forty-four when he died. In his obituary his school described him as an exemplary teacher. Actually he died of cancer, but they kept that a secret from me.

I was left all on my own. That was at the start of the Cultural Revolution, so I stayed on in the school. All the workshops and clinics for the blind were in such chaos they couldn't give us work.

I couldn't manage on my twelve-yuan monthly welfare benefit. My father's school had given me over 300 yuan after his death, but that soon got used up because I had to pay someone to light the stove, buy coal and do repairs around the house he'd left me. I even lost my twelve yuan for bare subsistence when organizations stopped functioning. Some of the neighbours helped, but our home was in a so-called "upper-class" district, where practically every family was in trouble, so none of them could do much. I didn't know where to turn. Just then, one of my first-year classmates saw me. He felt sorry for me, so he told me several of my old schoolfriends were keeping out of Red Guard activities and staying at home to make radios. They all lived in cramped workers' quarters, and would be pleased to come to my house where there was more space to assemble their transistors. In exchange they'd provide me with free meals. They hadn't much money themselves: to get transistor parts they'd raided the broadcasting room of a rebel Red Guard contingent. I only found out when they were caught and beaten up by the Red Guards. The next day the military control commission of the Public Security Bureau took me in for questioning too. I was arrested for hiding stolen goods. And besides, I'd slept with one of them. He'd confessed it. The police questioned me and kept me locked up for a few days, then they let me go. One of them told me I'd been let off lightly.

The school had been notified by the Public Security Bureau, and there was someone at the gate to meet me. Not long afterwards, at the end of 1968, I was assigned work. Since then I've been a masseuse in this clinic.

We talk about the same things as sighted people, but we also discuss things like whether it's better to be born blind and never have seen things, or to have seen then lost your sight. It's an argument that never gets settled.

I get my standard Beijing accent from the radio – our hearing's better than sighted people, so why shouldn't we speak better too? I read braille. Although the letters are the same as for foreign braille, we don't know what the foreign words mean. For example, the same letters "w-o-m-e-n" mean "us" in Chinese and "females" in English. And there isn't a Chinese–English braille dictionary, though I have got a Chinese–English phrasebook for blind tourists that was printed abroad.

I meet all sorts of people here. My pay is thirty-six yuan a month – it's not bad. ("*I'll say!*" *put in one of her colleagues.* "*In the old days how could the blind have earned thirty-six yuan? They sang in the streets or told fortunes or begged.")* But I don't save – what use would it be?

What I notice most is changes in moral standards. Old people can compare the old society with the new, but I can't. Nowadays I'm offered a seat in the bus and helped across the road. In the last few years there have been more and more people who treat us well. From our clients' talk we learn about social changes too, who's under fire and why, who's been commended and won a five-yuan bonus. So it seems the bonus system has come back. Sometimes they swear at the peasants for making so much money. One day, I heard some vehicle making a swishing noise. I asked what it was and I was told it was a mechanized roadsweeper. So I know the people who used to sweep the roads have gone. People are eating better than before, wearing better clothes. I can sense that too. I've bought some stylish clothes myself.

I can see everything. When the authorities gave me 132 yuan in back benefit for eleven months I saw that the Cultural Revolution had really ended. I didn't just hear it over the radio. The others asked me to describe Deng Xiaoping. Is he very short? I can't remember clearly. We blind people are funny that way, we like hearing what sighted people say, but we've got to hear one of our own describing things too . . . "I think Deng Xiaoping is rather short, but he's a great man!" And I meant that, every word.

There are people who jeer at the blind. Some kids yell, "Dump them in the river to feed the turtles." On a bus a man said in a loud voice, "This blind girl's quite a beauty. Too bad she's got glass eyes!" People shouldn't think the blind are deaf. How can you judge people just by their faces and figures? Plenty of sighted people are ugly. We know what is beautiful and what is ugly. Once someone at work bought an opera ticket and went off really happily to the theatre, but the ticket collector stopped him – some sighted person had palmed him off with a slip of paper. We don't forget something like that. *("In his next life he'll be born a monster!" one of her friends said.)* The doctor here was born blind. He can't control his face muscles and his face twitches. He doesn't look attractive but he has a heart of gold.

How do we manage? Our sticks help us to see our way. We walk at the edge of the lane for slow traffic, tapping the kerb. We hate it when lorries are parked by the roadside. You might bump smack into them before you know they're there. If you wear the new ultrasonic glasses with earphones you hear a warning buzz if there's something in your way. I don't like using them. They're too noisy.

I'm not married. I share the house my father left me with a friend from another clinic. She's single too. We turn on the light in the evening and remember to switch it off before we go to bed. We're human too. We can't live in the dark.

We know which banknotes are which by the paper and the size, but we can't tell which coupons are for 250 grammes of flour and which are for five kilos – they're no different to us. Coupons for rice and flour and oil feel the same too. But we ask sighted people to sort them out for us, putting the biggest ones at the back. Our hands are our eyes, so I don't approve of giving the blind heavy, rough work. It roughens their hands and that handicaps them more. Our hands are very sensitive, so we can cook and do housework just as well as people with sight. When we knit we feel what we're doing and can learn all sorts of stitches. One of my friends works in a bookbinding firm, which has roughened her hands so that she can't read.

I like going to the cinema. I can follow all the action. I'm not all that keen on operas. I can't understand the words when they're singing, and there's such a din. I know several people who work in cinemas, but when they get good tickets they don't think of me. I go and wait for tickets to be returned. There generally are some. Once they'd just started showing a good Japanese film when word got round it was to be withdrawn. I badly wanted to see it, but couldn't get a ticket. It happened to be my birthday, so I asked our accountant to write out a placard for me. It said, "Today is my birthday, please let me have a ticket." Very soon I saw people gathering round, and someone put a ticket in my hand. I felt the warmth of his hand.

Don't cry, don't cry.

Empty Burden

UN figures show that the disabled make up one-tenth of the world's population, although many of the people included in this frightening statistic might not regard themselves as disabled – for example, the severely myopic or manual workers who have lost a finger.

The proportion of disabled people in the People's Republic of China is lower than the world average. In recent years schools for the mentally handicapped have been set up in Beijing, Shanghai, Guangzhou, Hongkong, Taibei and many medium-sized cities. A few years before that, universities in both Beijing and Taibei set up crash courses in special education to train people who want to work in this field. Nonetheless, society should show more concern for the mentally handicapped, their families and those who teach them and work with them.

The entrance to a school for the mentally handicapped.

A mother who has just taken her son to school.

My husband and I are not close relatives.

It wasn't anything you would notice at first. We didn't realize until he was four years old and still couldn't say "Mummy" or "Daddy".

Why shouldn't I love him? Of course I love him very much. We spend more than half of what we earn on him every month, buying his food, clothes and toys, too. We've been to countless doctors but it's no use. I don't mind admitting I've even been to pray to Buddha.

He's seventeen now. He's been a bit better since he started this special reading class. Of course, teaching always does some good. It's not as if he couldn't understand anything.

We didn't dare have a second child. What if we had another one like him? Perhaps we are being too sensitive but we do feel under pressure. We can't look the world in the face.

We haven't had a happy day since . . . but you do get used to it, gradually. If you had a deaf-mute, for example, or a child with only one leg, the tongues wouldn't wag. But if you have a kid who's not too bright in the head then a lot of people will go on and on about you.

I'd give my life to make him normal, I would. You don't know how much we love him and how terrible the pressure is.

Woolly Hat

Xiao Fengzhen, thirty-six, female, a worker in a Peking electro-plating factory.

I never asked for anything in life apart from a good husband. I started work at this factory in 1966. When I was young quite a few men were interested in me. He came to our factory to repair machinery. He was from Jinan. You may find it strange when he came from so far away but we just clicked. I'd never really got on with anyone else but I did with him. It was fate. He had no father or mother because they'd fled to Taiwan. His class origin was bad. His factory was under the Fourth Ministry of Machine Building just like mine and we were both fourth-grade workers.

He's not much of a talker but he's very capable. I'm no good at sewing but I can knit and that's all I do at home. I start planning the next garment before I've even cast off the one I'm making. He takes care of everything else. Does the shopping, buys the coal, cooks and washes. He likes doing all that. A while ago he bought himself a washing machine. He said it was time to start mechanizing at home as well as at the factory.

Some time back the magazine *Modern Fashion* got together with Central Television to organize a hat-knitting competition. I got second place with a hat I'd knitted when I was off sick.

I got ill because I have too much drive and I fly off the handle easily. A job that other people do in two hours, I'll finish in one. That's all very well on a lathe – you can work at your own pace and you get the credit. But when there are seven of you working on an oxidizer, the pace depends on the group. However fast you work you still have to put in the same time. I can't take it easy and I can't suck up to people. I put up with the situation as long as I could. But if things go on like that for too long the work exhausts you in the end and you feel so angry inside. I told the management again and again that I just couldn't go on working in the oxidizer but they always said that experienced workers like me had to set an example. In May I got a sick-note from the clinic. Then I went home to rest which meant I lost my bonus. I didn't just sit around getting bored—I set to and knitted all the clothes the family will need this year and things for my friends, neighbours and colleagues as well. People kept asking me to knit hats and so on. I couldn't refuse. We've all got to get along together and everyone has to ask a favour at some time or other. When I'm invited somewhere I take one with me to give the hostess. Presents can be expensive and it's hard to choose the right thing. My hats are cheap and acceptable. I worked out last night that I knitted over fifty while I was off work, that's including the three I sent in for the competition.

I didn't know anything about the competition before he bought *Television News* and asked me if I thought I was good enough to go in for it. I wasn't sure. It was a national competition and people from Shanghai who really knew about style would be entering. My hats are really best for middle-aged women like me. We want something that suits us. It's a waste of time trying to make us wear anything too pretty or too way out.

The man from Central Television went to my mother's house to tell me I'd won. I'd given her address because this place is too hard to find. My sister came over with the message. A few days later I was invited to appear on the TV programme *At Your Service*. I got time off from the factory for it. We three prize-winners went on to show how we'd made the hats. They started shooting in Xuanwu Park but things kept going wrong and in the end they did it indoors. It took a whole week. I had my hair done at first but after a while I didn't bother.

People still recognize me. A couple of days ago some girls on the bus asked me to show them how to make my hat. They hadn't quite followed the demonstration on TV. I tried, but I'm not sure they got it. It's not difficult. The trouble is you need needles and wool to show people properly. You'll find the stitches I use in the pattern book but I vary them a bit to make them special, and I use a copper wire brush to fluff my wool. The other day I noticed woolly hats for sale on a street stall at five yuan apiece. At first glance they were quite like mine, but when I picked one up it was actually pretty crude. Each one costs me only 2.50 for the wool and if I set up shop beside him they'd all go for mine. Everyone in the factory who can knit is making them now. Some look okay until you stretch them over your hand, then you can see the tension is very poor. They'll lose their shape when they're washed, but mine won't. Oh well, we can't all be good at everything and anyway tastes differ.

I've liked pretty things since I was young, although of course I couldn't go in for that sort of thing then because of the Cultural Revolution and my bad class origins. My father was a Kuomintang army officer. He was sent to prison when I was a baby. When I was two, my mother remarried and took me and my brother with her. My new father was very good. My natural father is still alive, not that I would want anything to do with him, not even if he was rich. He never took any care of me and yet I had to take the blame for him. If you had a bad class origin you always felt as if you'd done something terrible. I used to hate filling in official forms because I had to put down "reactionary army officer" in the section for class origin. My mother's was bad too. I felt that everything and everybody was against me in those days: nobody would lend a hand when I had problems. My husband was the only one who was different. When we got married I said that we'd both had it tough and we'd have to depend on each other. Neither of us had a father so we could both care for my stepfather and my mother. My mother's had such a difficult life . . . That's enough. I can't bear talking about the past.

It didn't trouble me that we couldn't dress prettily in those days. A white shirt and beige trousers look quite neat. I didn't dare dress up for my wedding. One night they came hammering at our door to ask if I'd been to Tian'anmen.* That's right, it was 1976. So I got married in a khaki army jacket. My mother still uses it, says it's got plenty of wear left in it. Things change so fast now. Hats which everyone was wearing last year are out now. I like looking at the new styles in the street. But you've got to dress to suit yourself.

After I won the competition there was a big meeting in my honour. I was asked to teach a knitting course for women who were at home with children or on protracted sick leave. That way they can increase their

* On 5 April 1976, a meeting in memory of the recently dead premier, Zhou Enlai, was violently broken up by the authorities. Afterwards attempts were made to trace those who had attended it.

income and the factory's too. I was thinking of leaving my job but now I've decided to stay.

It may not sound very lofty but watching my daughter grow up is my real joy in life. That's where I get my confidence. I tell her my life hasn't been easy but I've given her a smoother path.

15

COMING AND GOING

Train Chief

Beijing, Zhengzhou, Xi'an, Lanzhou – Lanzhou, Xi'an, Zheng-
zhou, Beijing.

He said he hadn't achieved anything, apart from joining the
Communist Party and becoming the head of a train crew. He
agreed to talk to us only because he wanted more people to know
about the past.

I'm a year older than the People's Republic. In 1949, when I was one,
my whole family moved from Jinan to Harbin. My father was a
foreman on the railways, and railway people often get moved around.

We moved again in 1956, when I'd just started at the Railway
Primary School in Harbin. We went off to help the north-west. I hated
having to leave all my friends.

We settled in Xigu, near Lanzhou. The poverty of the peasants there
in the north-west made a deep impression on me – teenage girls with no
trousers, and whole villages taking their drinking water from filthy
ditches that people and animals pissed and shat into. It's different now.
Xigu is a satellite town of Lanzhou. The only thing that hasn't changed
is that the village girls around there still aren't keen on taking baths.
There are new bathhouses but some people won't use them. Some of
the temporary labourers on the railways hate bathing: they say it
weakens you and makes you tired.

I got into junior middle school in Lanzhou in 1962. The whole
country had been having a terrible time. After the Great Leap Forward
trees had been stripped of leaves and bark for food, and all the edible
grasses had been gathered too. People started making coarse buns from
husks and elm bark. Later they just ate the husks by themselves. Husks
don't fill you, so they had to eat grass. They even ate ailanthus leaves
although the smell of them is enough to make you feel sick. You had to

boil them then soak them for a few days first so they wouldn't stink quite so much and you could get them down.

Our teachers took us out looking for all kinds of edible things. Sometimes we found beancake crumbs by the railway tracks in the marshalling yards. We used to get down on the sleepers and the roadbed to lick up those crumbs. That beancake was being shipped from the north-east to Xinjiang to feed horses. We couldn't get hold of it for ourselves. We were different in those days. The meat the north-west sent to Beijing was loaded into trains here, but nobody stole any of it. Once I picked up a goat's tail, a hairy great thing, in the goods yard and took it home. It seems incredible now but my father insisted I should take it back, even though I hadn't eaten any meat for a year. He even forced me to confess it to my teacher. I still have a very clear memory of taking it back to the meat train.

Only the big stations had schools for us railway workers' kids. I went off to board at one when I was only seven, just a kid who still wet the bed. I went home once a week either by passenger train or by hitching a ride on a goods wagon. Deaths were very rare, but some were crippled in accidents – it's a dangerous business. I mastered it though; I can still get on and off a goods train going at about thirty kilometres an hour.

Some of us got as far as senior middle school or college, and some went to work after junior middle or even primary school, but we all had to start living independently at the age of seven. Our parents taught us only one thing: not to know the meaning of hardship.

After I started middle school in 1962, my parents moved further west, near Zhangye – too far for me to get home every weekend, even with my free rail pass. Because I'd been looking after myself since I was seven I was the class food monitor right through middle school. My job was to see the others got fed. I remember getting viciously beaten up by some of the other kids because I was neglecting them to study for the senior middle school entrance exams. I didn't squeal on them to the teachers. I already knew that people's teeth grow in their stomachs, not their mouths.

The Cultural Revolution started during my first year in senior middle school. Classes were suspended, and I joined the Red Guards for a while till I got fed up and went home. There were a lot of factories in the north-west – some built with Soviet aid, others we'd put up ourselves, and even though the Cultural Revolution had started they were still looking for people. I went into a chemical factory. I'd been there nearly a couple of years when I heard, in 1968, that I'd been assigned to an oil workers' technical school for further study. The chemical factory let me go, but as I left of my own accord I lost those two years of seniority. It was a good school, the successor to the Bailey School at Shandan started by Rewi Alley *(the New Zealander who was one of the founders of the Chinese Industrial Co-operatives during the Japanese War).* The graduates of the school are all in the oilfields of China.

My father died just as I graduated in 1970. I took up my right to succeed him in the railways because I thought it would help the family out. My qualification hasn't been any use, except in the last round of wage rises which you got only if you had a diploma.

I've been working in passenger trains ever since 1970. As a train chief, I ride for four days, then get seven days off, then spend the eighth day preparing for the next trip. It's a different schedule for the rest of the crew. This work never had novelty value for me, probably because my parents were on the railways before me – I knew all about it before I even started.

There have been endless campaigns on the railways these last few years. For example, there are regular drives to improve our ways of doing things, talk about "the people's railways must be for the people", talk about how we're not to ship or buy goods, talk about being polite to the passengers. The slogans change each time, but it's always the same message.

Sometimes they say it's bad for the railways' image if we're carrying all sorts of packages when we finish work, other times that buying goods along the route disturbs the economy, but whatever reason we're given, the real point is that we're not allowed to buy or ship things.

Train crews get on pretty well together. Once the train starts we become an entity. We look after each other, and do all we can to save the women comrades from having to look after the carriages with hard-class seats – they're too crowded. But you can't all have the soft-class sleeping car – there's only one. There are just too many people on the trains these days. We're always overcrowded. We often have over 200 people in a hard-class sitting carriage with only 128 places in it, but even then I still make the train crew take hot water to the passengers. Around Spring Festival, the train was so packed you couldn't even get your feet on the floor. Every time we got to a main station the crew were off with their big kettles to walk along the outside rapping on the train windows, asking the passengers if they wanted any hot water. Even though some of the windows were frozen up and couldn't be opened they still had to rap on them. We had to let the passengers know we cared.

As I see it the passengers aren't cattle: they've bought their tickets on a passenger train, and that gives them the right to expect service. That doesn't sound as good as those fancy slogans, but it's practical.

A lot of the serious overcrowding in the last few years has been because of people travelling to do business. It's fascinating to listen to them. But a train's a very special sort of community: the passengers are all pretty talkative because once you get to the station you never see each other again. What they say shouldn't be taken too seriously. If you acted on information picked up on trains you'd find the best part of it is nonsense. A few years back the luggage racks of trains from Beijing were always full, though going to Beijing it was quite different. There was a lot you couldn't get in the provinces in those days, even soap or matches. But the last few years the luggage racks have been weighed down with packages on trains going both ways.

I shouldn't really dislike any passengers, but I don't like people in their twenties who travel in soft-class sleepers. And I loathe journalists who flash their press cards and demand a sleeper from me as soon as they board the train, as if I owed them something. If they're journalists on provincial or national papers, I'll do what I can to fix them up, but I'll not lift a finger for ones from little rags I've never even heard of. Trainee journalists I won't give a sleeper to even if I've got some left: I'll keep them for the old folk.

Half the working time of a train chief is spent allocating sleepers, and it can drive you hopping mad. A few days ago I had a row with this guy from Hongkong who asked for a sleeper. I hadn't got any left, and did he look furious about it. Half an hour later a Japanese came to see me; he wanted a sleeper too. His documentation showed he was a technician inspecting some joint enterprise, and I reckoned that as he was a foreigner and here to work I ought to fix him up somehow. So I went to the soft sleeping car and persuaded a railway official travelling on a free pass to give up his berth to him and come into the train crew's sleeping compartment. Of course, only a top official would have had a pass for a soft sleeper. The upshot was that the Hongkong guy blew his top and accused me of crawling to foreigners and pushing Chinese around. He wouldn't listen to reason. He just said that his brown travel permit for returning Chinese didn't count for as much as a Japanese passport. I lost my cool too, and told him that he used his travel permit to buy tickets at the same rate as Chinese who earned a fraction of his Hongkong income, but that I'd made the Japanese pay the 70 per cent foreigners' surcharge in accordance with the regulations. The other passengers were all on my side. He wanted to be superior, but he wasn't going to pay the price. In the end I fixed him up with a hard-class sleeper when another passenger got off, and he apologized.

I was tough with him, but I'm not hard on people who really can't afford a ticket. We're supposed to make them pay a fine on top of the price of the ticket, but they're so pathetic, what's the point? They haven't got any money anyhow. So I just let them get wherever they want to for free. But keep that to yourselves, or all the fare dodgers will come on my train.

Golden October

*October is the ideal season for tourism and conferences in Beijing,
and on top of that 1984 was the thirty-fifth anniversary of the
founding of the People's Republic. Restrictions on entry into
Beijing began to be applied from the middle of September. So by
middle and late October . . .*

*Ten o'clock in the evening. In the ticket hall of Beijing
station "All tickets sold" signs hang at some thirty booking
windows for the lines to Harbin, Guangzhou, Shanghai, Baotou
and elsewhere.*

*People have to queue even to claim refunds on unused tickets at
a temporary ticket office in the open. The young tourist behind us
is wearing a striped brown suit over a sky-blue sweater and
carrying a wheeled suitcase made of simulated leather. He seems
rather upset.*

My wife has gone and disappeared. It was in the crush to get on the
train just now. We were just setting out on our journey home. I waited
for her at the ticket barrier until the train left, then I wandered around
the main hall. I was at my wits' end. I told an attendant I'd lost her
and he said I'd better get a refund right away, because if I hung around
the tickets would be invalid and I'd get nothing back on them. That'd
be twenty yuan down the drain. *(He opens his hand to show two
sweat-soaked tickets from Beijing to Handan on Train 307.)* I'm from
the Fengfeng Mining Bureau. We were in Beijing on our honeymoon.
We took the bus the twenty-five kilometres to Handan, and the train
from there. Counting the day on the journey, we've been away for six
days.

We knew that security's very strict in Beijing and we'd got all our
papers in order – our work cards, official letters of introduction, our

marriage licence and some national grain coupons.* We knew that without all that we wouldn't be allowed to stay in Beijing or even get anything to eat. My wife's useless. She's never been away before. She got sick on the bus and threw up all over the place. She was all right on the train.

As soon as we arrived in Beijing we asked where the hotel booking office was. "Over there," someone said, "the longest queue you can see." We queued for five hours, then just when it was going to be our turn they put up a sign: "All hotels in the city and the outskirts full." I didn't mind hunkering down for the night – I'm a man – but I couldn't ask her to. I remembered that one of my colleagues in the Mining Bureau had some kind of in-law who was something big in Beijing, so I made a long-distance call home. It took an hour to put the call through and then my colleague told me his in-law worked in the Coal Ministry. So we rushed over there and found them. They were real friendly and asked us to stay for supper, but I'd got no appetite. The first thing was to find a place to stay. They contacted the Coal Ministry hostel for us and I went to have a look. It was packed solid – there were even people sleeping on the landings. I thanked them for trying and went back to the hotel booking office at the station. I wanted to queue up to book into a hotel for the next night there and then. We couldn't sleep on a landing, not on our honeymoon. Besides, there wasn't even any bedding left in the Coal Ministry hostel.

That night my wife got terribly cold. I was okay – I had some liquor in the station canteen during the night – but she wouldn't, which was why she got so cold, and had to go to the canteen for a bowl of hot soup noodles every couple of hours. At dawn we were given tickets for accommodation the next night – in the guesthouse at the Hujialou bathhouse. We didn't know the way, but there was a computer whatsit by the hotel office. You put four cents in and out comes a piece of paper that even tells you where to change buses. When we got there it wasn't a guesthouse at all – it *was* the bathhouse. We'd been had. She had to stay in the women's baths, and I was in the men's baths. We didn't even need the papers we'd gone to all that trouble to get. People were bathing there during the day, so as soon as we'd signed in we had to clear off till

---

* People entitled to grain rations receive coupons valid only in their own locality. If they are travelling they may exchange some of these for the more valuable national coupons that are valid everywhere.

eight that night. So we changed our clothes and went out to see the town. We had to carry all our stuff about with us: they wouldn't look after it.

We had a street map, and with that we did the whole Forbidden City – Tian'anmen, the Palace, the Working People's Palace of Culture and Sun Yatsen Park. We'd planned to visit Chairman Mao's mausoleum, but it wasn't open that day. She was as useless as ever. She felt sick every time she got on a bus, and had to get off for a rest every three or four stops. "Stick it out for another couple of stops," I said to her. "If we get off now we'll never be able to fight our way back on again." We'd just got off in Wangfujing when she threw up all over the road. Then up comes some "hygiene cop" and fines us a yuan for the cost of getting it cleaned up. So we learned our lesson. We'd just have breakfast, go without a midday meal, and have some bread and tea when we got back to the bathhouse at night. That worked. We did several sights a day that way, and finished them all in four days. We had to give the Ming tombs and the Great Wall a miss: on a long bus ride like that she'd have spewed her guts out. Summer Palace? Didn't go there either. We knew from the map you have to change buses several times.

We brought over a thousand yuan with us – it's our honeymoon, and we were going to do some shopping in Beijing. But after milling up and down Wangfujing, Xidan and Qianmen Streets for ages we only got through about 300 yuan. I reckon there's better stuff in Beijing than in Handan, but it's not up to what you can get in Shijiazhuang. And what we did buy gave us a lot of worry. They leave the lights on all night in the bathhouse so the guests don't get anything stolen. Last night there was a power cut, so they issued us with candles. I had my money tucked in my shirt, some things in the little locker above my head, and some under my head as a pillow. I didn't sleep a wink. There were people leaving in the middle of the night to catch trains. At 1.20 yuan a night with a hot bath thrown in it was a bargain.

Why isn't this queue moving? In another couple of hours my tickets will be invalid and I won't be able to get refunds.

I'm a purchaser. I buy vegetables, rice and all that. My wife's the cook in our canteen.

I'm sure she'll cry – I did myself. I don't know whether she got pushed onto the train or what. Only the day before yesterday she said, "Everyone tells you that Beijing's full of terrific places to visit, but they're all so far apart. I never realized Beijing was so big." And she said that a honeymoon like this wasn't lucky. "We're on a honeymoon, but we're separated in that bathhouse. We can't even sleep together." She burst into tears. "It's the only time you've ever come here in your life," I said, trying to cheer her up. "A honeymoon in Beijing is something to remember." Me? It's the last time I'm coming to Beijing for a honeymoon!

We queued up for ages to buy the train tickets home. There were none left for the expresses that go via Handan, so we had to get tickets for Train 307, a slow train to Handan. We couldn't get seats, and on top of that the train gets into Handan at about four in the morning. It'd have been very cold when we got off. Never mind, we thought, we're going home: we'll take it anyway. Even then a lot of people couldn't get tickets.

When they opened the ticket barrier everyone surged through. The inspectors couldn't stop them, so they shut the barriers again and shouted, "Anyone who gets on a train without a ticket will be fined." My wife disappeared in the mad crush. I don't know whether she got past the barrier or not. I didn't move – I just stayed there behind the barrier till everyone else had gone through and they were going to close it again. "Are you coming through or not?" the girl checking tickets asked me. When I explained she said, "The train's leaving in three minutes. You'd better get over to the p.a. room and get them to make an announcement. If she's on the train or the platform she'll probably be able to get off." So I did that and then I stood by the barrier again. But there was no sign of her. The train had gone, so I went back to get them to make another announcement. "She wouldn't be likely to stay on the train by herself," they said, "but if she got off she wouldn't wait around here. She's probably rushing around the square outside." So I said, "Please, miss, make an announcement in the square." "You're out of luck," she said. "There's a drive against noise pollution. We've had a circular ordering the dismantling of all high-volume public-address systems. There's a total ban on announcements in the square. I'll give her another call in the waiting room, the station concourse and at the front of the station, but the sound won't carry right across the square." I listened to the announcement, then went to look for my wife in the square, but no sign of her. There were far too many people. So I went back to the main concourse. That's where the attendant advised me to cash the tickets back in.

She's got no ticket and no money, and I've got all our papers. All she's got is a couple of yuan for a late snack in the dining car. I've got the new clothes and shoes and things she bought here, she has our toothbrushes and hand-towels in her bag. Oh yes, she's got a personal seal too — that's something.* She could raise some money with her watch, I suppose. Or leave it as security till she pays for the ticket.

Only three people left ahead of us in the queue. When I've got the refund I'll go back to the p.a. room to see if she's turned up yet. Once she gets to Handan she'll be all right — our bureau's got an office there. She's twenty-three — she can find her way home from there easily enough. At least she hasn't been kidnapped.

They haven't given me the full amount — they took a service charge. Let's go to the police now. *(We accompany him to the police post in the station. "We'll work it out," the police officer tells him. "We'll find her somehow." After that we go to the station office, where the controller explains that they will do all they can to contact the stations that Train 307 will be stopping at. If his wife is on the train there'll be no problem.)*

Well, there's no point in getting upset. It's all up to the police and the railway people now. I think I'll spend the night in the waiting room. In a while I'll go back to the police to see if there's any news.

What's your address? Can I come and look you up next time I'm in Beijing?

* In China a small personal seal or "chop" bearing the owner's name is often used where a signature is employed for official purposes in the West.

Drinks and Smokes

A Beijing–Baotu express train. Hard-class sleeper. Five minutes after departure.

Have a smoke. One of mine, I insist. Not up to your standards? Drinks and smokes are for sharing. Okay, if you have one of mine, I'll have one of yours.

I'm thirty-six. Born in the Year of the Rat.* I'm a purchaser and salesman from Zhuoxian,† always on the road. We've got quite a lot of factories in Zhuoxian. Mostly they make parts for Beijing, Tianjin and Shijiazhuang. My factory does quite a lot of different lines. Mostly plastic mouldings: polyvinyl, polystyrene and fibreglass-reinforced plastics. We've never closed for a single day since we set up shop in the Cultural Revolution. There's always a rush on something. All the reforms and competition keep us busier than ever. We've got to hustle. And we've had to adjust to all the big changes going on. It used to be buyers that had to go down on bended knee. Now it's the sales people who get treated like dirt.

All that entertaining. All that flattery you have to lay on with a shovel. The man in charge of the procurement and sales department in the factory I'm going to in Baotou is a Zhuoxian man. Name of Zhang. So I spun him a yarn: "By today's standards we're many miles apart, but you're from the same commune as me. Your old man was called Zhang, so you must be descended from the great Zhang Fei.‡ No doubt about it." He lapped it up, and I soon had his official stamp on the contract. I told him he was right to be backing commune-run industry

---

* 1948.
† A county just south of Beijing.
‡ A legendary hero of the second century AD.

and getting the economy moving. "It's good for the country, good for the factory and good for our home. Could you do with some sesame oil? Good stuff – from home." Then he says no because he's scared of getting into trouble for breaking the rules. "Go on," I say, "try a couple of bottles." I went out and bought them there in Baotou. He was none the wiser.

Entertaining? Loads of it. I've even taken people to the Dasanyuan restaurant in Beijing: a meal for four cost 239.50 yuan, and that didn't include the cigarettes and booze. You've only got to mention negotiations and they'll come straight out with suggestions about a nice quiet restaurant – and quiet restaurants don't come cheap.

Of course it would be the end of socialism if everybody acted like that. But if nobody did, little factories like ours wouldn't stand a chance. We can't compete with state factories in quality, efficiency or anything else. There's only one thing we're good at: providing booze and cigs. Whatever you want we'll give you. State factories can't do that. That's why people buy our stuff, even though it's more expensive. Once the chopsticks start moving everything's possible. It's not their own money they're spending. There's no long-term future in doing things this way, but you won't get far trying to stop corruption single-handed. And where would the factory be without orders?

Do you think I enjoy it? Crap! I have to eat something before every banquet – I'd be sunk if the drink went to my head. Then I sit there looking at some huge spread that would make my wife's eyes pop out of her head, and casually I have to tell the waiters to take it all away and feed it to the pigs.

There's no way we can keep the Party rules, but we can't break the law. At worst we do things that are a bit bent and give you a bad conscience. Say the factory's just made a trial prototype of something we can't mass-produce yet, and we've got to go out and sell it. So what do we do? We buy other people's products and use them as our samples to get the orders. It's criminal fraud.

My childhood was very boring. I've never had the makings of a real farmer. My old man was a farmhand – even worse off than the poor peasants. They had a bit of their own land, but farmhands were just landlords' hired labour. We were liberated early and had land reform early.* That was when I was born, so they called me Baotian –

---

* His county came under communist control and went through the redivision of land before 1949.

[312]

"Landkeeper" – so we'd keep the land we were allocated in land reform. When I finished primary school I went home to be a commune member. It was a disaster year.* There were big floods, and I got together with people from the village to go begging in Beijing. We begged for a year until we were arrested and sent home. Later I took up slope-pulling. You got a length of rope, tied it to an iron hook, and stood at the bottom of a slope. When you saw a pedicab or pedicart wanting to go up you hooked it and pulled it up to the top, and they gave you a cent or two. It cost me quite a few fights to pull things up that slope. Once I pulled my brother-in-law's ear half off. To this day his ear still flaps. Mind you, I had no idea then I'd marry his sister.

When the Cultural Revolution came along I was in a "Peasants' Rebel Regiment". We went to stay in Beijing and ate for free at the reception centres for Red Guards who were travelling around the country then. Nobody dared interfere. We were the "revolutionary young warriors invited by Chairman Mao". I went to six of Chairman Mao's eight rallies for the Red Guards. Then we were told to go back to our own units to "struggle, repudiate and reform", so I went to Tianjin. And when they chucked people out of Tianjin I went to Baoding. Baoding was chaos – armed fighting. But there were lots of "reception centres" and "supply bases". One day you ate at the "Three Reds"† reception centre, and you agreed with them. The next day the Jinggangshan Army† supply base fed you, and you were for Jinggangshan. That's how I got by. When the 38th Army intervened to stop the fighting I took repatriation expenses and went home. I'd seen the world, and so when I got back I became a buyer.

Tricks of the trade? Plenty! I don't rely on a notebook. If you lose it you're sunk. I keep everything in my head – what everyone else's job is, what they like eating, what they want, what I can get from them. When I go to a new place I find out what's in short supply – it's scarcity makes things valuable. Isn't that what the national economy and the people's livelihood is all about? They look after the national economy with their state plans, and I sort out the people's livelihood – food, clothes, consumer goods, entertainment.

You ought to realize that we're all bullshitters. It's a hard life. And what have we got in store for us? Tongues worn out, shoes through to

* Around 1960–1.
† Rival coalitions in the factional wars in Baoding.

their uppers, a list of crimes as long as your arm, and the black house – the clink.

In 1960 more than half the people in the village, men and women, young and old, got "balloon sickness" – distended bellies. My dad died then. In 1970 the factional struggles were so bad that the harvest was ruined, but radio and TV lied and said it was a good one. In 1980 the contract system started, and things have been looking up since then. Honestly, commune members are better off than factory workers these days. But I can't leave. If I did, the factory would be one man short. Now you can see TV aerials going up over every house, and people can eat good-quality rice and white flour. Of course it's a good thing. But there's too much corruption about. That's why the Party's being purged.

Have another cig. I can claim it on expenses. Let's have a meal on expenses too. Is it true, what they say about it being possible to contract for commune-run enterprises? I'd love to do it – I could make it more profitable than it is now. If I contracted for it I wouldn't have a single buyer or sales rep. I'd let anyone who wanted to do the job for a short spell. I'd make them an allowance of so much a day to cover everything. I wouldn't give them a slush fund.

If an honest man tried to do this job he'd get nowhere. Do you know the people in the Baotou Industry Bureau? Or the Beijing one? Tell me how it's done and I'll pay you for the information.

My basic wage is thirty yuan, but the main thing is that the commission rate's good. They refund me what I actually spend when I'm away from home. Don't be fooled because I eat and dress well – I don't make as much hard cash as my old woman. No, no kids. She was married to another bloke, had a son by him then got sterilized. The bloke died, and she married me. But she had to leave the boy behind with the other family to keep it going. So my family dies out. She had a couple of operations, but they couldn't join the tubes up again. Let's not talk about my family. Why don't you two tell me something about yourselves? I've heard that authors can earn two or three hundred yuan for a night's writing. Is it true?

Zhangjiakou. Let's get out and stretch our legs.

The Sea

This 10,000-ton Shanghai-registered ocean-going freighter has been sailing the high seas and docking in the world's harbours for many years.
   A sailor of thirty-four.

Sure it's tough. You're at sea for days or weeks on end without seeing land, not even an island. Apart from the boat there's nothing . . . That's why you find yourself getting all sorts of ideas. Even "positive thinking" goes off. I'll give you an example: all those songs going on about the sea and how big and vast it is. It's true. We loathe it because it's too fucking big. You never get to the end of it.

Sometimes you get fed up to the back teeth with it, like when the main engine's gone and the auxiliary engine's bust too, and you can't fix them, and you're drifting at sea for days on end working extra shifts round the clock, trying to repair them. You're bushed, pissed off. That's when you want to tell the sea to get fucking lost because you're going home. Then you take a breather and carry on with the repairs. You even find yourself enjoying the misery.

What's so great about foreign travel? When I was a kid I was jealous of our neighbour because he took a bus to work every day. I thought being grown-up and going to work by bus every day was going to be terrific. But it was the last thing he wanted. He'd much rather have worked at home. Now though I really do envy people like him who can go home every night.

I'd already been abroad a lot of times before I joined the ocean shipping company. I spent over four years on an army farm in Yunnan. Our company was on the frontier, and we'd been so revolutionary there we were on our uppers. You couldn't buy anything – you had to

[315]

go over to the other side to do your shopping. Burma was just across the paddy-fields. No barbed wire, just a frontier marker, and frontier guards were few and far between – it's a peaceful frontier. You weren't even supposed to buy the stuff the Burmese brought over to our side to sell, let alone go to markets over there – but really nobody bothered. Even our company commander and political instructor were buying stuff – they had to eat too. They took Chinese money in Burmese markets. They like to buy factory-made goods on our side, because ours have always been cheaper than theirs. I got twenty-nine yuan a month, and half of it went over the border – all our oil, flour and monosodium glutamate came from the other side. Sometimes one of the frontier guards would see us and interfere because we were city kids, not local people. He'd shout at us to come back, and we'd just ignore him. We knew he had to shout, but he wouldn't shoot. We'd even yell back, "Don't get us wrong, captain. We're just going to buy oil."

Yes, I thought about going over for good, and I damn near did. But when I got to the border I felt terrible. It wasn't the same as all those quick trips across. I couldn't bring myself to do it. I'd have missed China. That was the time when we were still "struggling against self and repudiating revisionism", and like a stupid idiot I confessed. So I ended up being transferred to a rubber plantation in the mountains, over forty kilometres from the border. But I still made trips to the markets.

Our oil ration was only 150 grammes a month, that's five measly grammes a day. You never even saw a spot of it floating on your soup. We had a joke about oil: you could just get the spirit of it. There's a story behind that. We had to read something from Chairman Mao's works before work every day. One day the political instructor had a warning for us before we looked at the day's quotation: "There's no need to quibble over every word in Chairman Mao's directives: what matters is to get the spirit of it." That made us take notice all right. The "supreme directive" we were studying that day was about how we'd won the war even though the soldiers had it so tough with only fifteen grammes of oil and twenty-five grammes of salt a day, or something like that. So we did our sums. We were getting even less oil than the Red Army soldiers. Of course I know it was much tougher for the Red Army than for us. Apart from anything else, they didn't have a market to go to.

I had to pull a few strings before I got into the ocean shipping company.

There's a very rigid rank system on board — captain, chief officer, second officer, third officer, chief engineer, second engineer and all that. There's even a chief cook, second cook and third cook. There are ranks for the whole crew, and you have to climb the ladder a rung at a time. Getting a red light on promotion has never bothered me: I'm not a high-flyer. What does bother me is that as ordinary blokes we ocean-going sailors feel horny too — we've got all the usual desires and feelings, and we miss home. But the job we do isn't like ordinary ones.

It's all very well to say that women are dead keen to marry us, but if they do they become grass widows. They put up with that because they hope to get something out of it — they want the foreign goodies we bring back for them. But what's in it for us? D'you think we'd go through all this hell just for a colour TV? Is it worth it? Women aren't so wonderful either. My wife divorced me. She'd been messing around with someone else. The court gave our kid to her. Of course I miss him.

When we get back to Shanghai after six months at sea there aren't any berths for us, so we have to wait in the roadsteads for two or three days. You landlubbers don't have the faintest idea about what we have to put up with. I've come to hate landlubbers. It's hard even to see my kid. I did take him out for a western meal once. All those people in their fancy clothes made complete idiots of themselves. They dipped their knives in the soup and licked the serving spoons. Ignorant oafs.

Sometimes we go ashore when we're in a foreign port and sometimes we don't. We often see other Chinese around the docks and the cities. There's one difference you can see — mainlanders never ever go to brothels, and our Taiwan compatriots can whenever they like. We all get on fine, we have parties and visit each other's boats. There's not really anything to see in a boat. Their boats usually claim to be Chinese-built and they show us the "Made in China" plates on them, but their innards are usually foreign. We've got some completely China-built boats, but this one isn't. Everything except the hull is imported. Never mind. Roll on the day when all the ships in the world are Chinese.

Once a couple of overseas Chinese sailors from Saudi Arabia — they were on a Danish-registered boat — wanted to come aboard. We were in Kobe, Japan, pumping water. We brought them to the ship with us in our launch, they came aboard for a moment, then they went back ashore with the launch. What they said was, "We've never been back to China, so if we can just stand on your deck for a moment we'll have stood on Chinese territory." That really moved me. I'd been on Chinese territory all along.

You don't just get a sense of China's dignity, you get a sense of personal dignity too. I daresay that of all the ships in the world ours are the only ones where you won't find *Playboy*. Foreign sailors ask very rude questions about that, like "Aren't you human?" We've got an answer: "It's because we're human that we have to show a bit of human dignity." But those fucking idiots ashore keep sending us rubbish films – all politically correct. We know them backwards by now. When we were at anchor the other day they sent us a new movie they said hadn't been released yet – *The Girl in a Red Shirt*. She was wearing a shirt with no buttons – one she couldn't take off.

We feel very close to land, and very far away too. When we come back we're always asking people ashore about some news story. "Don't know." Then we ask about another one. "Don't know." Huh! They know even less about what's going on than we do. They don't listen to the radio or read the papers at all. But when we're at sea every day we strain to hear Radio Beijing through all the interference. You'd have to go on a long voyage to understand.

I've given you one long grumble, but for all that I'd really hate to have to leave the sea. How about that for a contradiction? We've all got these complaints, but we're really serious about modernizing the country: that's no contradiction.

If I really had to say things like "having the motherland at heart" I could, but we've heard a lot too much of that stuff. When you're in a force-twelve hurricane and feeling so sick you wish you were dead, when you haven't got the faintest idea what's happened to your family and don't even know if your wife's walked out on you, when you can see how poor we are from the contempt the foreign bosses show us – well, why the hell would we be putting up with all that if it wasn't for China? It's only when you've left the country behind that it fills your heart.

The sea's a right bastard but wonderful too. Don't think of it as blue. It can be any colour – red, white, blue, yellow – beautiful colours people ashore could never imagine. If you've never been to sea you've never lived. You're just tied to your hand-basin.

Hard-earned Money

Lanzhou. Wu Baosheng, twenty-nine, a worker in a construction company. His lean, dark features hint at energy and intelligence. A friend takes us to visit his flat, which has undergone "eight modernizations".

That's just a way they have of getting at me. My little flat with its "eight modernizations" probably won't even count as comfortable by the time China's four modernizations are finished.

Well, you've seen for yourselves what I've got here. The flat's the same size as an ordinary worker's and up here on the fifth floor it's cold in winter and hot in summer, which makes it the last place anyone would want to live. This block was jerry-built and the roof leaks, but it meets specifications. Just look at the ceilings – where the rain's got in they're as stained as a baby's pants. Could you get away with work like that abroad? Without decent housing, decent furnishings are a waste of money.

Laugh if you like, but I bought all my "eight big items" by cutting down on my food. When I was abroad I didn't waste money on cigs or drink. If I took a stroll round the town I'd look inside a restaurant and come straight out, then go into a fast-food place and be straight out of there too. Everything I saw was too expensive, so I simply cut out lunch and went back to the site canteen for supper. As I saved my money I had it all earmarked – so much for a fridge, so much for a nylon shirt, and so on. None of us came back empty-handed. We had all the foreign gear – fridges, colour TVs, radio cassettes, cameras, sewing machines, bikes, watches, calculators. Some of the lads even got motorbikes. All we missed out on were guns and atom bombs. You'd never get all that in half a lifetime here.

We weren't a foreign-aid project, helping our poor brothers in

[319]

Africa, Asia and Latin America. Anyhow, we saw that they don't live any worse than us. We were a labour export. The top foreigners provided the equipment and the advanced technology, and we provided labour power and the more basic technology. We were working as subcontractors on construction projects undertaken by advanced countries in developing countries. The country I went to was Iraq, to work on a civil engineering project. The bosses were French, the site managers were Germans and the foremen were Japanese. In fact it made no difference what country you were from. As far as the Iraqis were concerned, all the labour was supplied by the French contractors. It was all just a business transaction. We weren't supporting anyone, or being anyone's allies or kith and kin.

I went out there in 1982. It started with a rumour in our civil engineering brigade that there was going to be a job abroad. Everyone got very excited. Out of more than 400 of us not one had ever been in a plane. So we were all raring to take a look at the States or Japan. When we were told it was in the Third World, and Iraq at that, we lost interest. There was the heat, and there was the Iran–Iraq war, which was scary. Besides, though we hadn't been abroad we weren't ignorant. We helped Vietnam, and they attacked us. We helped Albania, and they badmouthed us. And then there was the TanZam Railway: we poured money into that like water, and what did we get to show for it but another burden? We're a poor country, and we go on spending our money like there was no tomorrow just to buy more obligations. Besides, the pay's lousy on foreign-aid projects and you can't afford to buy anything to bring home, apart from a watch or a bike at the most. Was it worth it?

Then the leadership held a meeting to mobilize us. We were told we'd be earning hard currency for the country, and keeping the brigade in work – our brigade hadn't had enough work for ages. Then he said, "This isn't a foreign-aid project, it's the export of labour, and the principle is that the country, the unit and the individual all do well out of it. Let me spell it out: you'll all be bringing colour TVs and fridges back with you. I can guarantee that everyone who goes will get himself modernized ahead of time." That really livened things up, and a lot of people volunteered.

Later, some of the volunteers backed out, with excuses like problems at home, the wife being sick, the kids being too young or their own health not being up to it. The first real reason was that the Iran–Iraq war was hotting up, and they were scared of getting killed and becoming ghosts far from home. The second was that they didn't set much store by what the leaders said – it would only need a circular from the Centre with red print at the top to put paid to their colour television, and they'd have spent two years being roasted in the sun for nothing. After the ten terrible years of the Cultural Revolution, people don't trust officials much. The third reason was that they'd seen a foreign film a few days earlier about what a dreadful time workers have working abroad, and they all took it as a warning of what to expect. I wasn't scared of getting killed, I didn't mind leaving home, and didn't give a damn about hardship and exhaustion. We're born to suffer and get exhausted. So I stayed with it. On top of that, things were bad at home – my old lady and I were always at each other. I wanted as much distance between us as possible so as to have some peace. When I went abroad she started carrying on with other men. I'm divorced now.

I wasn't bothered about political checks – there weren't any black marks on my record – and I was technically qualified. I'm a grade-four plumber and central-heating fitter. By the regulations you only needed to be grade two. Before we went we had a fortnight's study, learning the rules for dealing with foreigners and all that. Some of it came in handy later on, and some of it turned out to be completely useless. For instance, "Don't go to red-light areas" and "Don't speak on behalf of China". Could we afford to fool around in whorehouses and still get that colour television? Who would have taken me as representing China anyway? Only a complete idiot. But it was obvious to me in Iraq that the only way you can be sure of not disgracing yourself is by being rich. In that society the rich can do what they like. We were each given a clothing grant to get a smart new Sun Yatsen suit.* We had to put on a good show. We weren't representing the government, but we were Chinese. We didn't want them thinking we were going there as coolies because we were on our last legs.

There were sixty-eight of us. We had a group leader, three section leaders, a Party secretary, six members of the Party branch committee and three Party sub-branch heads. Apart from the group leader, who was in charge of all us Chinese and didn't work, all the other cadres worked with the rest of us.

The Germans twigged that our Party secretary was the man to come

---

* What foreigners call "Mao suits" were first popularized by Sun Yatsen.

and see about anything. They realized that the Communist Party's in charge.

When we left China they didn't even check the pictures in our passports – they just counted the passports and counted us, and we got on the plane. I'd expected that soaring through the clouds would be something terrific, but once we were airborne it was dead boring – a train's more interesting. You couldn't see a thing. When we refuelled at Rawalpindi the foreigners on the plane bought some Pakistani souvenirs, but we didn't have a cent in foreign currency, so all we could do was look. Baghdad was a shock. This was the capital? It wasn't even up to Lanzhou. People from our embassy met us at the airport, and our baggage wasn't searched. The customs officer just counted us, patted each of us on the shoulder, and said, "Friend, friend" in Chinese sixty-eight times over. He was supposed to know Chinese, but "friend" and "best good" were the only things he could say, and the second was wrong. I thought that if their half-educated people were dressed like field marshals, then ours, who are none too brilliant either, ought to be a bit better turned out, instead of looking like bales of raw cotton. But when I came back, blow me if our customs officers weren't dressed like field marshals too.

We had two days off after the journey, then we went to the worksite. It took us a whole day to get there by coach. The site was quite a shock, really bleak, like our Great Northern Waste. We called it the Great Southern Waste there and then. It was as hot at 40° centigrade above as the Great Northern Waste is cold at 40° below. You can keep out the cold by wearing more clothes but there's nothing you can do about heat: you can't rip off a layer of skin.

Was that work tiring! In China I was used to all the little freedoms you have in a big collective, but I tell you I got whacked out over there. But you get used to that after a while. Besides, I liked overtime: overtime rates abroad are really high, and I'd never have got my "big eight" without it. The wages were the equivalent of 800 US dollars a month but it nearly all went to the government. What we got was our usual pay in China, plus the same again in foreign currency, and various other allowances on top. We had to do overtime to earn more. I earned a heck of a lot more than I do in China, but by foreign standards . . . Well, it would depend where you made your comparisons.

We didn't get on well with the foreman. He was always itching to hit people. We Chinese stood together. The first time he hit one of us we all stopped work. We didn't call a strike – we just downed tools. In the end our leader called him a pig. After that he didn't lift a finger against any of us, but he went on swearing at us. He was wasting his breath. We couldn't understand – we just knew he was swearing.

Later on I came to see that we were in the wrong sometimes – we really did work sloppily, not giving it everything the way the Japanese and the Hongkongers did. Then our leader said, "It'll be a disgrace if our mainland group can't beat the Hongkong–Taiwan group." So without telling anyone we started competing with them, and of course we got ahead. The men from Hongkong and Taiwan were contract workers too. They were better paid than us, and got more work done too. Their overall productivity was higher than ours – they were highly mechanized.

It was synchronized building. In China we put the building up first, then do the plumbing, and install the equipment last of all. But they do it all at the same time. We made fools of ourselves when we were competing with the Hongkong–Taiwan group. One day our job on the worksheet was to build walls to the height of 1.75 metres. We did it by 4 p.m., talked it over and decided to overfulfil our quota. By the time we finished work we'd laid two extra courses of concrete blocks. At 2 a.m. our leader woke us all up and told us to take the two extra courses away again. We were hopping mad with the so-and-so till he explained: "In two hours the cranes will be lifting the equipment in over the walls. You've made them too high to get the stuff over. You've got to take the top layers off." We never realized how scientific it all was. So we had to remove the blocks, which took us till 3.50 a.m. At 4 a.m. the cranes arrived. They were finished by 7.30, and we put the blocks all back again. We learned our lesson from that: no more mindless overfulfilling of quotas! Their worksheets were produced by computer.

When I didn't have any plumbing to do, I worked as a brickie's mate; and when we had a lot of plumbing, the brickies helped us out. We're scientific too! We stick together and co-operate – that's where we're better. Other countries – and I'm not trying to run them down – really are pretty selfish. They won't help anyone. The other Chinese are all right. The men in the Hongkong–Taiwan group helped each other. The Taiwan lads more of course than the Hongkong ones: they treated each other right. With foreigners it's usually what's mine is mine, and what's yours is yours. With us Chinese, what's mine is yours, and what's yours is mine. Mind you, there are a few crooks who think what's mine is mine and what's yours is mine too. So we Chinese are the very best apart from the few of us who are the very worst. Well, no, that's only the workers. Foreign capitalists are really disgusting. They make their pile by ripping everyone off.

We got on just fine with the Taiwan lads: never mind the ideological differences, we were pals. Once one of the blokes in the Hongkong–Taiwan group said, "You mainlanders are brilliant – you built the Great Wall." "The Great Wall belongs to all us Chinese," I told him, "not just us mainlanders." Then he said he was a real Taiwanese, not someone who'd gone there from the mainland. That set me back – was he for Taiwan independence? He said he didn't think the Kuomintang's Three People's Principles* could unite China or that communism could unite Taiwan. I didn't think there was any point in arguing, so I said, "We're both workers, pal, so why argue about politics? Let's work together on the job for now. We'll see how it all turns out." Keep off politics and you can stay friends.

My money was earned the hard way. You'd never have been able to take the heat. Anywhere in the sun would burn your hand, and the sweat poured off you in buckets. But there was air-conditioning in the hostel and the food was great. So in two ways life was better than in China.

A rumour went round just before we came home. We'd bought all our stuff. Some of it we had out there, and some we were going to collect back here. The story was that we'd not be able to get it out through their customs. We all checked the list of things we'd be allowed to take out and found that we really were over the limit. Later the Taiwan lads told us that the customs there were very partial to bribery – all you had to do was slip them something. But what? The Taiwan lads said, "When we went home to visit our families we gave them Tiger Balm. That won't work now. You'll probably be okay if you give them Chinese fans." And it really did work!

When I got back to China I was a rich man.

My mum was a widow and I was her only kid, so I was spoiled. I was always shooting my mouth off, and I couldn't change my ways after Mum died. When I finished junior middle school I stoked the boiler in a theatre, but I couldn't take the theatrical atmosphere so I got myself transferred to the construction brigade.

Of course my standard of living's high. And my future plans? Marry a new wife, of course.

* Nationalism, democracy and people's livelihood, Sun Yatsen's summary of his political aims which became the official Kuomintang ideology.

16

SHOW BUSINESS

Song of Praise

*She was making pickles and her hands were covered in red chilli
powder. Young people in China might not recognize her name,
but they have all sung her songs.*
  Gu Jianfen, forty-eight years old, born in Japan.

I earned my first songwriting fee when I was still at university. I spent it
on a pair of leather shoes. I was a poor student but life was fun. Now I
have a certain political status and materially I'm quite well off. I do
better than most composers of my generation. I earn 110 yuan a month
and my husband is on about a hundred. If one of my songs appears in a
magazine, I get about ten yuan, or twenty if it's recorded, and a bit
more if I conduct it myself. I've earned over 3000 yuan in fees in the last
few years. That's not such a lot. Composers of film music get much
more. They can use a few simple bars over and over. I can't compete
with them. Some music is forgotten as soon as it's written, but my songs
have been very successful.

I spent my early childhood in Japan. We came back to China in 1942.
In 1958, I was branded a rightist. I was sent away from the Central
Song and Dance Ensemble to Liuhe county in Jiangsu province. It
didn't seem so terrible a prospect. We had a great send-off with drums
and gongs. As I did come from a bourgeois family and had some rightist
ideas, I felt at the time that I needed to reform. My husband was a
choreographer and his mother had been Japanese. That was another of
our crimes. In Jiangsu, with some colleagues, I set up a music school.

Then came another twist to the campaign. Our family was to be sent
to an ethnic-minority area in Guizhou province. Lucky we didn't go.
Small fry like us would have counted as big villains in a remote place
like that. We'd have been killed in some struggle in the Cultural
Revolution. Our director threatened to hand us over to the Public

Security Bureau because we wouldn't go. I got in touch with the Jiangsu Provincial Song and Dance Ensemble and they agreed to take us on but our director vetoed it. He said life in Jiangsu was too easy; we had to go somewhere really tough to be reformed. It wasn't a personal grudge. It's just the way things were then.

In the end, my husband was sent to Inner Mongolia while I went to Yunnan to collect folksongs. The dance troupe my husband directed had won a silver medal at an international youth festival in 1959. That made the Central Ensemble reluctant to let us go permanently because the medal would have gone with us. So in the end the decision was made to retain us under supervision although we weren't allowed to appear in public. A collection of my songs was put together in Shanghai – it got as far as being typeset – but it was suppressed before printing, so I lost the work of several years. When I made enquiries about it recently, I was told that even the publisher's editor hadn't survived, so there was no hope for the proofs. It brought home to me how lucky I'd been to get through.

Recently I wrote a humorous song about a woman of thirty who'd been married five years but still couldn't live with her husband because they didn't have a place of their own. When her factory finally allocated her a flat everyone was delighted and came to help her move. At the first performance the audience laughed so loudly they nearly lifted the roof off. Some people criticized me for using a song to expose social problems. In fact it does just the opposite. It's a song of praise. After all, she got her flat in the end. How many young people manage that? Precious few.

My most painful memory? My piano. We lived in Dalian at the time of the Japanese surrender in 1945. Soviet Red Army tanks were demolishing Japanese houses. Tins of food lay about in the streets along with the steelyards used to weigh things in the shops. We still use one of those as a rolling-pin at home. The Japanese just wanted to sell up and go home, so everything was very cheap. I asked my father for a piano. "How could we possibly afford anything so expensive?" he asked. "Go and have a look anyway," I begged. "The street's full of them." He came back with a Yamaha – the very best Japanese model – that he'd bought out of the money he took for the groceries.

It went with me everywhere. When my mother was seriously ill in the sixties we had to spend a lot on her treatment. Then she and my father died, and of course their funerals cost a lot. At one time the four of us had only thirty yuan. We sold everything except the piano. That was my life.

By 1966 we'd finally cleared our debts. Then the Cultural Revolution began and I couldn't play the piano again until 1973. If anybody heard you playing then you could be in big trouble and you can't play the piano soundlessly. In 1971, after Lin Biao's death, I "liberated" myself. I exchanged sheet music for recipe books and became a first-class cook. Later I took up knitting and spent hours poring over patterns.

I dusted the piano every day. Then I think I got a bit deranged. I couldn't bear the sight of it any more and I kept thinking about selling. My husband warned me I would regret it but I went ahead and did it.

I wanted it to be taken a long way away, and we arranged I shouldn't know who'd bought it. But I do know now and I do regret it. It was my fault: I wasn't tough enough.

Later, I couldn't bear life without a piano, so in the end my husband got hold of one which had been covered with posters. That's the one I have now. It's state property but it has been allocated for us to use.

My success came after the smashing of the Gang of Four. I couldn't compare with some of the younger composers but I wrote a lot. I was so glad I hadn't been killed or gone mad in the Cultural Revolution. Some people have said I write vulgar songs. Perhaps they mean popular songs – or perhaps not. I don't know. If one of my songs is criticized I'm the one held responsible, not the lyricist. My output has slowed in the past year because I am trying to write better. I think about 300 of my songs have been published.

Sixth Time Lucky

Guan Guimin. Singer, tenor. Born in 1946, Changzhi, Shanxi province.

I come from a family of vegetable farmers. We couldn't even afford a two-string Chinese fiddle. I made myself one out of a crate I picked up. I stole the strings too: I clipped some hairs from the tail of a horse that belonged to the collective. Only when I was in middle school did I earn enough money to buy a real instrument – a cut-price one that cost me two yuan. It took me a whole summer vacation to earn them.

After agricultural technical school, I went into a factory and played the Chinese fiddle and trumpet in its after-hours propaganda troupe. I was twenty-six when my solo singing talent was "discovered". The choirmaster of a Beijing song and dance ensemble who was back in Shanxi to visit his family recommended me for an audition with his ensemble.

I couldn't afford a ticket to Beijing, so I hitched a ride on a freight train from Changzhi to Taiyuan, at the start of 1973. That 800-kilometre trip through the mountains just about turned me to ice. And I was scared to death once I got to Beijing – a hick like me had never seen that many judges or pianos that big. They said my voice was pretty good, but I was too old. That was it, one sentence and I was sent home. When I got to Beijing the next summer, I'd learned my lesson. I auditioned for three troupes. But again I got nowhere. I had no "in", no big names behind me, not even a letter of introduction.

When I got back to Changzhi there was a big to-do about it. The boss criticized me for neglecting my work and my workmates ribbed me for wanting to go to Beijing. But I didn't let it get me down. "I'll try again next year," I said, very calmly.

When I went to Beijing for the third time, I made it into the troupe.

But when they tried to get me transferred, my factory asked them what right they had to transfer me, seeing we weren't under the same ministry. I kept on pleading with the boss, but when he finally agreed, the opening in the ensemble had gone. Fate was just playing around with me.

After the Gang of Four was smashed, I went to Beijing a fourth time and made it into two different troupes right away. But the factory boss who'd agreed to let me leave had now transferred out himself. The people from those two troupes who wanted me were given the cold shoulder. And, when the Shanxi Song and Dance Ensemble heard that Beijing was interested in me, they wanted me kept at home too. There went another year.

I refused to give up hope, and went to Beijing my fifth time at the end of '77. When I made it into the News and Documentary Film Ensemble, they went straight to the top men in the State Council for approval. Shanxi had to let me go then. But once I was back in Shanxi waiting for my transfer order, new problems cropped up. A whole lot of companies closed in on me – not to push me away this time, but to fight for me. There was one army ensemble that came and shoved a uniform at me: "Put this on right now, we want to get moving," they said. But it didn't work, I'd already agreed to join the other ensemble.

The sixth time I went to Beijing, it was on government money. I was twenty-nine and finally starting on my career. On my way to the capital, I kept thinking about my experience the previous five years – all my savings in that time had gone to "lay the railroad". I knew every park in Beijing as I'd had nowhere else to spend my lunch hours except to take siestas on park benches. The Ministry of Railroads and the Park Bureau owe me some thanks.

In 1979 I made it big with three hit songs, one of which was "Our Work Is Sweeter than Honey". The papers said I'd become a star overnight.

Now I'm doing further studies at the Music Academy. Working for a diploma.

Cabaret

There was an atmosphere of tremendous excitement while she was singing. People began to clap as soon as her act was announced. She wore an evening dress of shimmering lamé, real Hongkong style. It must have been bought for her by the hotel as it would have been paid for in foreign currency. Despite her slight reserve she seemed irrepressibly happy as, clasping her microphone with both hands, she thanked the audience repeatedly.

I'm nervous about speaking to reporters. To tell the truth I don't like them. We get some coming here, applauding us and then going back to write reviews which claim our floorshow is improper and frivolous. I was still making up when they told me that the assistant manager had brought you two in. I got pretty nervous, but once I started singing I forgot all about it.

I'm not much of a talker. Why don't you ask for the restaurant manager or the band leader? We share what we make. There are five in the band and five singers but one hasn't shown up tonight. If I say something wrong it could get everyone into trouble. The restaurant manager is very keen to have us here. In the daytime this place is a restaurant serving Chinese food, then at 9.30 p.m. it becomes a tea lounge with a cabaret. I don't understand politics and I'm afraid of annoying the manager if I say something wrong. I don't want to get the sack.

If you really like our music, please say something nice about us. Things aren't at all easy for us.

We're strict with ourselves because we want to keep this job. We lose pay if we're late, and if we don't show up at all, like that singer today, we lose several days' pay. That's a lot because we get about ten yuan a night each. If we sing badly we get hissed. A lot of the audience know their stuff: they can tell at once if you don't get it right. The guys in the band notice if you get a single note wrong and afterwards they tell you to watch it. When that happens I rush home and get on my earphones to check how the original singer recorded it.

It's not fair at all to say we flirt with the audience. We're very professional. Before the crackdown they had recently, the streets in Guangzhou had got quite nasty at night and one of the guys from the band had to see us home every evening. If any of us started sleeping around the rest of us would get on to them about it. We had one singer who was really terrific; she'd modelled her style on a famous star from Hongkong. But she was caught sleeping with a foreigner at the hotel so we had to get rid of her. Of course we felt for her and we believe that she'll change. But we had to kick her out because she would have affected the whole group's reputation. We want to stay in business.

We sing pop songs, so naturally our singing style and stage manner is more relaxed. The point is to communicate with the audience. In Shenzhen and Shenkou the cabarets are much freer . . . It's just like Hongkong. They're allowed to chat with the audience and to take requests. If a banned song gets requested they just have to make their apologies and that's an end to it. Teresa Teng's songs are mostly okay. Apart from the few which are specifically banned we're allowed to sing anything. I'd really like to go and sing there if I didn't have a daytime job here in Guangzhou. But I couldn't quit that. What if they decided to stop letting us sing? I'd be in a right mess then. We can't sway to the music too much here or people would say it was indecent. If we had too much eye contact with the audience they'd say we were flirting. Last year when they were searching for pornographic videos and that sort of thing in the campaign against "spiritual pollution", they closed all the cabarets down. It wasn't the first time either. Later the Cultural Bureau agreed to register us when they had checked to see that we met the required standard. We passed because our group is so professional and we work in a large respectable establishment like this.

We're only allowed to sing one foreign song to every four Chinese ones. It's too bad they don't count Taiwan and Hongkong ones as Chinese. After all they're meant to be part of China, aren't they? Anything should be okay so long as it isn't reactionary or porno-graphic, don't you think? Anyway the audience likes that sort of song and they like the way we sing, otherwise they wouldn't come. Most of the people who stay at the hotel are from Hongkong and Macao but the majority of our audience are local kids who run their own small businesses or street stalls. They're not making fortunes but they don't mind paying five yuan for a glass of coke and a couple of hours listening to us. It's not a bad deal, is it? When one of the other singers is on I like sitting at this table watching the audience. I watch their eyes and their expressions. I can't do that when I'm on stage myself, I wouldn't be able to take it all in. They're all so absorbed there's not a sound to be heard. I get a real kick out of it. Music's got such fantastic power. I never tire of watching them.

It's funny how I've turned out. I never sang as a child, absolutely never. No one in our family was into singing or guitar or anything. My parents work in a laundry. It was a world without music, even Cantonese music. I'm twenty-one this year, so I was three years old when the Cultural Revolution began. Then it was all revolutionary songs like "Sailing on the Seas Depends Upon the Helmsman". They were okay I think, but I was so young, I don't remember them very well. The songs I remember best are the ones about Chairman Mao that they played after National Day the year that Lin Biao died in a plane crash. There was a Mongolian one and a Korean one. I was in my first year at primary school and they were on the loudspeakers and the radio all the time. I thought they were wonderful.

It was my brother who got me started. He can't sing a note himself but he sells cassettes and records. At first he operated on the black market. He's got a permit now but he doesn't deal in the same stuff any more. In 1977 he was mostly selling Teresa Teng recordings. Sometimes he'd get cheated. He'd buy in tapes which had one decently recorded track at the start but the rest of the tape would be badly done or empty. The only way was to listen to the tapes right through. And then of course our customers would want to test them too. That's why I heard them over and over. I was in junior middle school then. All the girls got together to write down Teresa Teng's songs. Doing it from the radio we often got the words wrong. When I did her numbers everyone said I sounded just like her.

My brother said he wanted to see what one of his friends thought of my singing. He took me to see Teacher Lin, who plays the trumpet in the band. We all call him that because he teaches sports in a middle school. I sang pieces by five different singers with the guitar accompaniment. He said I had a feel for music and asked me which singer's style suited me best. I didn't know anything about style. I just copied anything I was given.

Teacher Lin was one of the first people to be involved in cabarets in Guangzhou. He's been at it four years, he's an old hand. One evening he took me for a trial with one of them. I got up on the stage in an outfit my brother had borrowed for me. The band began to play and I sang. Afterwards everyone clapped. I felt the thrill of performing for an audience for the first time. When we got home my brother asked me why I'd been gazing at the ceiling all through my song. I didn't even know I'd been doing it. I hadn't thought about anything but the song. No wonder I never thought to be scared.

That's how it all started. Later Teacher Lin gave me the score of a new song and asked me to sing it. I told him I couldn't sing something that I'd never heard. I didn't know what he meant by doing it straight from the score. Everyone in the band was astonished, but I'd never even heard of sight-reading. Anyway, Teacher Lin and the others say I've got a good ear for music and they've taught me to sight-read. Now they say I sing better than ever.

Some singers are young people out of work. Those of us who have got jobs do our eight-hour day and then work here until midnight. Of course it's exhausting, but it's great. If they closed us down life would be terribly boring with nowhere to sing and no audience. When we finish each night we go and have supper at a street stall. We talk about singing and all sorts of things. Even when I get home I can't get to sleep with all the songs still going round in my head. I keep thinking about how I could do them better. The professionals think we're too casual but actually we take our music just as seriously as they take theirs. We think they're dead old-fashioned. And how many of them could get an audience going in a huge place like this the way we do? How many young people would even want to listen to their boring old songs? Our band's always improvising so the music doesn't sound stale. Of course we use amplifiers – all pop bands do. A lot of our songs have to be sung in Cantonese to get the right effect.

I mostly sing in Zhen Ni's style nowadays. It suits me. I couldn't sing in my own style: the audience wouldn't go for it. They only like you if you sound like some big-name singer.

When they closed us down we hired a van and toured round the villages. We had bigger audiences than here. Our take was higher too because the peasants have more money than people in the cities. But it was too tiring. We were doing a round trip of a hundred kilometres every night. On the way home everyone except the driver would be asleep. The next day it would be work as usual. We can't afford to take it easy. The people we work with all know that we earn about 300 yuan more than they do, so we can't give them any excuse to complain.

My full-time job? I work in a shoe shop.

Sideline

*Wang Meng is twenty-nine. He is cheerful, always laughing, and chubby. The way he talks and behaves reminds you of a big-bellied Maitreya Buddha in a temple. He tells us that the work he now has in mind is designing the office that Monkey would have had when he was Protector of the Horses in heaven for the Jade Emperor.**

I'm a stage designer with the professional drama company of the Guangxi Autonomous Region. But I haven't done any serious work for the company: there's nothing to do. Hardly anyone wants to see spoken plays in Guangxi nowadays. There's nothing new, incisive or profound. What I'm concerned with is putting something on the stage that'll make the audience sit up. But all people want to see is Cantonese opera. When the Cantonese opera troupes go to the villages peasants who've had a good harvest will spend money like crazy to get operas – any operas – performed, and for nights on end. As long as there's plenty of noise they're happy. What if the troupe has only brought a couple of sets of costumes and props? No problem. Doesn't matter what period or which opera – just sing! They're even doing operas that have been banned for ages. And if you don't know the opera, just fake it. The audience don't care – they're enjoying themselves.

But with our spoken plays the more performances we give, the more money we lose. The best thing is for us not to perform at all. Every province in the country has a provincial spoken drama company, and on top of that some central government departments have got their own, as well as the armed forces and the Trade Union Federation. Below that there's a whole load of companies run by prefectures, cities and counties. If you ask me, they all ought to be closed down, apart from a few really good ones.

* An episode in the sixteenth-century fantasy novel *Journey to the West*.

I studied stage design at university, though I'd never been interested in that sort of thing when I was a kid. What I really liked was painting. I've planted rubber on Hainan Island. The same thing happened to all of us who left school and went down to the countryside. You ride in a truck across mountain after mountain for days on end without knowing where you are. Then they tell you to get out and suddenly a horde of bare-chested men in patterned shorts comes rushing out to welcome you with drums and gongs and slogans on red banners. That was the state farm. Later on, I remember lying in my thatched hut looking out through the window at a piece of clothing that had been hung out to dry as it blew in the wind. It looked just like a person. That's when I decided to take up painting again and get out of there.

I got out and became a dancer in a theatre company. Can you imagine it? Someone like me doing splits! I learned how to do the model ballets and performed in *The White-Haired Girl*.* I took the university entrance exams in 1977. That year stage design was the only subject on offer that had anything to do with art. After the exams I waited for days and days until finally someone told me there was a letter for me at the gate. I could see it was an official letter from the college. The people round me all said, "If you've passed you've got to stand us a meal." "Nothing doing," I said. "It's bound to be a rejection notice." I took the letter without showing any expression and without even letting my heart beat any faster, walked slowly back to my dormitory, climbed on the bed, pulled my quilt over me, tore the envelope open and lifted the quilt up to have a look: "Admitted". I let out a great sigh of relief and took it out in the sunlight to have another look at it. I really was in, damn it! Only then did I get happy. If you know what despair really feels like you'd best not bring it on yourself. I learned how to avoid that a long time ago. It's very easy: don't have any premature illusions.

I wasn't a very well-behaved student – and I didn't think much of the college's teaching methods. They issued the students with the texts of the lectures in advance, then the teachers read the lectures out. Was that teaching? There was one teacher they brought in from another province who knew nothing. He was really vicious. You had to paint with the colours he wanted. When he walked past he'd put his hand out

* During the Cultural Revolution years there were only a handful of officially approved "model" stage shows, of which two were ballets, *The White-Haired Girl* being one of them. This was based on an earlier and much better folksong-style opera of the same title.

and change one of my brushstrokes. As soon as he'd gone I'd change it back. Then he'd change it again, and I'd change it back again until he got fed up with me and told me to clear out. That suited me fine. If he'd been running a private school he could teach his students to hold their brushes upside down for all I cared. Colour sense is an artistic question. In the end that teacher cleared off and stopped teaching.

There are too many restrictions in stage design. You're like a woman with bound feet. There's the script, the director, technical considerations, and other things too. I got good marks in my own subject. Apart from one 4 in my first year from a teacher I quarrelled with I got 5 in all the other years.* My graduation design was for the Indian play *Sakuntala*. I set it in a theatre like a sports stadium with spectators all around, layer upon layer of them, three-dimensional. But we haven't got any theatres like that in China. It set the teachers quarrelling among themselves. Some of them liked it and some of them thought it was a load of rubbish. One of the teachers went to England for a conference not long ago. He took my designs with him and people had nice things to say about them.

I'll tell you a funny thing about the academy. One of the teachers had the nickname Mr England and we called another one Mr America. That was because they always talked about England and America. Because the teachers quarrelled I ended up being assigned a job back in Guangxi. My girlfriend threatened to break up with me, so we got married. The best assignment you can get after graduating is being kept on at the academy: you can get to see all sorts of new and interesting things, and you've got a chance of being sent abroad for further study. But I'm not one of those. There was no way I'd be kept on at the academy as a teacher. The only students the staff like are the ones who know that one plus one is two and not three.

Nanning's not so bad: you can make a lot of money. I've switched to traditional Chinese paintings, and I turn them out in batches. I pin a whole row of sheets of Chinese paper up on the wall, fill my brush with watery ink, and give each one a dab in turn. Then it's thick ink and the same stroke on each of them. That way I can do a whole batch of identical Gods of Longevity, cats, landscapes or whatever it is. Of course they sell. I have my paintings on show in a gallery in Guilin, and in the tourist season I pull in several hundred yuan. The low season is

---

* In this system of marking 5 is the highest mark.

my time for following my own interests and doing my own work. I do illustrations and comic books too. When I'm doing illustrations I read the beginning of the story and the last few lines, then start drawing. Eight yuan a picture. It doesn't matter if I get the picture wrong and it's nothing to do with the story. If they ask questions I can always find an explanation that'll keep everyone happy. Most fiction's no good: a silly story and rubbishy pictures to match. The plot's usually much worse than the lines in my drawings. The main thing in comic books is to make the characters good-looking, especially the men – they've got to be handsome. It's mostly women who read that sort of stuff when they're telling the story to children and amusing themselves at the same time. I've done some work for films and television too, but the scripts were pretty terrible. I made a bit of money, but only a bit. And I've got my own students as well. Lots of people want to learn how to paint. I don't know what they're after. Do they think there's a future in it? Is it to get into university? For education? I've never tried to find out. I set up a plaster cast or a still life and let them get on with it. I don't correct them much. Most of them would never have a clue even if you held their hands while they were painting for the rest of their lives. I charge them twenty yuan a month each. There are so many people wanting to learn that I can take my pick. I take the students who'll be useful to me in future. There are even a few with real talent. I don't take money from them.

University graduates only get fifty-four yuan a month in Guangxi. That's nowhere near enough to bring up a kid on. They're saying some people ought to get rich first now, aren't they? Well, I'm getting rich. We intellectuals ought to be making decent money and living well. But don't think of me as making good money, absolutely not. If you really wanted to pull it in there are some pretty shameless ways of doing it, like pestering foreign tourists with a bundle of scroll paintings and not leaving them alone till they've bought one. I've even seen a tourist buy one and tear it up on the spot.

I've got a son, and when he came I really didn't want him. When I was waiting for him to be born I was sitting outside the delivery room doing the designs for a television play. When they called me in I tore a strip of paper off the bottom of the picture I was doing, put a bit of red paint on his tiny feet and took his footprints. His first step in life! The little devil's just like me, always laughing. When we're bathing him or dressing him we always make a game of it, and he laughs as though he'd

[340]

never stop. I sing him lullabies to get him to sleep. I know lullabies from a lot of different places – Guangdong, Shanxi, Jiangsu, Anhui. Don't you believe me? Then listen . . . *(He sang the first lines of a whole string of songs in different dialects, like in an all-star singing programme on television.)* The longer you sing to him, the more awake he is. He just gazes at you with wide-open eyes to see what interesting thing you're going to do next. I've discovered that there's only one sound that'll get him to sleep – a low monotone like this, "mmm". When I was teaching him to say "Pa" to me I kept saying, "Pa, pa, pa" over and over again. He opened his eyes wide, held his breath for a long time, and then suddenly burst out with it: "Pa". I was so pleased I almost fainted. Whenever I've played with him since then he's kept on saying it over and over again. I'm his dad, but he's my boss: he costs me eighty yuan a month.

I do all right in Nanning. I'm quite well known in the local art world. I've joined the Zhi Gong Party* and pay twenty cents a month subscription. You can test me on "party history" if you like, but you won't catch me out. It used to be the Hong Bang,† but the party's constitution now says it "accepts the leadership of the Communist Party . . . and works for the four modernizations". It specializes in overseas Chinese work, and all our members come from overseas Chinese and intellectual circles. Think I've got it all off too pat? I could tell you a lot more than this.

Don't get the idea that just because I'm a bit of a joker all I'm interested in is food and bed. My interests in painting used to end with Impressionism. Now I'm into Picasso. I've been searching like hell through masses of Chinese and foreign stuff to find my own style. You get the feeling that people have gone about as far as they can, and that a lot of areas are worked out. You've got to make money, but you never stop experimenting and exploring. A lot of us painters are like that, probably because the really admirable great masters of the past were poor and crazy. A year and a half after graduating I visited the college again. I found that the top students who'd been kept on there were just painting the same old stuff. That made me feel a bit better. I may be stuck there out among those barbaric southerners, but I don't feel at all backward: my thoughts go a lot deeper. If everything were just right I'd

* One of China's minor political parties.
† A secret society with criminal connections.

find it dead boring. "Is that all there is to life?" I'd be asking myself. The thing that really counts is being able to see good art exhibitions from abroad. Of course, the only place they'll bother with is the National Art Gallery, but I'll go even though I have to pay my own train fares. Of course you often have to stand all the way to Beijing and all the way back to Nanning – a day and a half each way – but so what?

People are funny creatures. You can't live without money, but when you've got a bit of money it's not worth the trouble of earning even more. When life gets too comfortable you start trying to make things hard for yourself. That's why the moment my old teacher sent for me I came back here. I've worked it out, and I know I can't earn much here: it all has to be split seventy/thirty. Seventy per cent of what I make goes to the Guangxi authorities, and all I get is thirty or so yuan a month as an allowance for being away from home. But say what you will, this is the real thing for me, and I can get on with my painting and see what happens. There's a chance I may get a big exhibition. But if they mess it all up it'll be "bye bye"* for me. I'll go back to Nanning with a single somersault, like Monkey.

A few days ago I went back to Nanning to see my wife and the kid. I got quite a shock, I can tell you, when one of my painting students came to see me. I asked him what he was painting. He told me he wasn't doing any now, then asked me how much a year's advanced study at the Central Academy would set him back. A thousand, I told him. Okay, he said, he was planning to buy himself a place to live in Beijing and take an advanced course. The way he talked really made me sit up. He told me he'd given up painting for trade. How much had he made? I can't tell you straight out, but . . . but he's already a ten-thousander. How true the saying is, "After a few mere days in your cave you find a thousand years have passed outside." I'd only been away for about six months and I could hardly recognize the place any more. I got the impression in the theatre company that half the staff had become deputy managers or board members of some company or other. The moment you meet them they whip out their cards. Even when everyone was celebrating at a wedding reception they were all talking business. But here I am, still talking about art and complaining about how this is wrong, and I'm fed up with that. Basically, I'm fed up with myself. Why bother? I'd do much better sitting in a café and talking business like

* The speaker used the English expression.

those people, what we call "pig-feeding" in that part of the world. If you make a go of it you can pull money in by the handful, and for no effort at all. Art will never make you a ten-thousander, not even if you bust your gut. If they can all make money, I reckon that I could do just as well as a lot of them by really having a go at it. But I still don't want to go in for business – I'm not that broke yet.

17

YOUTH

Dreams

A girl met on a road in southern Jiangsu.

My name's Wu Liyao. I'm seventeen and in my second year at senior middle school. I've got loads of ideas, but I don't know whether they're crazy or not, and I can't talk about them to my parents. They're always going on about ideas, but if I open my mouth they both jump down my throat: "Children should mind what they're saying or they'll be in trouble!" I don't dare talk to my teacher either. Once, when I said something to her, she told me I'd got too many notions for my own good. But I only said what I thought. Now I keep it all to myself, and they all say I'm making great progress. I don't mind talking to you: you've got nothing to do with me.

Both my parents are doctors; they're very busy. As soon as I was weaned they sent me back to the village, and my grandmother brought me up. I had a great time with my friends – catching locusts, baking them in clay and eating them; swimming in the river and fishing for tiddlers; stealing beans from the fields. My clothes were always torn and dirty. I didn't have a care in the world then. If the sky'd fallen in it wouldn't have bothered me. The sad thing is, once all that's gone you never get it back again.

I'm not saying I go round with a long face all the time now, or I'm especially unhappy. I'll be weeping one minute and laughing the next. Everything interests me, that's my problem. But frankly I don't want to change. In our class, if you do very well without really trying they say you're smug and self-satisfied. If you do badly, that's one black mark less. And if you worked really hard but your marks are only average they praise you for being a conscientious student. Big deal!

My main worry was getting into the Communist Youth League. It looks good if you can, but not everyone who deserves to manages it.

Universities still assess you by whether you're a member, and whether you're a "three-good" student. That means good health, good politics and good marks. If people get the same marks in the university entrance exam they give Youth League members priority, and the "three-good" students can even get in with lower marks. How do they tell if your politics are good? By whether you're in the League, of course! Seeing as how your future depends on it, everyone at middle school's trying to join. I'm all right now. I've finally made it.

I realized pretty quickly what a pushover it is for some people to get in, and just how hard for the rest of us. Some people have just the right sort of personality – nothing special about them, but nothing you could pick on either. But not me. Every time we had a discussion about joining the Youth League the others all said I was smug and self-satisfied, and that I was stand-offish and only ever spent time with a few of the girls. It's not fair. I do care about the class, my work's good, and I'm always helping the others with their homework. Why should they say I'm smug?

There was a girl I was really good friends with – but not any more. We were always sharing things: rulers, pencils – everything. We used to walk home after school and revise for exams together. She wasn't that good at Chinese. But it was a mistake getting involved with her. She got this little calendar with photographs of film stars on it, and everyone crowded round after school to have a look at it. She promised to give it to me, but then a few days later I saw our Youth League secretary sneaking a look at it under her desk. So she'd been sucking up to the cadres! I didn't mind about the calendar especially, but I thought that was pretty low. Anyway, after school, I waited at the gates for her to see if she'd still walk home with me, but she pretended she hadn't seen me – she came out laughing and chattering with a crowd of girls. I was really hurt. And after that she was always talking with them in the breaks between classes. I felt left out, but when I got closer to listen it was all the same boring old stuff: a nice dress one of them had seen; some freak born with two heads; which girls were seeing which boys – who'd looked at whom, who'd touched whom. You've only to look at one of them and they all scream, "Ooh, disgusting!" and giggle. Is that what they mean by not being stand-offish? We used to scoff at them being so silly. So I honestly can't believe she really found it so funny. Anyway, she joined the Youth League after that. It'll serve her right if she fails her Chinese at the end of term.

That turned me off joining the League for a while. But in the end I made it when they started letting the brightest ones in. School kids are really boring, aren't they? So petty!

Everyone thinks if you don't go to university you're a wash-out. They've dropped music and art classes at senior middle school. The teachers are always at us to read more and write more essays. And our parents won't let us watch television or see a film. We're stuck in the same old place all the time and can't even go on a trip anywhere. It's always: "Get to university first; there'll be plenty to see and do later on. You've all the time in the world!" It's crazy! They don't understand me, but I understand them all right: they want us to do well. And okay, I can see why they feel like that, but when we're both working under so much pressure the results aren't all that good. And sometimes you get sick of your parents and teachers, and even society – only of things like that, of course, not with the whole system. Is getting to university honestly the be-all and end-all of our lives? Is that what we have to slave away for? What's the point in a life ruled by exams? If only they'd take our interests and tastes into account in our education. Then we could drop the subjects we don't like and are never going to get anywhere with, and spend the time on what we're good at. That way they'd get the best out of everyone, and the success rate would be high as well.

No, I'm not satisfied with the way we're taught at present. I feel like there's this net around us, holding us in, and cramping our intelligence and abilities.

I wish I could yell at the top of my voice: Let us run our own lives! No doubt in the big cities they'd say, "Teaching here's been adapted to individuals' needs for a long time; we can't see the problem." But just think what a tiny proportion schools like that represent. We haven't got children's centres or youth centres or anything here. Nor have most places. If you wrote a story based on our lives, people would say it gave a depressing picture. But that's exactly how it is. You can't always make young people look at problems historically. There's been progress compared to the past – I accept that. But there's a lot I'm not happy with now. Mind, if you had a society where even the middle-school kids were perfectly content, I'd say it was a society on its last legs.

The teachers are always going on at us about China's long history and glorious civilization, and how we're a brave and hard-working people; and how none of us know how lucky we are being born into a socialist society. Of course I don't take everything we've got for granted. I know socialism's superior to capitalism. But there's good and bad in both systems. I wrote these two essays at junior middle school. One was about a couple always rowing over stupid little things. The point I was making was we should all try and get along together, and love and respect each other. Not just for our own good, but for the country's good and the children's good, and society's good as well. The other was about children who are treated badly by their parents, so they end up being afraid of adults and won't communicate with them. After she'd read them the teacher came to have a word with me. She told me I'd dwelt on the dark side – she wanted something positive. But I don't see anything wrong with writing about what I see going on all around me. Writing about heroes and heroines may set a good example, but if you write about what's wrong with life it makes people think. Anyway, after that I wrote an essay called "Spring Silkworms" praising teachers to the skies – and she gave me a really good grade.

I've started keeping a diary and I write in it every day – but I won't let my father see it. The problem is finding somewhere to hide it: there just isn't anywhere. I'm worried my wild ideas will freak him out if he sees it.

I've had a more practical idea recently: teaching. If I were a teacher and one of my pupils fell asleep in class, I wouldn't tell their parents – they'd only lose out on their bonus taking time off to come and see me. I'd tap the kid on the shoulder and say, "Fallen asleep, have you? Was I being boring?" If I was a teacher I'd know everything my pupils were thinking. Or would I? I'm always thinking, if I were a mother I wouldn't treat my children's ideas and the things they're into the way I'm treated, even if they were wrong. But maybe I'll forget that when the time comes.

I've got confidence in myself and in what I can do – the same way I'm confident we can achieve modernization. And I'm already beginning to get to know myself.

I could go on talking like this for ages, but I reckon I've gone on long enough.

Fly in a Bottle

Nanjing's best hotel, the Jinling, has just been completed and is still practically empty. It is ten in the evening and the attendant is sleepy. "If you want to chat, try the Victory; its coffee bar is open to the public." A smile lights up her tired face. "Go on, you'll find some real Nanjing people there!"

The Victory Hotel coffee bar sells beer too. People are dancing between the tables. The admission charge is one yuan.

Luo Bin, male, nineteen, is holding a glass of beer and smoking a good cigarette.

The Jinling Hotel's got a really top-class coffee shop – it even rotates – but we're not allowed in. This is the only fucking place in the whole city where we can have a bit of fun. The Friendship Store isn't friendly to us Chinese: we're banned. The bloody Jinling Hotel's the same. Smash the place, I say.

Yes, yes, I know all that – the country's short of capital, it brings in foreign exchange, foreigners have to be protected. Heard it all before. In Nanjing, in our own country, why can't we go where foreigners go? We're not allowed into the Dingshan Hotel, the Shuangmenlou or the Jinling. Even the bloody antique shop has a foreigners-only section. Ordinary people can't go into the overseas Chinese shop – and the people who can go there can't get into the Friendship Store. But the foreigners who go there can go to any hotel. It's wrong. My old man's a Party member, but when I ask him if it squares with his Marxism–Leninism he goes dumb.

Of course some places are out of bounds to foreigners, but I'm not allowed in the restricted zones either. Foreigners cruising on the Yangtse aren't allowed to photograph Nanjing Bridge, but neither am I. Besides, I've got no camera.

[351]

I'm waiting for a job. I'm not keeping a stall with a trading licence like some young people – they've got something to do. Not me. I live off my family. Some time ago a foreign woman came here and asked me, "Waiting for a job – does that mean out of work?" She spoke fucking good Chinese, with no bloody foreign twang. I knew she was just acting stupid so I told her, "Out of work means you've lost a job; waiting for a job means waiting for work. It's not the same." That floored her. She said, "You've got a tongue in your head." So I told her, "You ask too many questions!" I couldn't be bothered with her. "You're not my wife," I was thinking. "I don't have to waste my time talking rubbish to you." But I kept a smile on my face to look friendly. Hell, I know some foreigners come here to make friends, and some are spies here to gather secret intelligence. Most of them just come for fun, and ask all sorts of questions. When they go home they write articles to cover their air fare and get famous. That's the way it is. But whatever I think, you disagree with me. We're not on the same wavelength. You're a writer out to make money, so you don't say what you think. Anyone who can put a few fucking words on paper thinks they're a writer and a cut above me. I've got no time for any of them, the liars. As I see it, Liu Binyan's just about the only honest writer around.* Keep your hair on – I'm not getting at you.

Swearing's a habit of mine. It's one of the pleasures of life.

The people who have it toughest in China are the youngsters waiting for jobs. Even by their standards I'm screwed up. Some are doing all right, studying and making something of themselves, being useful to society, and all that. Not me. In this life it doesn't pay to be too much of a goody-goody, or even fairly good. But crime's out – it doesn't pay. The clink's no joy. So I'm a fucking drifter. You're right – as jobless youngsters go, I'm backward.

To be honest, I don't want to go on drifting. I'd like to work. But they all want fucking graduates, not the likes of me. I didn't even graduate from senior middle. Failed six of the seven subjects I took. I only passed in physical education, and a fat lot of use that is.

I've nothing to do, can't even have a good moan. That's why I come here, to dance, shoot the breeze with people I know or strangers, do some drinking. I can't do without it now, even if I've got to borrow the money. My old man only gives me ten yuan a month. That won't even

* See note on p. 268

cover my smokes. So how can I afford to come here? Don't worry – I'm not a burglar or a mugger. I'm a dealer. "Cooking" the Cantonese call it. Not smuggling. Reselling. Take jeans for instance. You can get Chinese-made fake foreign ones at four yuan the pair in Guangzhou. The lads bring a few dozen pairs up here and I resell 'em at ten yuan. If people want to be suckers that's their look-out. Speculation? Perhaps. I don't let my old man know. He's a Party member, working like an ox for the people. I'd be an ox, but where's the fucking cart? So I'm a wild ox.

Of course I believe in communism. The mess I'm in is one thing, but there's nothing wrong with communism. And I'm all for Deng. But for him, we'd have been sent to the bloody countryside. With all these reforms the peasants have divided up all the land, so they can't send us to the countryside any more. I may be down and out, but I'll be damned if I'll go and live in a village! Besides, China's really turned the corner these last few years, and things have loosened up, all thanks to Deng and his Third Plenum.

My name's Luo. I was born in 1964. I'll be twenty this year: my birthday's next month. At school I was like the other kinds, nothing special. I've been waiting for a job for nearly two fucking wasted years now, since September 1982. The residents' committee fixed me up last year as a casual labourer boiling water. I quit after two months – I was wasting my time, pulling in a lousy fifty yuan or so a month. There was no chance in that job of becoming a regular worker. And as a teaboy I had everybody looking down their noses at me. I was better off out of work. I've asked around, but it's hopeless – I've no power and no money. My dad's only a grade-twenty cadre, not even a section chief, so who's going to help me? Hell, I've had a lousy deal, born into a shitty family like that. When factory workers retire their kids can step into their shoes, but that doesn't go for cadres.

Self-reliance? Fine. But how many people actually make it on their own? It's all down to knowing the right people, and having something other people want. But I'm at the bottom of the heap! A girl down here might always catch someone's eye, marry him and make it overnight. But not a hope for me.

A girl would have to be blind to take me. Even if I find a job next year, I'll still have three years to do as an apprentice, so I'll only be earning thirty-eight yuan a month by the end of 1987 or the start of 1988. No one is going to marry me before that.

The government's finding jobs for us all in batches. Next year's bound to be my turn. But I've no proper qualifications, only a school-attendance certificate saying that after three years' study I flunked the final exams. Maybe no one will take me. *(A girl invites him to dance. "Go and find someone else. Can't you see we're talking business?" She looks at him and swears, then moves away.)* She's a tramp! Chucked out of her school. That's how it is in Nanjing, it's always the girls who ask the men to dance. Fucking unnatural. I'm not scared of her! Her bloody boyfriend's a pal of mine. This place has done me no good, which is why I don't let my kid sister come here. She might get up to anything.

There's no hope for me. I just hope the country can get rich, then my life'll be a bit better. I'm proud of being Chinese. I've got the vote. I'm a citizen. It gets up my nose when Chinese crawl to foreigners.

I had some fucking stupid dreams as a kid. Like driving a tank. What an idiot! Mind you, I'd still like to fight in the next fucking world war, defending home and country. I know, I know, everyone wants peace, so why should I want a war? I'm bored out of my mind. If useful people like scientists and engineers die, it's a big loss to the country. If I die, so much the better for China. And at least I'd have done something with my life.

I often think I'm a fly in a glass bottle, with light but no future. I can't open the bottle and let myself out. I don't even fucking know whether I could still do a proper day's work in a factory. It's as well there aren't many like me, or the country'd be in a real mess.

Forty Minutes

The Number 44 bus runs along the old city wall, making a complete circuit of Beijing. The stops have the names of the old city gates, some of which still stand, and others which have gone – Desheng Gate, Xizhi Gate, Chongwen Gate . . . Vehicle Number 3715 is a big, three-door bus with sixty-nine seats. When full it can take over 120 passengers. The two bus conductresses, dressed in identical grey, padded greatcoats, were at the ticket counter in the bus.

The complete circuit takes an hour and five minutes. We got on halfway round, so we had forty minutes with them. Their names were Wang Lian and Bao Mujie. They were both twenty years old.

I've been on the buses for over a year now. My mother used to do the same job. She started in the Great Leap Forward in 1958. She retired at fifty so that I could inherit her job.

These days the bus company doesn't recruit workers from outside. Any vacancies go to the unemployed children of its employees. My father used to be a bus driver. He's always lived in Beijing.

At first my mother didn't want me to take this kind of job. I applied to go to university when I finished school. But then we heard they were going to abolish the system of children stepping into their parents' jobs, so I took over from my mother at once. I probably wouldn't have passed the entrance exam anyway, still . . .

I've been on the buses four years. At first I was on the Number 1 route. It goes past Xidan, Tian'anmen and Wangfujing and along Changan Avenue, so of course it's always full. All day long the bus would be so packed you could hardly breathe. We used to change shifts midway along the route. I could only just squeeze myself on board, and getting to the ticket counter was harder still. I came off shift at eleven o'clock at night. My elder brother and sister took it in turns to meet me because we live down rather an out-of-the-way lane.

The Number 44 is a new route. Six crews have been transferred on to it. We're quite lucky here because we have slack times. There aren't too many passengers at all between 10 a.m. and 1.00 p.m., from 2 till 4 in the afternoon or in the evening. Each bus has eight conductors, split into two shifts. The early one is from 5.30 to midday and the other is midday to 8.00 p.m. We make five circuits of the city each day. We're always on the late shift, so we never get to watch television. We only get home in time for the late evening repeat of the news. I don't go to the cinema much. The company gives us tickets once every three months.

Sometimes I go to buy my own tickets for a morning show. But by the time I've got up, tidied around the place and bought some food and cooked it, it's time for work.

Show your ticket please, if you're getting off. Yes, I'm talking to you. (*A woman in a red jacket who had already moved a few feet away slowly drew her monthly pass out of her pocket and showed it with a look of disdain.*) Disgusting! People assume we get a bonus for catching fare-dodgers, but we don't.

It's easy to spot them. They always go to the most crowded part of the bus. And when they get off, they run. Or sometimes they wait until you are just closing the door to slip off. People from outside Beijing are honest and buy tickets. Some soldiers don't, though. You have to go on and on at them to get them to pay. Maybe they don't get much money. Then the young girls from Anhui who come here to work as maids act stupid and pretend they don't know they have to pay. Pedlars from the free markets tend to be stingy. They try riding for free too. You have to be sure before you go after them. If I nab them I never get it wrong, but I don't usually bother. See this stretch? A year ago there were no houses here, and those saplings hadn't been planted. It was just waste ground. Now look at those lights.

At the beginning of the month you have to check the tickets particularly carefully because people are supposed to buy new monthly passes. If you catch someone who hasn't bought one, they have to buy a return ticket for the whole route. If they use a faked pass, they have to buy a new one valid for a daily return journey along the whole route –

that's six yuan. If the inspector finds passengers on the bus who haven't paid, our bonus is cut.

(A quarrel breaks out towards the front of the bus. One passenger is accusing another of pushing.) We hardly ever argue with the passengers. In fact we've got an award for courtesy. It's on that sign on the front of the bus. It's a matter of the way you speak to people. If the door pinches someone as it's closing, you can apologize nicely and that'll be that. If you're in a bad mood and don't feel like apologizing when someone complains, a row can easily blow up and go on until the passenger gets off. That's just stupid.

It's when we're fed up we have rows. Always the same little group of us coming to work, and knocking off at the end of the shift. Nothing different ever happens. Sometimes you feel everyone you see comes from the same mould.

We can't find boyfriends on the job. Some of the passengers do try to talk to us. We get to know the regulars. Men sometimes try to shoot us a line. There was this young guy we used to see every day on the bus. He never gave up. Even when we ignored him, he would keep talking away. He was good-looking. He said he worked in a song and dance company. It was true too – he showed us his identity card. But it's no good, no good at all. You can't trust people you meet on a bus.

Conductors and conductresses usually go out together or with the drivers. Then they can help each other out. See the conductor up at the front door? He isn't actually one of our crew. He's finished work already on his own bus but he came to take over from his girlfriend so that she could go home early. But we're on our own – we take care of ourselves.

After work I read novels and magazines. I buy them for myself. *The Younger Generation* is my favourite magazine. We both pay about six yuan a month to go to dressmaking classes. Including bonus and allowances for hairdressing and transport, my wage comes to about seventy yuan. I give it to my mother and when I ask, she gives me some back. It's not as much as I need. I'm closest to my mum and dad. At work it's another member of our crew.

I look after my own money. I save twenty yuan a month. For when I get married? Well, not exactly.

[357]

I'd like to get promotion to be a driver or despatcher. A lot of drivers started as conductors. Some people get promoted after only one year, and others never manage it. My ideal husband? I'm still too young. I'd like to find someone who is better than I am. I'd sooner he wasn't doing the same job. He should be better than I am, but I don't necessarily think he's got to have a better job.

We can't help getting dirty. If you look at your shoulders after just one run, you'll see a layer of dust. The bath attendants start and finish at the same time as we do so we can't go to the bathhouse. We get 5.50 yuan a month hairdressing allowance. That won't get you to the best hairdressers, but it's enough for an ordinary place.

Of course we can't have real hairdos or even use haircream. We'd just get our hair full of dust. See how dry my hair is. The job's tough the whole year round. In summer it's terribly hot. The bus is roasting to start with and the people make it even hotter. In spring it's very windy, and in winter it's cold. I bought this coat myself. The company issues us with uniform for spring and autumn. We get a lot of passengers in late spring and early autumn. Young lads bring their girlfriends to ride round and round the city. They have monthly passes. Look at our Beijing. It's so beautiful. Each season is different. *(The reflection of lights outside the bus kept flickering across her back.)*

We can't really get to know anyone on the buses. People come and people go.

Goodbye! Goodbye!

List of Translators, Chinese Titles and Sources

ABBREVIATIONS

BJR *Beijingren* (Shanghai, 1986)

CLF Cheng Lingfang

CM Carole Murray

DD Delia Davin

GB Geremie Barmé

GY Gladys Yang

JB Judy Burrows

JCK Jeffrey C. Kinkley

WJFJ W. J. F. Jenner

For each piece the Chinese title and the version or versions on which our translations are based are given. Where no periodical source is given the translation is based only on the book version. In some cases the authors changed the title between periodical and book publication; we have given the title used in the book.

PART ONE: LIVINGS

Popcorn	"放地雷"的小男孩儿	Tr. by WJFJ
	Shanghai wenxue No. 7, 1985; *Beijingren* (Shanghai, 1986), p.548.	
Ten Thousand Yuan	万元户主	Tr. by WJFJ
	Shouhuo No. 1, 1985; *BJR*, p.83.	
Dr Yang	杨大夫	Tr. by DD/CLF
	Shanghai wenxue No. 1, 1985; *BJR*, p.553.	
Bandit Turned Housewife	看电话的老太太	Tr. by JB
	Zhongshan No. 1, 1985; *BJR*, p.45.	

PART TWO: LOOKING BACK

Ancient Footprints	陈迹	Tr. by WJFJ
	BJR, p.277.	
Her Past	旧雨新知	Tr. by DD/CLF
	Zuojia No. 1, 1985; *BJR*, p.52.	
Last of a Kind	昨天的职业	Tr. by JCK
	Zuojia No. 1, 1985; *BJR*, p.50.	
Banker	老人	Tr. by WJFJ
	Shouhuo No. 1, 1985; *BJR*, p.61.	

PART THREE: WAYS UP

Newly-weds	上只角，下只角	Tr. by WJFJ
	Shanghai wenxue No. 7, 1985; *BJR*, p.535.	
Diploma	文凭	Tr. by DD/CLF
	Shouhuo No. 1, 1985; *BJR*, p.414.	
Second Try	待到来年九月八	Tr. by WJFJ
	manuscript.	
Hitting the Jackpot	中奖	Tr. by WJFJ
	Zhuomuniao No. 4, 1985; *BJR*, p.452.	

PART FOUR: STATES OF MARRIAGE

Virtuous Wife, Good Mother	临街的窗口	Tr. by WJFJ
	BJR, p.17.	
Whirlpool	流中的旋涡	Tr. by DD/CLF
	Shanghai wenxue No. 7, 1985.	
Staying a Widow	守寡	Tr. by DD/CLF
	Wenxuejia No. 1, 1985; *BJR*, p.296.	

PART FIVE: REFORMERS

Builder	盖楼人的脚下	Tr. by WJFJ
	Zuojia No. 3, 1985; *BJR*, p.123.	

Joining Forces	呼兰河归海	Tr. by CM
	Zuojia No. 3, 1985; *BJR*, p.159.	
Bridges and Rabbits	龙门阵	Tr. by WJFJ
	Shanghai wenxue No. 1, 1985; *BJR*, p.90.	
Twenty-seven Days and Three Days	二十七天与三天	Tr. by DD/CLF
	Shanghai wenxue No. 1, 1985; *BJR*, p.130.	

PART SIX: PEASANTS

Land	两山之间一棵树	Tr. by WJFJ
	Zhongshan No. 1, 1985; *BJR*, p.1.	
Deep in the Mountains	太行云深不知处	Tr. by DD/CLF
	Zhuomuniao No. 4, 1985; *BJR*, p.68.	
Boring But Glorious	请笑一笑......	Tr. by WJFJ
	Shanghai wenxue No. 7, 1985; *BJR*, p.449.	
Planning Her Family	多子多福	Tr. by DD/CLF
	Zuojia No. 1, 1985; *BJR*, p.280.	

PART SEVEN: WORKERS

| Mr Average | 青工 | Tr. by GB |
| | *Wenxuejia* No. 1, 1985; *BJR*, p.207. | |

Street corner PhD	马路博士:	Tr. by GY
	Zhongshan No. 1, 1985; *BJR*, p.465.	
Gold Miners	新的金山勇士	Tr. by WJFJ
	manuscript.	
Cyclist	骑车人	Tr. by GY
	Zhongshan No. 1, 1985; *BJR*, p.437.	
The Human Factor	小乔，和他欢乐的伙伴们	Tr. by WJFJ
	Shouhuo No. 1, 1985; *BJR*, p.164.	

PART EIGHT: SERVICE

Mail	最佳路线四公里	Tr. by DD/CLF
	Wenxuejia No. 1, 1985; *BJR*, p.332.	
At Your Service	为您服务	Tr. by GY
	Zhongshan No. 1, 1985; *BJR*, p.318.	
Vieux Paris	老巴黎	Tr. by WJFJ
	Zuojia No. 1, 1985; *BJR*, p.339.	
Schoolfriends	校友	Tr. by DD/CLF
	Wenxuejia No. 1, 1985; *BJR*, p.398.	

PART NINE: OFFICIALDOM

Jargon	标准话	Tr. by WJFJ
	BJR, p.13.	
Section Chief	小组长	Tr. by GY
	Zhongshan No. 1, 1985; *BJR*, p.170.	
Lawyer	迟到的孩子，你早！	Tr. by WJFJ
	Shanghai wenxue No. 7, 1985; *BJR*, p.239.	
United Front	学而优 仕而优	Tr. by JCK
	Zhongshan No. 1, 1985; *BJR*, p.264.	

PART TEN: LONERS

Irreproachable Conduct	"风纪典范"	Tr. by DD
	BJR, p.289.	
Misfit	离群雁	Tr. by JB
	Shouhuo No. 1, 1985; *BJR*, p.270.	
On the Road	"为什么，为什么流浪"	Tr. by GY
	Shanghai wenxue No. 1, 1985; *BJR*, p.219.	
Good Looks	漂亮的三丫头	Tr. by DD/CLF
	Shouhuo No. 1, 1985; *BJR*, p.300.	

PART ELEVEN: CRIME AND PUNISHMENT

Inside	在同一堵高墙后面	Tr. by WJFJ
	Zhuomuniao No. 4, 1985; *BJR*, p.363.	
Son	儿子	Tr. by WJFJ
	Wenxuejia No. 1, 1985; *BJR*, p.432.	
Hero	英雄	Tr. by WJFJ
	Zhuomuniao No. 4, 1985; *BJR*, p.254.	
Self-help	"生活，教会了我证明我自己"	Tr. by WJFJ
	BJR, p.457.	

PART TWELVE: GETTING ON

Avionics	头·批顾客	Tr. by WJFJ
	Shouhuo No. 1, 1985; *BJR*, p.20.	
Selling Flowers	买花吗？买花吧！	Tr. by JB
	Shouhuo No. 1, 1985; *BJR*, p.283.	

PART THIRTEEN: SECOND THOUGHTS

Going Back	长满丛林的山岗	Tr. by WJFJ
	Wenxuejia No. 1, 1985; *BJR*, p.377.	
Philosophy of Life	却道天凉好个秋	Tr. by WJFJ
	Zhuomuniao No. 4, 1985; *BJR*, p.259.	

Red Guard	夜来风雨声声慢	Tr. by CM
	Shanghai wenxue No. 7, 1985; *BJR*, p.309.	

PART FOURTEEN: HANDICAPS

A World of Colours	缤纷的世界	Tr. by GY
	Zhongshan No. 1, 1985; *BJR*, p.593.	
Empty Burden	空白的重荷	Tr. by DD/CLF
	Shanghai wenxue No. 7, 1985; *BJR*, p.489.	
Woolly Hat	绒线帽	Tr. by DD
	Shanghai wenxue No. 1, 1985; *BJR*, p.500.	

PART FIFTEEN: COMING AND GOING

Train Chief	七岁的单身男子汉	Tr. by WJFJ
	BJR, p.345.	
Golden October	旅游	Tr. by WJFJ
	Shouhuo No. 1, 1985; *BJR*, p.358.	
Drinks and Smokes	烟酒不分家	Tr. by WJFJ
	Wenxuejia No. 1, 1985; *BJR*, p.393.	
The Sea	大海—你真坏，又真好	Tr. by WJFJ
	BJR, p.409.	

Hard-earned Money	钱，可不是白来的	Tr. by WJFJ
	Zhuomuniao No. 4, 1985; *BJR*, p.189.	

PART SIXTEEN: SHOW BUSINESS

Song of Praise	翅膀	Tr. by DD/CLF
	Zhongshan No. 1, 1985; *BJR*, p.442.	
Sixth Time Lucky	一路不顺风	Tr. by JCK
	Zuojia No. 1, 1985; *BJR*, p.529.	
Cabaret	"酒干倘卖无"	Tr. by DD/CLF
	Wenxuejia No. 1, 1985; *BJR*, p.145.	
Sideline	副业	Tr. by WJFJ
	Zhongshan No. 1, 1985; *BJR*, p.179.	

PART SEVENTEEN: YOUTH

Dreams	多梦时节	Tr. by JB
	Zhongshan No. 1, 1985; *BJR*, p.196.	
Fly in a Bottle	我，"瓶中的苍蝇"	Tr. by GY
	Zhongshan No. 1, 1985; *BJR*, p.202.	
Forty Minutes	四十分钟的夜	Tr. by DD/CLF
	Wenxuejia No. 1, 1985; *BJR*, p.353.	

ABOUT THE AUTHORS

Zhang Xinxin was born in Nanking in 1953. She was in the People's Liberation Army for two years, and was a nurse and a factory worker before entering college. She is now on the staff of the Beijing People's Art Theater and has produced several television shows based on her own journalism.

Sang Ye, born in Beijing in 1955, is a working journalist and a researcher in modern Chinese history.